# Managing Corporate Responsibility in the Real World

AF166843

Jouko Kuisma

# Managing Corporate Responsibility in the Real World

## Lessons from the frontline of CSR

Jouko Kuisma
Helsinki, Finland

ISBN 978-3-319-85311-6        ISBN 978-3-319-54078-8 (eBook)
DOI 10.1007/978-3-319-54078-8

Printed on acid-free paper

This Palgrave Macmillan imprint is published by Springer Nature
The registered company is Springer International Publishing AG
The registered company address is: Gewerbestrasse 11, 6330 Cham, Switzerland

# Foreword

My own exciting journey in the corporate responsibility world started in 1990, when I participated in defining K-group's first environmental policy. I worked then in the K-retailers' association and moved to the parent company Kesko in 1995. In those days, the logistics department of Kesko Food – the market leader in Finland – was ahead of its time as concerned environmental actions, also in the eyes of the authorities. Kesko Food's environmental team wanted namely to start collecting corrugated board for recovery from K-food stores in Kesko Food's delivery trucks. Health authorities opposed the plan first, because 'for health reasons it is not allowed to transport waste in cars that are meant for distributing foodstuffs'. Kesko Food got a one-year licence for their Northern Finland distribution area to test collecting corrugated board – the same packaging material in which the foodstuffs had been distributed to the K-stores. During that test year, nobody died due to this 'health risk' or even got sick, and the collecting became permissible in the whole country.

From there, we moved on step by step: replaced cardboard boxes with reusable plastic boxes, built internal recycling centres into K-food stores, added a recycling terminal to the central warehouse complex, started an ISO 14001 environmental management system, carried out energy reviews on premises, developed an environmental store concept for K-stores and published the first environmental report in 1997. The next steps were a system for responsible sourcing, updating of corporate values and various HR projects. In 2000, we started reporting on corporate responsibility and succeeded in being the first company in Finland to follow Global Reporting Initiative (GRI) guidelines. A little later, we bought reporting software, engaged a third party to perform assurance on the report and joined a European organization to promote audits on labour conditions at our suppliers in risk countries.

In a large corporation, compiling such a manifold out of numerous small acts took over ten years and continues still, always aiming at better results. So much time was needed, as in the 1990s no clear systematics was available for managing, measuring and reporting of corporate responsibility. Even the terminology on the subject was quite mixed for a long time. The definitions included soft and green values, ethics, megatrends and philosophies of saving the world, and links to the normal everyday management were difficult to find and explain.

Times have changed since those days. Corporate responsibility has become a natural, necessary, often inevitable part of corporate values, strategy, risk management, competitive weaponry and profit seeking. Stakeholders have become much more interested in company actions and they require open, transparent disclosure of actions and results. It is by all means still allowed to seek a good economic result, which is the basis of responsible business, but the profit has to be made responsibly, supporting sustainable development and proving it. Well managed corporate responsibility improves profitability; irresponsible behaviour destroys it, sometimes extremely fast.

In this book, I present experiences of managing corporate responsibility and offer a simple development model that can be introduced in SMEs and also in larger companies in a relatively short time. Since I retired from the Head of CR position at Kesko Corporation, I have had the opportunity of assisting over 20 companies and one sectoral association in developing responsible sourcing, CR management and reporting. Finnish companies are usually fundamentally responsible, and typically plenty of single pieces of responsibility already exist, as well as know-how. The next step is to develop systematics with which the pieces are brought together and integrated into the overall management, not as a separate function as such, but first as a support function completing business functions and step by step as an essential part of the management system and everyday work. Creating the systematics is not difficult, and it will cost practically nothing. Commitment and toughness are certainly needed, but that is nothing new.

My management model is based on the Global Reporting Initiative (GRI) Guidelines. Identifying the stakeholders and their expectations is important, and the responses to them are given in the promises of the management principles and in a concrete action plan. All promises and actions must be measurable, otherwise one cannot manage. And even though corporate responsibility covers the whole company, one has to concentrate on material issues. In order to discover them, I go through all GRI indicators, not to instruct how to use them, but to present my experiences and views – sometimes also to criticize them. I also present some opinions with which the readers may not necessarily always agree.

I use plenty of pages for responsible sourcing, as I have not seen too much thorough briefing on this subject yet.

For those who have not yet developed systematics for corporate responsibility, my book offers a development model in stages which can be accomplished in about six months. The last part of the model – reporting – is an important part of the transparency of operations. It is useful to start reporting soon after the development project has been carried out – in the future, the quality of reporting can be improved year in, year out. I suggest that the relationship between corporate responsibility and profitability is monitored closely from the beginning.

More advanced colleagues can compare their own results and plans with my experiences and observations. For NGOs and other parties with a side view on companies, the book discloses 'inside information', which, I believe, will increase understanding on company aspirations. For those students entering working life, the book introduces interesting future topics in the corporate world, changes that everybody will inevitably face and that will affect the attractiveness of companies among young job seekers.

Helsinki, August 2016                                                    Jouko Kuisma
Comments and suggestions are welcomed:
jouko.kuisma@gmail.com

# Acknowledgements

I first go back in time and thank the top management of Kesko at the time – **Timo Karake, Juhani Järvi, Matti Honkala, Matti Halmesmäki** – for giving me a pretty free hand and adequate resources to develop corporate responsibility and take up many interesting subjects. The commissions of the International Chamber of Commerce were very beneficial for my work, thanks to **Timo Vuori**, Chief Executive of ICC Finland. My membership of the Finnish Business and Society Network has kept me up-to-date – thanks to Executive Director **Mikko Routti** and his team for interesting and useful events. And last but not least, many thanks to my wife **Maija-Liisa** who looked over the correctness of my language when I wrote the Finnish edition of this book, published in 2015, and showed remarkable patience both then and again during my work with this English language edition, as I often had to regard my writing as more important than gardening or picking berries.

# Contents

| | | |
|---|---|---|
| **1** | **The Lay of the Land** | 1 |
| 1.1 | Responsibility Ensures and Improves Profits | 1 |
| 1.2 | Four Stages of Stakeholder Influence | 3 |
| | 1.2.1 Believe Me, When I Say | 3 |
| | 1.2.2 Tell Me, When I Ask | 3 |
| | 1.2.3 Prove Your Claims | 3 |
| | 1.2.4 Involve Me | 4 |
| 1.3 | New Concepts for Management | 4 |
| | 1.3.1 'Triple Bottom Line' Covers More Than the Traditional Income Statement | 4 |
| | 1.3.2 Terms Are Still a Bit Lost | 6 |
| 1.4 | Plenty of Subjects in the Public Eye | 7 |
| | 1.4.1 Climate Change, Carbon Footprint | 8 |
| | 1.4.2 Energy Efficiency | 10 |
| | 1.4.3 Material Efficiency | 10 |
| | 1.4.4 Water Footprint | 11 |
| | 1.4.5 Responsible Supply Chain | 12 |
| | 1.4.6 Human Rights | 12 |
| | 1.4.7 Tax Footprint | 13 |
| | 1.4.8 Chemicals | 14 |
| | 1.4.9 Well-Being at Work | 15 |
| | 1.4.10 Corruption, Bribery and the Grey Economy | 16 |
| | 1.4.11 Animal Welfare | 16 |
| 1.5 | Plenty of Organizations Involved | 17 |
| | 1.5.1 The United Nations | 17 |
| | 1.5.2 The UN Global Compact | 20 |

|       | 1.5.3 | UN Guiding Principles on Business and Human Rights | 21 |
|       | 1.5.4 | ILO and Other UN Suborganizations | 22 |
|       | 1.5.5 | The UN Principles for Responsible Investment | 23 |
|       | 1.5.6 | Global Reporting Initiative | 24 |
|       | 1.5.7 | OECD | 25 |
|       | 1.5.8 | International Organization for Standardization (ISO) | 26 |
|       | 1.5.9 | The International Chamber of Commerce | 26 |
|       | 1.5.10 | European Union | 28 |
|       | 1.5.11 | BusinessEurope, CSR Europe | 31 |
|       | 1.5.12 | Finland as a Country Case | 32 |
| 1.6 | How to Follow the Development of Corporate Responsibility | | 33 |
| 1.7 | Features of a Responsible Company | | 35 |

**2 Developing a Management Model for Corporate Responsibility**    **37**

| 2.1 | A Simplified Model for Managing Corporate Responsibility | | 38 |
| 2.2 | Setting up a Steering Group | | 39 |
|     | 2.2.1 | Members of the Steering Group | 39 |
|     | 2.2.2 | Working Programme of the Steering Group | 40 |
|     | 2.2.3 | Timing of the Steering Group's Work | 41 |
|     | 2.2.4 | The CR Organization After the Development Project Phase | 41 |
| 2.3 | Overall Basis for CR Management | | 43 |
|     | 2.3.1 | Corporate Values | 43 |
|     | 2.3.2 | Vision of Corporate Responsibility | 47 |
|     | 2.3.3 | Corporate Responsibility in Corporate Strategy | 50 |
| 2.4 | Stakeholder Assessment | | 52 |
|     | 2.4.1 | Identifying the Key Stakeholders | 52 |
|     | 2.4.2 | Examining the Stakeholders' Expectations and Requirements | 53 |
|     | 2.4.3 | Company's Own Actions in Response to the Expectations and Requirements | 54 |
|     | 2.4.4 | Indicators for Monitoring the Success of the Actions | 54 |
|     | 2.4.5 | Our Expectations of the Stakeholders | 55 |
|     | 2.4.6 | Indicators for Measuring Success of Stakeholder Cooperation | 55 |

2.5  Risk Assessment                                                   56
2.6  SWOT Analysis                                                     60
2.7  Evaluation of Own Present State and Comparison with
     Competitors                                                       60
2.8  Identifying Material Aspects of Own Responsibility                62
     2.8.1  Materiality Assessment, Defining the Boundaries            64
     2.8.2  The Order of Importance of Performance
            Indicators                                                 66
     2.8.3  Essential Issues in Materiality Assessment                 67

3  Economic Responsibility                                            69
   3.1  Economic Value Generated and Distributed to
        Stakeholders (EC1)                                            70
   3.2  Financial Implications and Other Risks and
        Opportunities Due to Climate Change (EC2)                     72
   3.3  Standard Entry Level Wage by Gender Compared to
        Local Minimum Wage (EC5)                                      72
   3.4  Proportion of Spending on Local Suppliers at Significant
        Locations of Operation (EC9)                                  73

4  Environmental Responsibility                                       77
   4.1  Materials used (EN1), Share of Recycled Materials
        (EN2)                                                         78
        4.1.1  Reporting on Materials Used is Still Small-Scale        79
        4.1.2  Chemicals Should Be Included                            79
   4.2  Use of Energy, Energy Efficiency, Greenhouse Gas
        Emissions (EN3EN7, EN15–19)                                   80
        4.2.1  Energy Companies Are Too Slow in Counting
               Their Environmental Profile                            82
        4.2.2  It Makes Sense to Calculate Your Own Emissions         83
        4.2.3  How Carbon-Free Is the So-Called 'Carbon-Free
               Electricity'                                           84
        4.2.4  Environmental Label for Electricity                    85
        4.2.5  Carbon Compensations                                   86
        4.2.6  Reducing Emissions                                     87
        4.2.7  The Material on Climate Change is Endless on
               the Internet                                           89
   4.3  Biodiversity Issues                                           89
   4.4  Use, Recycling, Reuse of Water EN8–10, Water
        Discharge EN22                                                90

4.5     Other Significant Air Emissions EN20 and EN21     90
4.6     Handling of Waste and Hazardous Waste EN23 and
        EN25, Significant Spills EN24     91
4.7     Environmental Impacts of Products and Services EN27–28     93
        4.7.1     More Thorough Information for Professionals     93
        4.7.2     Easy-to-Adopt Environmental Labels for
                  Consumers     94
        4.7.3     Results Through Product Development     95
4.8     Carbon and Water Footprint in Product Labelling     97
        4.8.1     Carbon Footprint     97
        4.8.2     Water Footprint     100
        4.8.3     Environmental Criteria in Public Procurement     101
4.9     Transport of Materials, Products and Employees EN30     101
        4.9.1     Purchase Delivery Transport     102
        4.9.2     Delivery Transport     102
        4.9.3     Transport Is Only Part of the Life Cycle     104
4.10    Screening of Suppliers Using Environmental Criteria
        EN32 and EN33     105

5   Responsible Managing of Own Human Resources     107
5.1     Job Satisfaction     108
        5.1.1     Job Satisfaction Indicators     109
5.2     Basic Data About Employees (LA1)     110
5.3     Employee Turnover (Part of LA1)     111
5.4     Health and Safety (LA6)     112
        5.4.1     Sick Days     112
        5.4.2     Accidents     113
        5.4.3     GRI Indicators Emphasize Injuries at Work     114
5.5     Training (LA9), Skills Management, Lifelong Learning
        (LA10)     114
5.6     Performance and Career Development Reviews (LA11)     116
5.7     Equal Remuneration for Women and Men (LA13)     116
5.8     Labour/Management Relations (LA4), Health and Safety
        Committees (LA5)     117
5.9     The Company's Attractiveness as a Workplace     118
5.10    Other HR Indicators of GRI     118

6   Responsible Supply Chain     121
6.1     In the European Union the Workers' Rights Are
        Respected – at Least in Theory     122

6.2 In Developing Countries the Control of Labour
Legislation is Insufficient                                         123
6.3 The Partners Have to Obey the National Laws and ILO
Conventions – Nothing Special in That!                             124
6.4 Minimum Requirements for Working Conditions
and Terms                                                          125
   6.4.1 Freedom of Association and Right to Collective
Bargaining                                                         125
   6.4.2 Equality, Discrimination, Treatment
of Employees                                                       128
   6.4.3 Working Hours                                    128
   6.4.4 Remuneration                                     129
   6.4.5 The Importance of a Living Wage                  130
   6.4.6 Health and Safety at Work                        133
   6.4.7 Child Labour                                     134
   6.4.8 Forced Labour and Disciplinary Measures          135
   6.4.9 Controlling Must Be Plausible                    136
6.5 Social Auditing Schemes                                        138
   6.5.1 Social Accountability SA 8000 Standard
(www.sa-intl.org)                                                  138
   6.5.2 Ethical Trading Initiative (ETI), SEDEX Database
(www.ethicaltrade.org, www.sedexglobal.com)                        139
   6.5.3 Business Social Compliance Initiative (BSCI)
(www.bsci-intl.org)                                                140
   6.5.4 Fair Wear Foundation (FWF) (www.fairwear.org)     141
   6.5.5 Fair Trade Labelling (www.fairtrade.net)          141
   6.5.6 Other Schemes for Monitoring Labour Rights       142
6.6 Summary of Responsible Sourcing                                144
6.7 How to Proceed in Developing Responsible Sourcing?             146
   6.7.1 GRI's Instructions for Screening Suppliers Are
Non-specific                                                       150
6.8 Human Rights Related to Sourcing                               151

7 Social Impacts                                                   155
7.1 Relations with Local Community SO1, SO2                        155
7.2 Corruption and Bribery SO3–5                                   156
7.3 Political Contributions SO6                                    159
   7.3.1 A Company as a Political Donator                 160
7.4 Breaches of Legislation                                        160

**8    Product Responsibility**                                                                     163

**9    Materiality Assessment in a Matrix**                                                  165

**10   Management Principles Guiding Corporate Responsibility**      169
    10.1   Public Management Principles Are Important                      169
          10.1.1   Code of Conduct                                                    171
          10.1.2   International Commitments of Corporate
                   Responsibility                                                      172
    10.2   Environmental Policy                                                          172
          10.2.1   HR Policy                                                            173
          10.2.2   Principles of Responsible Sourcing                   174
          10.2.3   Principles of Risk Management                       175
          10.2.4   Product Policy, Product Statements               176
          10.2.5   Communications Policy                                   177
          10.2.6   Sponsoring Principles                                   177
    10.3   Standards Assisting Management Principles                    178
          10.3.1   Product Certifications                                     182

**11   Drawing up the CR Action Plan**                                               183

**12   Reporting on Performance**                                                          187
    12.1   Outline of the GRI Guidelines                                          187
          12.1.1   Standard Disclosures of the GRI
                   Recommendations                                          189
          12.1.2   Fundamental Issues of Management             191
          12.1.3   The Pain of Starting the Reporting               191
          12.1.4   Reporting Software Saves Work                    192
          12.1.5   Profitability Aspects Are Worth Taking Along   192
          12.1.6   Indicator Protocols                                       194
          12.1.7   Style of Reporting                                         195
          12.1.8   So, Who Would Read the CR Reports?         196
          12.1.9   Assurance of the Report                              198
          12.1.10   GRI Content Index                                     199
          12.1.11   How to Use the Report                            200
    12.2   The Future of CR Reporting                                             201
          12.2.1   EU Directive on Non-Financial Reporting     201
          12.2.2   Next Steps for GRI                                       203
          12.2.3   Integrated Reporting                                     204

**13   Communicating Corporate Responsibility**                                209
 13.1 Corporate Responsibility on the Company's Website         209
 13.2 Communicating to Stakeholders                              212
 13.3 Introduce Persons in Charge                                213
 13.4 Corporate Responsibility in Marketing                      214

**14   Stakeholder Cooperation Revisited**                                     217
 14.1 Typical Weaknesses of Stakeholder Cooperation              219
  14.1.1 Stakeholder Definitions Are Too Narrow             219
  14.1.2 No Balance Has Been Found Between
    'Defence' (Complying with the Norms)
    and 'Offence' (Strategic Opportunities)            220
  14.1.3 The Company Takes the Defensive Position
    Too Early                                          220
  14.1.4 Own Efforts Are Concealed                          220
  14.1.5 Communications Fail                                221

**15   New Year Resolutions**                                                  223
 15.1 Spend Quality Time with Friends                           223
 15.2 Learn New and Exciting Skills                             223
 15.3 Lose Weight                                               224
 15.4 Be more Honest                                            224
 15.5 Get Rid of Old Bad Habits                                 224
 15.6 Improve Grades                                            224
 15.7 Become More Organized                                     224
 15.8 Reduce Stress                                             225
 15.9 Save Money                                                225

**16   Summary**                                                               227

**List of interviewees**                                                       229

**List of useful web pages**                                                   231

**List of people I have quoted in my book**                                    241

**Index**                                                                      243

# About the Author

Jouko Kuisma graduated from Helsinki School of Economics as M.Sc. (Econ.) in 1971. In 1985, he took the eight weeks' management course at the Business Management Institute (LIFIM). He served Kesko Corporation – a listed Finnish retail group with annual turnover of 10 billion euros – from 1976 until his retirement in 2007. From 1995 to 2001, Kuisma was Senior Adviser on EU public affairs and international trade organizations. From 2001 to 2007, he was Head of Corporate Responsibility (CR), reporting to the Deputy CEO. He had participated in Kesko's CR development since 1990 and was later responsible for introducing ISO 14001, social auditing of suppliers and environmental reporting – and since 2000, CR (GRI) reporting.

During his Kesko years, Jouko Kuisma was active in national and international business organizations. He was a member of the EU Multistakeholder Committee on CSR (Brussels), the Environment Commission and the Business in Society Commission of the International Chamber of Commerce (Paris), and the Board of Business Social Compliance Initiative (Brussels). In Finland, he chaired the CR Working Group of the Confederation of Finnish Industries and the Responsible Importers Network of the Central Chamber of Commerce.

During Kuisma's Head of CR years, Kesko became a leading company in the CR sector in Finland, as well as in Europe and globally, and Kesko also received the UNEP/ICC Business Award for Most Sustainable Partnerships, Johannesburg Summit in 2002 (K-environmental store concept, together with the Finnish Association for Nature Conservation).

After having retired from Kesko, Jouko Kuisma worked as an independent CR consultant, developing his customers' management model for CR with the same principles and practices that he now presents in this book. He has had 20 customers from 12 different sectors: food industry, clothing industry, construction, publishing, restaurants, hotels, banking, furniture industry, waste management, energy, technical trade and department stores. Among his customers, about one third has been big companies, the rest SMEs. The management model Kuisma offers is universal, not dependent on the size or sector of the company. He has over 25 years of all-round experience in developing CR – his favourite areas are responsible sourcing, reporting and combining profitability and responsibility.

For Jouko Kuisma, corporate responsibility is a very practical issue, which cannot be managed by depending on theories. He may be the first author of a CR book who has been in practical charge of the CR issues in a large corporation, with excellent results. As he has also consulted plenty of companies and been very close to their daily operations in this work, his experience of the subject is very wide and practical.

Jouko Kuisma's personal awards include Knight of the Order of Lion of Finland (governmental award) and the Environmental Award of the Pekka Kuusi Foundation.

# List of Figures

Fig. 2.1   Assessing the importance of stakeholders                              53
Fig. 4.1   The waste hierarchy                                                   92
Fig. 4.2   Product assortment grouped by environmental quality                   96
Fig. 9.1   Presenting the results of the materiality assessment                 166

# List of Tables

| Table 2.1 | Stakeholder assessment | 56 |
|---|---|---|
| Table 2.2 | Risk assessment on corporate responsibility | 59 |
| Table 2.3 | SWOT analysis | 60 |
| Table 2.4 | Materiality assessment of performance indicators | 66 |
| Table 3.1 | Kesko's purchases by operating country in 2015 | 74 |
| Table 4.1 | Ethical and unethical low prices | 97 |
| Table 6.1 | Living wage calculations | 132 |
| Table 6.2 | Suggested action plan for responsible purchasing management | 147 |
| Table 11.1 | Action plan | 185 |

# 1

# The Lay of the Land

## 1.1 Responsibility Ensures and Improves Profits

Corporate responsibility is a familiar subject in principle as well as in practice, and companies have already done much for it. The actions have, however, been too separate and random, and the big picture has been difficult to perceive. Companies lack an explicit system with which their responsibility can be managed and the results measured. As this is the case, it is difficult to manage responsibility efficiently and make the most of its benefits.

And after all, responsibility consists of *ordinary everyday work, nothing special nor exotic*. By being responsible, managing this now better recognized feature of everyday work in a systematic way, it is possible to save money, improve reputation and find many new business ideas for creating future growth. My claim is that developing corporate responsibility does not cost anything in the end; the savings and other positive changes will outweigh the costs.

Sometimes, top management retards the plans for developing corporate responsibility, because they have the wrong impression that such a project would mean much extra work and high costs. Therefore, in such companies it is psychologically not a good idea to start the development initiative by presenting environmental indicators and the plans for improving them. A better plan is to count the financial impacts of the environmental improvements and start selling the idea to the Chief Financial Officer and the rest of the management team by showing the expected savings. I have an example of this from the 1990s.

© The Author(s) 2017
J. Kuisma, *Managing Corporate Responsibility in the Real World*,
DOI 10.1007/978-3-319-54078-8_1

Kesko Food used to recycle a huge amount of wooden pallets, on which goods were delivered to the stores in delivery trucks. The pallets could be recycled 20–25 times before they got broken, and there was a huge pile of broken pallets on the backyard of the warehouse. The broken pallets were transported in trucks to a company that could use the wood for some other purpose. The transport costs were high, as there was lot of air in the load between the boards. The environmental manager suggested that the company should buy a crusher which would crush the boards into small pieces. It would save so much space in the load that only one transport out of four would be needed. That would decrease the emissions of the transports by 75 per cent and of course the transport costs by the same 75 per cent. The crusher cost 30,000 euros. Counting the emission decrease was not the best way of justifying this investment, but giving the CFO the financial calculation – the payback time for this investment will be 11 months and the interest on the invested capital will be 33 per cent – he thought this is a very profitable investment, to be carried out right away.

There are plenty of examples of how responsibility saves money: carrying out energy efficiency reviews on premises, training truck drivers to adopt a more economical driving style, investing in precautionary health care and welfare at work, preventing accidents and so on. I will return to such examples later in this book.

*I suggest that the readers of this book do not concentrate on just becoming more responsible, but rather on becoming more profitable by being more responsible in a systematic, transparent, measurable way.*

I support this development by presenting a simple, practical management system that will help in organizing corporate responsibility work, identifying the stakeholders and material aspects, defining the management principles, measuring the results and reporting on them.

I use very few quotations and have marked them in my text without making footnotes, and I have not made a list of references at the end of the book, as I do not refer to any books. *This is not an academic book, but a practical book*, based on my own work, experiences and opinions since the beginning of the 1990s. Corporate responsibility is a relatively new subject in the academic world, and I have been so busy developing operations in practical life that I have not had too much time to follow and search for what academic researchers have found out. I have not even cited Michael Porter, who seems to be included in the references of almost all books in this field – I mention one of his books, though. This does not mean that I do not respect him, I am just not used to citing professors.

# 1.2 Four Stages of Stakeholder Influence

In my home country Finland, and in most developed countries, the business culture has always been based on responsibility. Companies comply with laws and keep to contracts, even though they are based on handshake only. The goods are delivered and invoices paid on time, nobody gets cheated.

The world has however changed, become much harder in many ways, and stakeholder trust in companies has declined. Complying with laws and agreements is not enough to make a company responsible – every company must comply with them anyhow. If a company wants to call itself responsible, it has to exceed such minimum requirements. And a company's own reassurances about its responsible actions are no longer enough; proof is needed, facts on the table. This development has had four stages:

## 1.2.1 Believe Me, When I Say

Companies used to write or speak about what they were doing, thinking that 'Believe me' was convincing enough. When the purchasing contract included the clause 'Child labour is forbidden' and the supplier had signed the contract, it was accepted that everything was in order. Or when the company brochure announced that our garden furniture is made of 'hardwood', it was understood that they did not have anything to do with rainforests.

## 1.2.2 Tell Me, When I Ask

As soon as this reassurance was no longer enough, stakeholders started to place more targeted questions: 'Tell me'. Where does this timber come from? Is it from a legally logged forest? Are there gene-modified ingredients in this product? Do they give antibiotics to these rainbow trouts? Under what sort of conditions are these eggs produced?

## 1.2.3 Prove Your Claims

From the first two stages to the third, still valid stage is short: 'Prove it to me'. Does your company have environmental certification? Do you use certified timber? How much energy do you consume and what have you done to save energy? How many part-time workers do you have and what is your employee turnover? Do you report on the results of corporate responsibility and has the report been independently assured?

### 1.2.4  Involve Me

At the fourth stage, the stakeholders are satisfied with the information they have received, but they want to get involved in what the company plans to do: 'Involve me'. There are many ways of cooperating: changing the company's behaviour according to the feedback received, involving employees and contractors in planning, organizing joint projects and events with environmental and development aid associations. And the cooperation will be even more successful if the results can be measured.

## 1.3  New Concepts for Management

### 1.3.1  'Triple Bottom Line' Covers More Than the Traditional Income Statement

Decent companies have always acted responsibly in their relations with society, as well as with other stakeholders, but this has been neither emphasized nor measured in their management. As globalization started to progress, and competition became more and more intense, stakeholders began to lose their trust in companies and the criticism especially against the big multinational corporations grew visibly stronger in the 1990s. Stakeholders felt that the big corporations were taking advantage of cheap labour and weak public administration in poor countries and that the environment was suffering from the severe fight for profit.

Before this, companies had mainly disclosed their financial results. Now, their operations were required to become transparent in every respect. Making profit is by all means still acceptable, as long as stakeholders can be convinced that the profit has been made responsibly, supporting and promoting sustainable development in all its fields. In addition to shareholder value, a new concept of 'stakeholder value' was introduced and started to have a significant effect on company operations and behaviour. The new approach was clarified by the famous British consultant **John Elkington**, who created the concept 'Triple Bottom Line', according to which companies should disclose the results of economic, social and environmental responsibility side-by-side and explain their interrelationships.

Triple Bottom Line has already celebrated its twentieth anniversary. John Elkington's latest book is called *The Breakthrough Challenge*, in which he speculates, together with his co-writer **Jochen Zeitz**, on necessary future actions. In the attached interview, John gives a few thoughts on their topic.

### John Elkington: Most Businesses Are Very Far from Full Transparency

John Elkington is the co-founder of four companies, including Volans Ventures and SustainAbility Ltd. He is a founding member of the B Team advisory board, an initiative uniting leaders in sustainability. He is also the author or co-author of 19 books – the latest with Jochen Zeitz is called *The Breakthrough Challenge*. John lives in London.

**Your book explains the B Team's listing of ten key steps needed to respond to your subtitle 'How to connect today's profits with tomorrow's bottom line'. (Information on B Team: bteam.org.) Here are some questions I think will be most interesting for my readers.**

**Do you see any frontrunners already following 'Apply True Accounting Principles'?**
Well, the obvious example is Puma, the German sportswear brand. The process broke the surface in 2011, when the company reported its Environmental Profit & Loss (EP&L) for the first time. Jochen Zeitz was Chairman and CEO at the time – and the bulk of the work was done by Trucost and PwC. I think the loss reported was 145 million euros, almost half their profits for 2010.
Last time I spoke to Richard Mattison, Trucost's CEO, he told me that they had been working with some 40 companies in this area.
I know Novo Nordisk in Denmark have also pushed forward with a similar approach. And Puma's parent company, now called Kering, is requiring all its brands to complete an EP&L process by 2016. But Puma has throttled back since Jochen left – and I'm not sure how deep the Kering process really runs.

**Does the next step 'Calculate True Returns' differ from your 20-year old Triple Bottom Line (TBL) concept?**
Not really, at least for those who properly understood what the TBL implied. The notion of what Jed Emerson later called 'Blended Value' was always part of the TBL approach. Jochen has said that he always saw the EP&L as a way of completing one dimension of a TBL accounting process.
But a lot has changed since I coined the TBL term and outlined the concept in 1997 with *Cannibals with Forks: The Triple Bottom Line of 21st Century Business*. New concepts (or brandings) have come along, among them the Circular Economy, Integrated Reporting, Impact Investment and Shared Value. So we have a better idea today of how to do some of this stuff – but also of how difficult some parts of this can be.

One of the steps is 'Pursue Full Transparency'. Which business actions are lacking transparency?

What a question! Where to begin? Despite people like Don Tapscott talking of 'naked corporations', most businesses are still very far from the point of full transparency. This can be because they are privately owned (like family businesses), or state-owned, which can mean lower pressures to disclose. It can be because they are hyper-sensitive about protecting key aspects of their intellectual property and/or business model. Or it may mean that they simply don't know what is going on, particularly deeper down in their supply chains. Still, the longer term trajectory is increasingly clear, particularly now that each of us – including employees of companies that would prefer to keep quiet – have cameras in our cell phones, and take them with us everywhere.

When do you think the Asian clothing industry will take the 'Embrace well-being' step seriously?

High profile suppliers operating with major brands are under increasing pressure, particularly since the Rana Plaza disaster. But supplier countries like India, China or Russia will sadly escape much of the necessary scrutiny for some time and, to use a quaint but unfortunately apt English term, sometimes get away with murder.

## 1.3.2  Terms Are Still a Bit Lost

*Environmental responsibility* started to become more exact in the 1990s, due to the introduction of environmental management principles and systems. Environmental management standard ISO 14001 was introduced in 1997, and some environmental reports were published in the 1990s, though there was no common scheme for such reporting yet. As soon as environmental responsibility was followed by other responsibility areas, this wider entity was named *'corporate social responsibility'* (CSR).

The term 'social' created confusion, as it was difficult to know whether the term referred to human resource management or to relations with society – and it was not too easy, either, to define company responsibility towards society. The Commission on Business and Society of the International Chamber of Commerce (ICC) – today called the Commission on Corporate Responsibility and Anti-Corruption – had already agreed at the start of the 2000s that the correct term for such a way of acting was 'responsible business conduct' and the common term in use should be *'corporate responsibility'* (CR).

More new terms were introduced when the reporting scheme Global Reporting Initiative (GRI) was published in 2000. As the scheme was called Sustainability Reporting Guidelines, some companies started to use the term

'*Corporate Sustainability*'. GRI Guidelines are a recommendation, including Triple Bottom Line performance indicators of economic, social and environmental responsibility, product responsibility and safety, as well as relations with society and plenty of management description.

As corporate governance has been much emphasized lately, GRI now calls their reporting scheme ESG-reporting (*Environmental, Social and Governance Reporting*). Where financial reporting describes the company's economic success ('financial performance'), ESG-reporting covers all other activities and results ('non-financial performance'), which very much affect the financial result and the company's value. This *financial/non-financial performance*-combination probably describes best, which results can be reached by good, responsible management, but again this terminology is difficult in use.

And there are still more terms. Some people talk about *corporate ethics, business ethics* and *ethical management*. In my opinion, ethics is a comprehensive and difficult concept, and I would not take it as the basis for responsible management.

In some cases, ethics surely is useful. It is much more natural to include ethical aspects in discrimination, child labour, freedom of association or animal welfare than in purchase of waste press, actions against material loss or personnel training days.

Some people place *green values* on top, but those values focus mainly on the environment and, in addition to the desirable matters, they seem to involve both politics and feelings. *Soft values* are also often called for, but I would not connect them to defining responsible management. In my opinion, all issues included in corporate responsibility are today part of developing risk management, financial results and the company as a whole – that is, they are very *hard values*.

*All issues included in corporate responsibility are today very hard values.*

My aim in this book is to consistently use the terms 'corporate responsibility', 'responsibility', 'responsible business' and 'responsible management'. Terms referring to society and ethics will appear every now and then, however.

## 1.4  Plenty of Subjects in the Public Eye

As corporate responsibility covers all sectors and functions of business, the amount of subjects linked to it is almost innumerable. Luckily, only a few companies have to find procedures and solutions for them all.

As a warm-up exercise, I comment briefly on some large-scale subjects that have been in the public eye for some time now and are predicted to stay in view for a long time. I will return to all of them later, when I explain different parts of corporate responsibility and performance indicators, of which each company should choose the crucial ones through materiality assessment.

## 1.4.1  Climate Change, Carbon Footprint

Controlling greenhouse gas emissions and with that, slowing down and stopping global warming, came strongly to the fore in the United Nations Conference on Environment and Development (Earth Summit) in Rio de Janeiro in 1992. One of the major results of this conference was Agenda 21, the Rio Declaration on Environment and Development. The next step was taken in Kyoto in 1997 with the Kyoto Protocol, in which targets for greenhouse gas reduction were set for industrialized countries. The Kyoto Protocol is legally binding, and it has been called the most demanding environmental agreement of all time. The emission targets have, however, been modest, as political consensus has been difficult to reach – unfortunately efforts to control climate change have been steered more by politics than by science. Therefore, company actions are urgently needed, as companies have the capacity to act much quicker than governments.

The negotiations started in Kyoto have continued in many intergovernmental meetings over the years. As said, politics has been a big barrier to progression, and developing countries have had difficulty accepting restrictions that they should be facing in their pursuit of a better standard of living. The US and China have been in a critical position, and they finally agreed on cooperation in tackling climate change and gave corresponding promises at the UN Climate Summit in New York in September 2014.

So far, the results of various negotiations and agreements have not been promising. However, in 2014 global emissions from energy production diminished by 6 per cent.

In December 2015, the UN Climate Change Conference was held in Paris. The conference negotiated the Paris Agreement, a global agreement to combat climate change, the text of which represented a consensus of the representatives of the 196 parties attending. The agreement was to become legally binding if joined by at least 55 countries, which together represent at least 55 per cent of global greenhouse emissions. Such parties would need to sign the agreement in New York between 22 April 2016 (Earth Day) and 21

April 2017, and also adopt it within their own legal systems (through ratification, acceptance, approval or accession). There were already enough signatories in October 2016 and the agreement came into effect at the beginning of November 2016.

The expected key result of the Paris Conference was an agreement to set a goal of limiting global warming to less than 2°C compared to pre-industrial levels. The parties will also 'pursue efforts' to limit the temperature increase to 1.5°C. The 1.5°C goal will require zero emissions sometime between 2030 and 2050, according to some scientists. The agreement is predicated upon an assumption that the high polluters such as China, the US, India, Brazil, Canada, Russia, Indonesia and Australia, which generate more than half of the world's greenhouse gas emissions, will somehow drive down their carbon emissions voluntarily. There will be neither a mechanism to force a country to set a target by a specific date nor enforcement measures should a set target not be met. There will be only a 'name and shame' system, and many experts doubt whether efforts will be made in practice, though the theoretical consensus in Paris was pretty promising. Some experts are very pessimistic and say that the fight to stay under two degrees' warming has already been lost, and that we just have to adapt ourselves to such a future, to a totally new economic system, based very much on energy.

Ordinary consumers are still pretty carefree in their consumption habits. Chatham House's survey 'Livestock – Climate Change's Forgotten Sector', published in December 2014, points out that the production of meat and dairy products accounts for 14.5 per cent of greenhouse gas emissions. The consumption of these products grows continuously, and as consumers do not take into account their climate change effects and do not change their consumption habits, it will be very difficult to keep global warming under two degrees.

The link to the survey: http://www.chathamhouse.org/publication/live stock-%E2%80%93-climate-change%E2%80%99s-forgotten-sector-global-public-opinion-meat-and-dairy

As climate change is a very serious matter from the point of view of global living conditions, no company can think of ignoring this problem. Every company and every individual has to take responsibility for controlling climate change. It is clear that energy intensive industry sectors have a much bigger responsibility than for instance accounting offices or car repair services.

There is an international ISO 14064 standard for the counting and reporting of greenhouse gas emissions – I will return to this later.

## 1.4.2   Energy Efficiency

In Finland, as in most countries of the northern hemisphere, about three quarters of greenhouse gas emissions originate from energy. Approximately half of this is generated in energy production at power plants, 20 per cent in the industry's own energy production and construction and about 25 per cent in traffic. The share from households is less than 10 per cent, in which living, traffic and food are the biggest emission sources. Emissions are caused by fossil fuels, which need to be gradually replaced by renewable energy sources.

Changes in energy production are very slow, whereas it is possible to gain quick results both in companies as well as in households by improving energy efficiency: innovations in production, energy reviews of premises, geothermal heating, planning of lighting and many other savings measures. The best combination is probably to switch to renewable energy whenever possible and to consume energy as little as possible. And that saves money as well!

Years ago, **L. Hunter Lovins** and **Amory Lovins** of the Rocky Mountain Institute in the US, and **Professor Ernst von Weizsäcker** of the Wuppertal Institute in Germany, wrote the book *Factor Four*, and later **Friedrich Schmidt-Bleek** of Wuppertal published the theory 'Factor Ten'. The basic idea of Factor Four was that as production will presumably double from the present in some timeframe, it has to be managed with half of the raw materials and energy used today, in order to ensure sustainable development. Factor Ten went even further and suggested that the inputs needed for the present amount of production should be squeezed out to one tenth of the present production. It seems that Factor Four and Factor Ten have disappeared, at least from energy policy discussions, as the need for energy is estimated to grow continuously also in developed, high technology countries.

*Factor Four and Factor Ten seem to have disappeared, at least from energy policy discussions.*

## 1.4.3   Material Efficiency

The basic principle of sustainable development is that we satisfy the needs of today's population without risking the possibility of future generations satisfying their needs. Thus, we have to be careful not to use renewable raw materials more than they can be renewed and take a very critical position on using non-renewable raw materials, in order to prevent their coming to an end.

It is commonly known that we consume natural resources much faster than nature can regenerate itself. To avoid such development, we need to improve both energy efficiency and material efficiency: how to use less raw materials with respect to output, how to reduce loss, how to recycle raw materials, how to change the existing materials to those with less environmental impacts, and so on. For example, recycling has become more common in many sectors, both voluntarily and by law, and this development will definitely continue. As in many other affairs, money is a good consultant in promoting material efficiency, which in most cases saves a lot of costs.

## 1.4.4  Water Footprint

Water, especially pure drinking water, is a scarce natural resource and it is becoming more and more scarce. At the moment, farming accounts for 70 per cent of the world's water consumption, industry accounts for 20 per cent and households for 10 per cent. In Europe, industry's share is about 53 per cent, farming accounts for 25 per cent and households for 22 per cent.

Estimated population growth means that farm production has to grow by 60 per cent by the year 2050. More grain, meat and milk products will be needed, and their production will use plenty of water. Special attention has to be given to those crops that are common around the world and that consume plenty of water per produced ton ('water footprint'). Such plants are, among others, sugar cane, maize, wheat, rice, sorghum, millet and cotton.

The demand for water grows also in industries and energy production. The International Energy Agency estimates that by the year 2035 water use in energy production will double, due to growing use of coal and biofuels. Lack of water has already caused production breaks for example in France, the US, China, India, Sri Lanka and Brazil. The water demand from industry is estimated to double by 2030.

Household water consumption will increase with urbanization. About half of the world's population lived in cities in 2010, and the World Health Organisation (WHO) estimates that the share of city dwellers will rise to 70 per cent by 2050.

You can find a lot of information on water by downloading the report 'Evaporating Asset: Water Scarcity and Innovations for the Future', SustainAbility Ltd, Aug.2014, http://www.sustainability.com/library/evapor ating-asset#.V5HMkbEkqM8

ISO has published the international water footprint standard ISO 14046 – I will return to this later.

### 1.4.5  Responsible Supply Chain

Labour conditions in the supply chain have raised interest all over the world. As production has been moved from the developed high wage level countries to developing low wage level countries, reputation risks of supply chains have grown. In many developing countries, labour laws may comply with the minimum requirements, which are the ILO conventions, but there are no proper resources for controlling the compliance of laws, or the control is neglected even on purpose, so that companies in these countries can be priced competitively on the world market.

Child labour has always been discussed in this connection, but actually child labour is detected very seldom when monitoring factories that produce for imports. Most non-compliances are found in remuneration, working hours and work safety.

Control of a production plant or primary production in a poor country far away from the buyer is extremely difficult, especially as the production is often organized in complicated networks and there are plenty of contractors and their subcontractors. If a single company tries to examine the working conditions of its own suppliers or contractors alone, the resources for this work are undoubtedly scarce, the know-how insufficient and the bargaining position unfavourable.

It is possible to obtain better results by cooperating within the industry. For example Business Social Compliance Initiative (BSCI), set up by European retail groups, is already, due to its 1,700 members, a true market force and the suppliers wanting to sell to these members need to comply with BSCI requirements. Audits against the BSCI audit scheme are always carried out by an independent ('third party') certification body that is present in the country in question. The local auditors speak the local language and know the national labour legislation, as well as the practical problems. It is very difficult to prove the accountability of the buyers' own audits, no matter how seriously they have taken that task.

### 1.4.6  Human Rights

Companies that source or run businesses in developing countries – and sometimes elsewhere – can now and then get involved in violations of human rights. Human rights were defined in the United Nations' Universal Declaration of Human Rights (1948) and the complementing conventions on civil and political rights and on economic, social and cultural rights. The ILO Declaration on fundamental principles and rights at work also belongs to this category.

Companies do not usually regard themselves as responsible for all possible human rights; they want to concentrate mainly on labour rights that are easier for them to control. Also on this subject, the focus is on controlling the supply chain extending to countries with low wage levels.

The United Nations Global Compact Initiative includes promoting human rights as well as basic labour rights. In 2011, the United Nations Human Rights Council endorsed the 'Guiding Principles on Business and Human Rights', which were developed by the Special Representative of the Secretary-General on the issue of human rights and transnational corporations and other business enterprises. National governments have then decided on the national implementation of the principles. The company view on the principles is that they transfer too much of the state's responsibilities to companies. It is important for a company's business and risk management that they take their own share of responsibility for human rights, but that should not obscure the state's primary responsibility.

*It is important that companies take their own share of responsibility for human rights, but that should not obscure the state's primary responsibility.*

## 1.4.7  Tax Footprint

As everybody knows, corporate and personal taxation – both direct and indirect – are used for financing the public sector, which then organizes the basic public services. Tax legislation is different from country to country, which easily leads to tax competition. For example in the European Union, it is extremely difficult to unify tax legislation as the decision would need unanimity of all member states.

Many developing countries have not been able to organize taxation properly, which means that those states do not get enough money to finance their public services and infrastructure. Then there are the so-called tax havens that have become heavily criticized lately. Income that should be taxed in the home country is transferred abroad, out of the tax authorities' reach, sometimes legally, sometimes illegally. It has been estimated that from the European Union around 1,000 billion euros are transferred annually to countries where that money is taxed very lightly or not at all. For comparison: EU countries spend altogether 950 billion euros on healthcare. The annual money transfers from developing countries are, according to the World Bank, about 550 billion euros, consisting of illegal transfers by corrupted politicians and of transfers by multinational companies. Again for comparison: the global aid to developing countries is somewhat over 95 billion euros; that is, development aid would not be needed if the money transfers abroad could be blocked or at least restricted. And in April 2016, *The Guardian* presented Oxfam's report, according to which some of the biggest US companies have hidden over 1,200 billion US dollars in tax havens. In 2008–2014, the total sum of taxes paid by the 50 biggest US companies was 1,000 billion US dollars.

The so-called Panama-scandal news in spring 2016 led to serious negotiations in many countries and in the European Commission. Before the scandal, the Commission had already published an 'Anti-tax avoidance package', and the OECD also has plans to block undesirable money transfers. A probable solution in the EU is that companies operating in many countries will have to publicly report their tax footprint – the profits earned and taxes paid in each country of operation.

## 1.4.8   Chemicals

In 2007, the EU tightened control on chemicals with its REACH regulation (Registration, Evaluation, Authorisation and Restriction of Chemicals). The most important target in the regulation is to ensure the high standard of protecting health and environment, to improve the competitiveness of the chemical industry in the EU, and to ensure free movement of goods in the EU internal market.

The European Chemicals Agency (ECHA), located in Helsinki, Finland, registers in the REACH database all substances that are manufactured in the EU or imported to the EU at an annual volume of over one ton. There are approximately 30,000 such chemicals in use in Europe, and about 300 new substances enter the EU market every year. The registrations will be accomplished by 2018 in three stages. Neither manufacturing nor importing of unregistered substances is permitted.

Registration requires that the manufacturers and importers of chemicals provide information on the hazards, risks and safe use of chemical substances. Today, there is not enough information on the health nor environmental impacts of most of the 30,000 substances in use. ECHA also requires declarations of ingredients in various items and appliances if those ingredients are supposed to be released from the items or if they are especially hazardous. All safety information has to be passed on to all parties in the supply chain, so that the companies using chemicals in their own production can act safely and responsibly.

Consumers know very little about the use and impacts of chemicals. Few people have, for example, heard that a quarter of all pesticides in the world are used in growing cotton, or that a quarter of all chemicals in the world are used in manufacturing clothes and textiles. As these quantities are huge, consumer concern will definitely increase in the future, along with their growing consciousness, and they will require much more undisputed transparency from the companies on this issue.

## 1.4.9 Well-Being at Work

Investing in employees' well-being is a profitable investment. According to the research of The Finnish Institute of Occupational Health, investing in precautionary healthcare and other well-being at work will significantly reduce sick days and employee turnover, and the cost savings outweigh many times the money invested. Well-being affects productivity as well: loss will decrease, quality will improve, as well as the financial result all in all. It is very rare to meet a company that yields significant profits even though the employees feel bad. In Asia, many entrepreneurs indeed still believe that they earn best when the workers have as low wages as possible, long working hours without overtime compensation, and poor working conditions in many other ways. How much more would these entrepreneurs earn if they invested in their workers' well-being?

*How much more would Asian entrepreneurs earn if they invested in their workers' well-being?*

One day, when labour shortage finally becomes a reality – though sometimes one thinks that will never happen – a company's reputation as a good employer will be a crucial competitive weapon in recruiting. The importance of well-being at work has been seen for a long time in 'The Best Place to Work'-type of survey that examines the attractiveness of companies as workplace.

## 1.4.10   Corruption, Bribery and the Grey Economy

The best-known international organization dealing with corruption and bribery is Transparency International (www.transparency.org), which publishes, among other things, an annual Corruption Perception Index and National Integrity System Assessments. In the 2015 Index, the ten least corrupt countries were Denmark, Finland, Sweden, New Zealand, Netherlands, Norway, Switzerland, Singapore, Canada and Germany. Most of the developing countries suffer from corruption and bribery, which implicates big challenges for companies buying from those countries, especially as such companies usually have zero tolerance against corruption and bribery.

The national assessments are useful reading for companies, especially when searching for new business partners in unfamiliar countries. For example, of the Eastern European countries that have joined the European Union in the last few years, Transparency reports reveal that corruption is especially apparent in public procurement and tends to raise purchasing prices by 20–25 per cent.

Money laundering is part of the grey economy from which the responsible companies have to dissociate without fail. My only personal experience of the issue dates back to the 1990s, when I was active in a European trade association. We had the annual conference that year in Vienna, ending with the traditional conference dinner. Beside me sat a young man, who escorted one of the female participants, sitting opposite us. The other persons around the table were mostly CEOs of big retail groups. The youngster did not feel too comfortable in this company; he said he had had to borrow the jacket and tie from one of his friends as he does not own such clothes. As I had never met him before, I started asking questions, finally about his work. He moved his chair closer to me and said quietly: 'I'm in the paper business'. Coming from a country famous for its paper industry, I became interested and wanted to know more. He then told me, confidentially, that he sells invoices and receipts. At that time, it sounded like a joke, but of course it raised serious thoughts after the dinner, and I believe (and hope) that his business turned out to be unsuccessful very soon.

## 1.4.11   Animal Welfare

Treatment and welfare of animals grown for food raises plenty of discussion, including mink and fox farms, piggeries, chicken yards, broiler hatcheries, animal transports and use of hormones.

The EU Parliament has set up an animal welfare task force, focusing on improving the living conditions of livestock, reducing animal transports (in the EU, a million animals are transported daily), keeping cloning away from food production and developing a general directive on animal welfare.

*In the EU, a million animals are transported daily.*

In Finland, as well as in many other countries, the Ministry of Agriculture has set up an advisory board which follows and assesses the standard of livestock welfare, makes proposals for developing the welfare and gives statements on motions and plans on it.

Down is an important component in producing outdoor apparel, and Patagonia – a well-known company in this sector – has wanted to ensure that the birds are not live-plucked for that purpose. For Patagonia's principles of traceable down, see http://www.patagonia.com/us/patagonia.go?assetid= 37607. On the front page there is a link to the video, 'What the pluck – conventional down is a scary business' (cannot be seen everywhere, due to some copyright reasons).

HKScan Group is active in nine Northern European countries. It is the fifth largest company in the meat sector in Europe and it has net sales of more than two billion euros. Here is a link to their animal welfare policy: http://www2.hkscan.com/attachments/animal_welfare_policy.pdf

# 1.5 Plenty of Organizations Involved

Corporate responsibility is part of the global development of international economy, hence there are very few national characteristics involved. The best way to predict the development is to keep track of the agreements and recommendations of international organizations and legislation and recommendations of the European Union. Many industry sectors also have their own international cooperation schemes, like Responsible Care for the chemical industry, ICTI CARE in the toy industry (International Council of Toy Industries), International Cocoa Initiative, Roundtable on Sustainable Palm Oil, and so on.

## 1.5.1 The United Nations

The UN is an intergovernmental organization that covers practically the whole world. At the UN, decisions are made by government representatives of the member states. The decisions are agreements, commitments and declarations. For example, the Millennium Declaration approved in 2000 included these development goals for the twenty-first century:

1) To eradicate extreme poverty and hunger
2) To achieve universal primary education
3) To promote gender equality and empower women
4) To reduce child mortality
5) To improve maternal health
6) To combat HIV/AIDS, malaria and other diseases
7) To ensure environmental sustainability
8) To develop a global partnership for development

Progress towards reaching the goals has been uneven across countries. The major successful countries include China (whose poverty population declined from 452 million to 278 million) and India. The World Bank estimated that MDG 1A (halving the proportion of people living on less than $1 a day) was achieved in 2008, mainly due to the results from these two countries and East Asia.

In the early 1990s, Nepal was one of the world's poorest countries and remains South Asia's poorest country. Doubling health spending and concentrating on its poorest areas halved maternal mortality between 1998 and 2006. Its Multidimensional Poverty Index has seen the largest falls of any tracked country. Bangladesh has made some of the greatest improvements in infant and maternal mortality ever seen, despite modest income growth. However, the child mortality and maternal mortality rate are globally down by less than half. Sanitation and education targets will also be missed.

The Sustainable Development Committee of the UN was replaced in 2012 by the High-level Political Forum on Sustainable Development (HLPF). The Forum will assemble every four years at the head of state level in connection with the UN General Assembly, and annually in connection with the UN Economic and Social Council (ECOSOC).

Many NGOs criticize the UN for not listening to citizens, as power has been given to government representatives. These NGOs would like to regulate the operations of multinational companies by developing the UN into a legislature that could prescribe binding regulations covering all member states. So far, member states have wanted to keep legislation under the decision-making power of national parliaments, and the thought of accomplishing laws between around 200 states and putting them into effect and controlling them seems utopian.

*Many NGOs would like to regulate the operations of multinational companies by developing the UN into a legislature.*

In 2015, the UN decided on the 2030 Agenda for Sustainable Development, which consists of 17 new Global Goals (SDG, Sustainable Development Goals). They are:

1. *No Poverty* – End poverty in all its forms everywhere
2. *Zero Hunger* – End hunger, achieve food security and improved nutrition and promote sustainable agriculture.
3. *Good Health and Well-being* – Ensure healthy lives and promote well-being for all at all ages.
4. *Quality Education* – Ensure inclusive and equitable quality education and promote lifelong learning opportunities for all.
5. *Gender Equality* – Achieve gender equality and empower all women and girls.
6. *Clean Water and Sanitation* – Ensure availability and sustainable management of water and sanitation for all.
7. *Affordable and Clean Energy* – Ensure access to affordable, reliable, sustainable and clean energy for all.
8. *Decent Work and Economic Growth* – Promote sustained, inclusive and sustainable economic growth, full and productive employment and decent work for all.
9. *Industry, Innovation and Infrastructure* – Build resilient infrastructure, promote inclusive and sustainable industrialization and foster innovation.
10. *Reduced Inequalities* – Reduce inequality within and among countries.
11. *Sustainable Cities and Communities* – Make cities and human settlements inclusive, safe, resilient and sustainable.
12. *Responsible Consumption and Production* – Ensure sustainable consumption and production patterns.
13. *Climate Action* – Take urgent action to combat climate change and its impacts.
14. *Life Below Water* – Conserve and sustainably use the oceans, seas and marine resources for sustainable development.
15. *Life on Land* – Protect, restore and promote sustainable use of terrestrial ecosystems, sustainably manage forests, combat desertification, and halt and reverse land degradation and halt biodiversity loss.
16. *Peace, Justice and Strong Institutions* – Promote peaceful and inclusive societies for sustainable development, provide access to justice for all and build effective, accountable and inclusive institutions at all levels.
17. *Partnerships for the Goals* – Strengthen the means of implementation and revitalize the global partnership for sustainable development.

You can read about the goals in more detail on the UNDP's (United Nations Development Programme) website: http://www.undp.org/content/undp/en/ home/sdgoverview/post-2015-development-agenda.html

## 1.5.2  The UN Global Compact

In 1999, the then UN Secretary-General Kofi Annan challenged companies to promote the realization of nine universally important principles. Later, anti-corruption was added as the tenth principle. The UN Global Compact is the world's largest sustainability initiative with 13,000 corporate participants and other stakeholders over 170 countries. There are over 50 local networks, where members exchange experiences of implementing the principles: www.unglobal compact.org

These are the ten principles:

### 1.5.2.1  Human Rights

Businesses should:

- Principle 1: Support and respect the protection of internationally pro-claimed human rights; and
- Principle 2: Make sure that they are not complicit in human rights abuses.

### 1.5.2.2  Labour Standards

Businesses should uphold:

- Principle 3: the freedom of association and the effective recognition of the right to collective bargaining;
- Principle 4: the elimination of all forms of forced and compulsory labour;
- Principle 5: the effective abolition of child labour; and
- Principle 6: the elimination of discrimination in employment and occupation.

### 1.5.2.3  Environment

Businesses should:

- Principle 7: support a precautionary approach to environmental challenges;
- Principle 8: undertake initiatives to promote environmental responsibility; and

- Principle 9: encourage the development and diffusion of environmentally friendly technologies.

### 1.5.2.4 Anti-Corruption

- Principle 10: Businesses should work against corruption in all its forms, including extortion and bribery.

It is not possible to measure compliance with the principles accurately, but the pressure from publicity takes care for its part that the companies do not damage their reputation by committing to Global Compact and then neglecting all efforts to implement it. The signatory companies have to send an annual report – usually their corporate responsibility report – the so-called Communication on Progress to the Global Compact office in New York. If a company does not send the report by the deadline, Global Compact first registers the company as 'non-communicating' and after having waited for 12 months, finally deletes it from the member list.

## 1.5.3 UN Guiding Principles on Business and Human Rights

John Ruggie, the Special Representative of the UN Secretary-General developed Guiding Principles on Business and Human Rights, which were endorsed by the UN Human Rights Council in June 2011. After this, states have been expected to develop and publish their national action plans for the Principles.

The Principles are based on three pillars: the state's responsibility to protect human rights, a company's responsibility to respect human rights, and the availability of remedial actions.

The complete text of the Principles is available here: http://www.ohchr.org/Documents/Publications/GuidingPrinciplesBusinessHR_EN.pdf    and here is more information material on the implementation http://business-humanrights.org/en/un-guiding-principles

By July 2016, only seven countries had released their national action plans (NAPs): the UK, the Netherlands, Denmark, Finland, Lithuania, Sweden, and Norway: http://business-humanrights.org/en/updated-assessments-of-national-action-plans

Business has criticized the Principles and the NAPs for tending to increase company responsibility for human rights to reach the level of the states and to make the companies responsible for the violations of their collaborators. The companies certainly do their best, especially for putting the labour rights in effect, but the influence of individual companies is very limited in countries where human rights are poorly fulfilled. Therefore, it is important to further highlight the state's responsibility. I return to the subject in Chapter 6.

## 1.5.4   ILO and Other UN Suborganizations

The conventions of the International Labour Organization (ILO) are very close to corporate responsibility in practice, as national labour laws are based on them. The procedure is tripartite: representatives of states, employer organizations and employee organizations negotiate the conventions, which should then be ratified by the states, meaning that they should adapt the conventions into their own national legislation. I wrote 'should', because the problem is that in many countries the legislation remains unfinished or differs from the ILO conventions, or particularly, that the laws exist but there are no resources – and in some cases no will – to control their conformance. It is useful to visit ILO's website: http://www.ilo.org/dyn/normlex/en/f?p=1000:10015:0::NO:10015:P10015_DISPLAY_BY,
P10015_CONVENTION_TYPE_CODE:1,U and study which countries have ratified which conventions. The less ratifications, the more probable it is to find violations of labour rights in such countries.

ILO's fundamental conventions on labour rights are freedom of association and right to collective bargaining, elimination of forced and compulsory labour, abolition of child labour and elimination of discrimination. There are two conventions on each of these, which makes eight altogether. These conventions have all been ratified by 138 states. Freedom of association seems to be the most difficult convention: 17 countries have ratified neither of the two conventions – these are all the countries on the Arabian Peninsula, Afghanistan, Iran, Lao, Thailand, Vietnam, China, India, South Korea, the US and the small island states of the Marshall Islands, Palau and Tuvalu, which have not ratified any other conventions either.

China has not ratified the forced labour convention, India has not ratified the child labour convention, the US has not ratified the prohibition of discrimination. The US has never been too excited about ILO conventions – while European states have typically ratified around 100 conventions, the US had 14 ratifications in April 2016, China 26, Vietnam 21, India 46,

Bangladesh 35 and Russia 74. As a curiosity, Burkina Faso has ratified 43 conventions, Central African Republic 46 and United Arab Emirates 9.

*Of the ILO conventions, European countries have typically ratified around 100, Burkina Faso 43 and the US 14.*

The other UN suborganizations associated with corporate responsibility are UNEP (United Nations Environmental Programme), UNDP, WHO, UNICEF (United Nations Children's Fund) and UNCTAD (United Nations Conference on Trade and Development).

## 1.5.5   The UN Principles for Responsible Investment

At the beginning of 2005, Kofi Annan, then Secretary-General of the UN, assembled the world's biggest institutional investors – especially big pension funds – to develop common Principles for Responsible Investment (www. unpri.org). UNEP FI (Finance Initiative) acted as secretariat of the initiative, and Global Compact participated as well. The Principles were published in New York in April 2006, and it was estimated that at that time around 40 per cent of the world's pension funds were behind the principles – since then, the number has become much bigger. In April 2016, the amount of signatories was over 1,500.

The six Principles whose content has been specified by examples of possible practical actions, are:

*Principle 1*

We will incorporate ESG issues (= Environmental, Social and Governance issues) into investment analysis and decision-making processes.

*Principle 2*

We will be active owners and incorporate ESG issues into our ownership policies and practices.

*Principle 3*

We will seek appropriate disclosure on ESG issues by the entities in which we invest.

*Principle 4*

We will promote acceptance and implementation of the Principles within the investment industry.

*Principle 5*

We will work together to enhance our effectiveness in implementing the Principles.

*Principle 6*

We will each report on our activities and progress towards implementing the Principles.

In the recent expert surveys (like those by GlobeScan and SustainAbility) the investors that are signatories of the UN Principles for Responsible Investment are clearly the stakeholders that have the biggest effect on the development of corporate responsibility.

## 1.5.6  Global Reporting Initiative

International cooperation for reporting on sustainable development got started at the end of the 1990s, when the GRI was established on the initiative of UNEP and funded by the UN Foundation. GRI (www.globalreporting.org) is a multistakeholder scheme, meaning that many experts with different backgrounds have participated in the work from the beginning: academics, accountants, consultants, environmental and other non-governmental organizations, trade unions, companies, research institutes and so on.

This diversity of experts has been fruitful: when those usually critical stakeholders have had an influence on the 'standardized' contents of company reporting, they no longer need to criticize the reporting scheme. But the more people with their diverse opinions get together (in some GRI meetings there have been 300 participants), the more difficult it is of course to draw up punctual, unambiguous and practical guidelines for reporting.

GRI published their first Sustainability Reporting Guidelines in the summer of 2000. After that, the Guidelines have been updated regularly, every three years or so. The latest version called GRI G4 was published in 2013. The recommendations have also been renamed, sustainability reporting has been replaced by ESG-reporting (Environmental, Social and Governance Reporting). The companies had wanted GRI G4 to become relatively compact and simple, so that reporting would not be too laborious for the preparers, and the readers would easily find the issues that were the most material and interesting to them. Even though materiality has been strongly emphasized in the recommendations, the content of reporting has been further extended and thorough compliance with the recommendations has become more difficult.

I return to GRI as a management tool in 2.8 and to GRI reporting in Chapter 12. GRI Guidelines will be replaced by GRI Standards in 2018 – I will comment on this in 12.2.2.

## 1.5.7 OECD

The OECD (Organisation for Economic Co-operation and Development) has been publishing OECD Guidelines for multinational companies since 1976 – a corporation that operates in two countries is already multinational. The latest update dates from 2011. The Guidelines introduce the voluntary principles of responsible business, as well as the legal norms and international standards prevailing in the international operational environment. The Guidelines aim at ensuring that company operations are in line with government policies, strengthening trust between parties, encouraging foreign investments and promoting sustainable development. OECD Guidelines are the only comprehensive multilateral code on responsible business conduct that the states have pledged to promote. In addition to states, representatives of business, employee organizations and NGOs have participated in preparing the Guidelines.

*A corporation that operates in two countries is already multinational.*

The Guidelines are supported by the National Contact Points (NCP) set up by governments. NCPs enhance the conspicuousness of the Guidelines, adapt them to national circumstances and help companies and their stakeholders to implement them in practice. They also act as an arbitration forum if any practical problems arise.

The OECD case archive contains three resolutions by NCP Finland. In 2006, NCP Finland dealt with the appeal against the pulp factory of the Finnish company Botnia SA in Uruguay, on their environmental actions and communication and against the actions of Botnia's financier Finnvera. In 2012, the appeal was against the consulting company Poyry Ltd, on their share of the environmental and human rights violations in the Xayaburi dam project in Laos. NCP disclosed in its statements that neither Botnia nor Finnvera had acted against the OECD Guidelines, and neither had Poyry, which however 'should have more actively recognized its standing in the project'.

## 1.5.8  International Organization for Standardization (ISO)

As the requirements for corporate responsibility grow stronger, the international standards and certification against them become more important, because then the companies will have independent, qualified proof of applying certain management systems. The environmental management standard ISO 14001, developed by the International Organization for Standardization (www.iso.org), has been in use since 1977. Today, it is estimated that there are around 300,000 ISO 14001 certifications in the world. The ISO 14001 certificate proves that a company complies with the standard's requirements for an environmental management system, but the standard does not have any requirements for environmental performance. The latest environmental ISO standards are ISO 14064 (carbon footprint) and ISO 14046 (water footprint).

The ISO 26000 Social Responsibility standard, published in 2010 (for some reason, ISO uses the term 'Social', even though there are also environmental topics included), differs from other ISO standards in the sense that it was developed into a guidance standard, so it does not include any performance indicators and it cannot be certified. In spite of this, many companies say that they comply with ISO 26000, and there have been efforts in some countries to certify this compliance, even though ISO has strictly forbidden this.

I return to ISO 26000 in 10.2.

## 1.5.9  The International Chamber of Commerce

The ICC (www.iccwbo.org) is the only global business organization covering all sectors. It has a total of 6.5 million members – companies and associations – in over 140 countries, and local offices on all continents in 92 countries such as Brazil, India, China, Russia and the US. ICC strengthens a company's global prerequisites for operation by influencing the regulation environment, developing tools for foreign trade and offering services linked to them. ICC wants to make global business easy.

ICC represents companies in connection with the UN and its suborganizations, and with the OECD and WTO (World Trade Organisation). ICC Commissions such as 'Corporate Responsibility and Anti-Corruption' and 'Energy and Environment' have produced plenty of statements, recommendations and guidelines in the area of corporate responsibility. The ICC Business Charter for Sustainable Development dates back to 1996 (revised in 2000), and thousands of companies are committed to the Charter. Later, guidelines and codes were issued on corporate responsibility, responsible sourcing, responsible marketing and fighting corruption. Though ICC has members from all over the world, the commission members are mostly representative of large European and American companies. The fact that the headquarters are based in Paris may affect participation, as it is too troublesome to travel from Tokyo or Buenos Aires for a one-day meeting in Paris. As with international organizations generally, formulating statements and decision-making tend to be very slow at the ICC.

Timo Vuori, Chief Executive of ICC Finland, comments on a couple of topical subjects on ICC's agenda in the following interview.

### Timo Vuori: ICC has been Critical of Compulsory CR Reporting

Timo Vuori is Chief Executive of ICC (International Chamber of Commerce), Finland.

**Can we expect any new position papers or recommendations from ICC?**
*Compliance* and *SDG* (Sustainable Development Goals) have been high on the agenda lately.
Risk management of companies has been enhanced by compulsory norms like the UK Bribery Act and by voluntary recommendations like the UN Principles on Business and Human Rights. Companies have strengthened their compliance actions in order to manage the risks connected with the regulations – non-compliance may at worst lead to criminal liability. Compliance has become more important as part of corporate responsibility and ICC has published instructions for companies, such as ICC Antitrust Compliance Toolkit and ICC Anticorruption Third Part Due Diligence, ICC Guidelines on Gifts and Hospitality and ICC Ethics and Compliance Toolkit. ICC is now working on a position paper on the social responsibility and tax payments of multinational companies and potential instructions on due diligence in supply chains.
The ICC has worked towards sustainable development since the UN Rio Conference in 1992 and highlighted the companies' role in this work. ICC Business Charter for Sustainable Development was published at that time, recommending common environmental management principles. In 2015, a social responsibility dimension was added to the Business Charter. After the UN updated their Sustainable Development Goals in 2015, many companies have taken all or part of these SDG goals into their own targets of sustainable business. ICC finds the private sector crucial in solving resource and emission problems and reminds companies of their role and responsibilities.

**What has been ICC's stand on the UN Principles on Business and Human Rights?**
UN Secretary-General's Special Representative John Ruggie had regular contacts with the business world when he drew up his recommendations. For companies, human rights are on the one hand a clear and on the other hand

a challenging subject. The companies can take human rights into account in the employer's role. More challenging is to take responsibility of the other actors' and partners' actions in the markets where national legislation and culture do not support human rights. In ordinary life, companies will face problems, to which it is not easy to find solutions, not even by implementing the UN Principles. Human rights can be discussed beautifully in international conferences and cabinets, but clearing up everyday challenges in the countries of weak governance needs deep understanding and experience of field work.

It is important that human rights get a new kind of attention in the business world, but at the same time companies should not be strained with unreasonable obligations on governance and reporting, which do not solve the everyday problems of human rights. Results are more important than administrative processes. ICC will consider case by case whether new recommendations on human rights would be needed. The latest is the ICC-IOE-BIAC recommendation, 'Role of Business in Weak Governance Zones', which appraises the companies' role among local uncertain political development.

**What about the development of CR reporting?**
ICC has wished that the various reporting schemes were as uniform as possible in order to get comparable information. On the other hand ICC has enhanced individuality in order to make understanding of company-specific differences easier. ICC has not taken a position in favour of any reporting scheme, though GRI has been regarded as very useful. ICC has been critical of compulsory reporting, fearing that it would stiffen the actions, and the information produced would not be understandable enough.

## 1.5.10 European Union

### 1.5.10.1 EU Commission and EU Parliament

The EU Commission organized thorough committee work on corporate responsibility (the EU still calls it corporate social responsibility) in 2002–2004. The EU Multistakeholder Forum on CSR was chaired by commissioners Erkki Liikanen (Finland) and Anna Diamantopoulou (Greece) – my role was to represent EuroCommerce. The Forum decided to promote company voluntary work for corporate responsibility, as both the Forum and the EU Commission were of the opinion that all necessary laws exist already. After the final report of the Forum was published, many NGOs, especially environmental NGOs that had participated in the work, announced that they wanted binding legislation for companies, but they did not express what kind of legislation that should be.

During the last decade, the EU Commission has produced new environmental and chemical legislation, published guide books on environmental (2008/2011) and social criteria (2011) in public procurement and updated their corporate responsibility strategy. After many years of tough negotiations, the Commission finally in 2013 made a proposal for a directive on non-financial reporting, which the EU Parliament approved in April 2014. The directive applies rather to big companies: public interest entities (listed companies, banks, insurance companies) with more than 500 employees. This definition is in the directive, but at a national level I have seen that two of these three limits have been outweighed: 500 employees, turnover 40 million euros, balance sheet 20 million euros. I suggest that everybody checks the national legislation enacted before December 2016 to make sure what the final limits will be.

The member states have to include the reporting directive in their own legislation by December 2016. The companies involved must report according to the directive for the first time from the financial year 2017. They have to add a 'non-financial report' to the annual report, informing at least about their environmental performance, social and worker issues, respect of human rights and issues of preventing corruption and bribery. In addition to this, they have to give a short description of the business model and operation principles that the company follows in the issues to be reported. The report also has to explain which non-financial performance indicators have been found material for the company.

The instructions for how to comply with the reporting directive have so far been vague. The directive has met lots of justified criticism as it lets the companies choose what kind of information about the responsibility they decide to disclose. If a company gives out a GRI report, this is sufficient for fulfilling the requirements of the directive, which is understandable as GRI calls for exact performance indicators. Instead, it is difficult to understand and accept that a company could announce Global Compact, OECD Guidelines or ISO 26000 standard as the basis of their reporting, as it is not possible to measure compliance with any of those schemes.

Partly this vagueness has been supported by the companies, as the EU Commission has received many such statements on the directive, in which all the other suggested schemes in addition to GRI can be approved as a basis of reporting. It seems that the companies have not wanted the EU Commission to draw up exact reporting instructions, but they want to align their own reporting content and basis as flexibly as possible. The weight of the reporting directive may remain minor in practice if there are no stricter instructions for the content in future development.

I return to the directive in 12.2.1.

The EU Commission has regularly published their corporate responsibility strategy. The latest is valid from 2015 until 2020: http://ec. europa.eu/growth/industry/corporate-social-responsibility/index_en.htm. Before it was published, the Commission received 525 statements on the draft. The summary of the statements can be found here: http://ec. europa.eu/growth/tools-databases/newsroom/cf/itemdetail.cfm?item_id= 7490&lang=en&title=The-European-Commission%E2%80%99s-strat egy-on-CSR-2011-2014%3A-achievements%2C-shortcomings-and-future-challenges

Sirpa Pietikäinen, an active Finnish member of the European Parliament and Minister of Environment in the Finnish Council of State from 1991 to 1995, comments in her attached interview on what is expected from the EU in the next few years as to corporate responsibility.

---

**Sirpa Pietikäinen: Directives on Financial Statements and Eco-design Are Topical Subjects in the EU Work**

Sirpa Pietikäinen is a member of the European Parliament.

**What subjects of corporate responsibility do you see as topical in the EU work in the next few years?**
Corporate responsibility and transparency have become more important in the European Union, and new requirements on reporting have been added. The directive on financial statements will improve the social and environmental accounting of companies and enhance integrated reporting. It has also obliged the banks as well as the mining and forest industry to disclose their financial statements by their countries of operations. Such reporting makes avoidance more difficult and is thus a crucial issue, as concerns corporate responsibility.

The EU Commission launched an initiative in the spring of 2016 stating that reporting by countries should be extended to other sectors, too. I am in favour of such an initiative and will work for it in Parliament. Another subject that will be topical in the next few years is the directive on eco-design. The existing directive on ecological design should include more requirements for the recyclability of the products and the manufacturers should carry this responsibility. A maximum carbon footprint should be defined for products and untouched natural resources should not be allowed into the production chain if recycled material is available.

Additionally, I believe that the debate on how to transfer to using sustainable raw materials in the production of biofuels will continue.

**In what subjects do you wish companies should invest in developing their responsibility?**
I wish they would develop functioning models for 'responsibility accounting'. Some company representatives say that reasonable, accountable CR reporting is just not possible. I think the problem is that we still have not been able to agree on the global standard. We have to find the solution – we have been able to decide on accounting standards and auditing rules long ago.

**Are the EU's actions for cutting down $CO_2$ emissions and increasing the share of renewable energy sources sufficient? Do you think the Paris Agreement will bear fruit?**
No, they are not sufficient. If we want to keep global warming under two degrees, we should stop using coal totally in all parts of the world by 2050. The European Union is committed to cut down the greenhouse gas emissions by 40 per cent by 2030, but we have not yet seen the promise of giving up coal.
The Paris Agreement was historical and important, but we will see the final results only after having seen how the parties implement the decisions in practice. For example the emission trading system of the EU, which has been said to be the major tool in reaching for the goal, does not function well enough.

**The EU Directive on non-financial reporting will come into force in 2017. Do you think it will bring forth decent reporting?**
I do not believe it will. I think the requirements on reporting should be stricter and more accurate. The CR reports should be audited in the same way as financial reports, according to binding standards. In addition to that, the boards of companies have to be responsible for the CR reports just like they are responsible of the financial reports.

## 1.5.11 BusinessEurope, CSR Europe

BusinessEurope (www.businesseurope.eu) is the central organization of European industries and employers, located in Brussels. It has 41 business federations from 35 European countries as members. It lobbies for company interests, also as concerns corporate responsibility in the EU, though it has no permanent committee for that purpose – the environmental issues are dealt in the Industrial Affairs Committee and the labour issues in the Social Affairs Committee.

BusinessEurope encourages its member companies to develop corporate responsibility voluntarily and keeps a list of companies that are committed to the voluntary network 'European Alliance for CSR', established by the EU Commission in 2006. In recent years, we have not heard much of the CSR Alliance, and actually there were not many who wanted to work for it in the beginning. In July 2016, there were only 173 companies on the list. The EU

Commissioners in charge of enterprises have every now and then invited CEOs of big companies to Brussels to discuss the subject, and it seems that the Alliance has thus been regarded as active.

In Brussels, there are many sectoral EU organizations (e.g. EuroCommerce, Euratex, European Chemical Industry Council, FoodDrinkEurope) that follow the EU legislation of their own sector and cooperate with BusinessEurope whenever needed. Corporate responsibility issues are permanently on their agenda.

CSR Europe (www.csreurope.org), also located in Brussels, is a European network specializing in corporate responsibility. CSR Europe's network of 45 national partner organizations reaches out to more than 10,000 companies in Europe, and their corporate membership brings together 50 multinational companies across sectors and regions. CSR Europe mediates best practices between members and maintains close contact with the EU institutions and civil society to promote CSR objectives, to ensure close policy insights and to advance opportunities for collaboration. CSR Europe's views on responsible business have been summarized in the Enterprise 2020 strategy and programme, which is the only business initiative embedded in the EU CSR strategy.

## 1.5.12   Finland as a Country Case

### 1.5.12.1   Finnish Government and Ministries

In the Finnish government, corporate responsibility issues are coordinated by the Ministry of Employment and the Economy. The Ministry's website gives a lot of information about corporate responsibility, for example about Global Compact, OECD Guidelines, ILO conventions and human rights.

The Ministry is supported by The Committee on Corporate Social Responsibility, which is a consultative body that supports administrative decision-making. Its 15 members represent various authorities, trade and industry, labour market and civic organizations.

The Committee on Corporate Social Responsibility functions in pursuit of a stronger national and international social responsibility policy, and economically, socially and ecologically responsible operation and production methods among enterprises and other organizations. The Committee also acts as the Finnish NCP for the implementation of the OECD Guidelines for Multinational Enterprises. The Committee's term of office extends from 30 December 2014 to 30 December 2017.

The Finnish government decided on its corporate responsibility principles in November 2012. The government's target is to help Finnish companies and public administration forerunners of corporate responsibility. This target was already in the government programme earlier than this date. The government also wants to take responsibility aspects more into account in industrial policy, public procurement and the administration's own operations. It is stated in the principles that many small- and medium-sized enterprises are interested in assessing and developing their own responsibility, but they lack the tools for doing it. The government looks for solutions to this challenge, together with organizations representing SMEs.

Sustainable development and environmental legislation are the responsibilities of the Ministry of Environment. The government has established the National Committee on Sustainable Development, which promotes cooperation to reach the targets of sustainable development and strives to get sustainable development included in the national politics, administration and social practices. The Committee consists of representatives from the Council of State, Parliament, administration, business, municipalities and regions, trade unions, universities, NGOs, arts and science sectors and churches. The Secretariat of the Committee is placed in the Ministry of Environment, and there is a network of contact persons in all ministries.

## 1.6   How to Follow the Development of Corporate Responsibility

**Membership of the sector organization**
The easiest way of being continuously informed about corporate responsibility issues as well as other important issues is belonging to the own sector association. This also provides possibilities to influence development.

**Membership of an organization specializing in corporate responsibility**
CSR Europe and its member organizations specialize in corporate responsibility, and their monthly newsletters offer useful and actual information about the development in legislation, voluntary initiatives and best practices. There are plenty of seminars and workshops on actual subjects and good possibilities for networking with other members. There are over 200 other organizations inside and outside Europe, like Business in the Community in the UK (www.bitc.org.uk), Business for Social Responsibility in the US

(www.bsr.org) and The Business Ethics Network of Africa (headquarters in South Africa, members in 25 African countries) www.benafrica.org.

Plenty of CR news from all over the world can be found at www.csrwire.com.

## Websites of ministries in charge of corporate responsibility

Although sector associations communicate actively about CR development, it is useful to follow what information the ministries present on their websites, especially about government and EU decisions. Their web pages usually offer guidance and tools, particularly for SMEs.

Finnish Ministry of Employment and the Economy: http://www.tem.fi/en/enterprises/corporate_social_responsibility_(csr)

Danish Ministry of the Environment: http://web.archive.org/web/20140703201148/http://eng.mim.dk/the-ministry/

Dutch Ministry of Infrastructure and the Environment: https://www.government.nl/topics/corporate-social-responsibility-csr

## 'The big four'

The four biggest auditing/consulting companies PwC, KPMG, Deloitte and EY all have departments for consulting their clients on CR and for assurance of CR reports. They publish development reports at a global and national level. It is easier to find CR material on PwC's and KPMG's websites – Deloitte's and EY's global websites are more difficult in that sense, and it is better to try their office in your home country. http://www.pwc.com/gx/en/services/sustainability/sustainable-development-goals/sdg-research-results.html https://home.kpmg.com/xx/en/home/insights/2014/10/materiality-assessment.html

## CR literature and topical articles

There are not too many training programs offered for CR as a whole. Therefore, it is useful to participate in shorter seminars on more narrow topics, usually organized by the specialist CR associations. It is also useful to read the newest books on CR. as well as follow the national press and some international article publishers, for example: http://www.theguardian.com/uk/sustainable-business and http://www.mckinsey.com/insights/.

In the LinkedIn network (www.linkedin.com), there are many discussion groups worth following.

Plenty of CR news from all over the world can be found at www.csrwire.com.

# 1.7 Features of a Responsible Company

No authority has clearly defined when and why a company can be called responsible.

The definition has been discussed, for example, in the ICC Commission on Business in Society and in the EU Multistakeholder Forum on CSR. Their position was that corporate responsibility goes voluntarily beyond legislation in fulfilling stakeholder expectations. There is plenty of legislation on the subject – economic, social and environmental legislation – and new laws are not needed. Some NGOs have required new laws, but they have not been able to make concrete proposals. Compulsory reporting is the only subject that seems to develop through legislation.

**The EU Commission** has defined CSR as the responsibility of enterprises for their impact on society. CSR should be company led. Public authorities can play a supporting role through a smart mix of voluntary policy measures and, where necessary, complementary regulation.

Companies can become socially responsible by: following the law; integrating social, environmental, ethical, consumer and human rights concerns into their business strategy and operations.

**The Confederation of Finnish Industries** has this definition:

'Responsibility is part of the business skills of a successful company. A responsible company operates as sustainably as possible and combines the targets and expectations of the company and its stakeholders. Responsibility actualizes best when the company commits itself voluntarily to develop it as a part of normal operations. Reporting should be voluntary and informal, so that the company can best tackle the issues material to its own business and to the stakeholders'. (This was before the EU Directive on non-financial reporting.)

The CSR Compass of the **Finnish Ministry of Employment and the Economy** has used this definition:

'The starting point for corporate responsibility is respecting the laws and exceeding the minimum legal requirements, such as:

1. the requirements for suppliers on respecting the labour and human rights at work;
2. cooperation with suppliers in order to improve social and environmental conditions, like agreeing on decent working hours;
3. systematic environmental and climate management;

4. improving working conditions and working environment;
5. developing products or services that are related to environmental or social issues.

**My own summary of the** basic features of a responsible company **includes the following:**

- Responsibility is part of the corporate philosophy: values, vision, strategy;
- The company has clear management principles, models and instructions guiding responsibility;
- Top management is committed to the subject and has ensured that the employees are also committed;
- The performance of corporate responsibility is monitored reliably and reported openly and transparently (the GRI international reporting recommendations);
- Measuring and reporting concentrate on material issues;
- Development is goal-directed;
- The company works in regular interaction with its stakeholders.

# 2

# Developing a Management Model for Corporate Responsibility

Managing corporate responsibility (CR) is not different from managing the company as a whole. The main difference is that when adding CR into corporate management, there will be more subjects to be managed. For a long time, managing CR and measuring CR performance used to be separate from other management, unstructured issues that were difficult to master. The reason for this confusion may have been that during the introduction of the subject, the term used was corporate *social* responsibility – the term *social* misled the discussion quite a bit. Later, it was noticed that CR was actually a matter of developing the company's performance and ways of working, although partly in new areas and much more than before in interaction with various stakeholders.

**And above all, a major requirement when introducing CR is to increase the transparency of the company's activities.**

Listed companies are used to the fact that they have to inform openly and quickly about even small issues that may affect the company's financial results and future expectations. Smaller unlisted companies usually do not have such an open communication culture – many of them do not even disclose their financial results, nor even their owners, never mind corporate responsibility. However, in the last few years, CR has more and more often earned its own section on company websites.

In the long run, CR management will be integrated into the company's overall management system. As CR is a pretty new subject for most companies – part of it may be familiar, but it has not been systematically managed – it is wise to start developing it first as a separate process. This process, as I will show next, is very simple and easy to master.

© The Author(s) 2017

J. Kuisma, *Managing Corporate Responsibility in the Real World*,
DOI 10.1007/978-3-319-54078-8_2

# 2.1 A Simplified Model for Managing Corporate Responsibility

### Basis for Management

Managing corporate responsibility is built on the same basis as management in general: on corporate values, vision and business strategy. This basis may already include some substances associated with corporate responsibility, and they can be updated during the CR development process.

### Expectations and Requirements

It is necessary to examine what stakeholders want from the company as concerns CR, and how we today comply with these expectations and requirements. At the same time, it is useful to compare our efforts to those of our main competitors and the best practice companies in our sector.

### Material Issues

Before we can start the systematic CR development process, we need to assess which are the material and most important CR issues for us, as it is neither possible nor reasonable to try to cover everything.

### Promises

We have to give promises on how we will develop our CR, taking our stakeholders' expectations into account. Corporate values and strategy are such promises, but in addition to them, managing principles guiding corporate responsibility as well as commitments to national and/or international initiatives are needed. Before giving promises, it is important to define own value chain: what are the limits of our responsibility (does it cover for example our suppliers, disposing of our products after use and so on).

### Actions

Promises are fulfilled through actions in practice. For that purpose, systematic action plans are needed, both at corporate level and in detail in each department.

### Measuring and Reporting on Performance

It is important to measure performance of the action plans reliably, so that setting targets and managing development is possible. In measuring, as well as of course in actions, it is necessary to concentrate on material issues. It is also important to recognize the connections between responsibility and financial results and capitalize on such connections.
Public reporting on material results compared with set targets should take place at least once a year.

### Return to the Beginning

New targets should be set according to the results achieved, following the principles of continuous improvement.

## 2.2 Setting up a Steering Group

In order to work systematically and take all necessary issues into account when building a management system for corporate responsibility, it is useful to set up a *steering group* which will take responsibility for the development work. After having completed the management system phase, this group can continue until the CR work becomes so established that it can be included in the company's common management system. I will return to the tasks of the steering group and to the roles of particular persons and organs when I present the different stages of the management model.

### 2.2.1 Members of the Steering Group

*The recorder and practical operator of the steering group* should be the person who will hereafter be named the company's CR manager – responsible for developing, coordinating and reporting. If such a person is not hired from outside of the company, this job is usually given to an existing specialist working in either quality, environmental or development functions. Sometimes the appropriate person can also be found among the HR or communications specialists. As the CR manager's job is crucially important for future development, the elected person should be devoted and committed to this job – a 'just right' personality.

The *chair of the steering group* fits best to that member of the management board who will be named responsible for this area. Very often this person is a development director in charge of strategy and planning. It is clear that the chair also needs to be committed to developing corporate responsibility and presenting the plans successfully to the management board.

As *members of the steering group*, 4–5 persons should be invited, representing different functions of the company as experts, so that all important areas concerning corporate responsibility are represented.

Typical such functions are production, procurement, marketing and/or communications, real estate and/or environmental operations and human resources. As soon as the development project has proceeded to choosing performance indicators and further to the action plan, the steering group should invite representatives of finance and IT departments and other similar units outside of the steering group to share their views on the development.

Having had the opportunity to assist over 20 such steering groups as their consultant, I of course recommend cooperation with one of the consultants available in your country. The more practical experience the consultant has of the CR work in big as well as smaller companies, the better. Such a consultant could support the chair and the recorder in guiding the steering group's work. You do not need to be afraid of the costs – the consultants are very efficient and will not spend too much chargeable time on your project, and you will finally save a lot of time and money, as the project will progress smoothly and common mistakes can be avoided.

## 2.2.2  Working Programme of the Steering Group

In the start-up phase, the working programme of the steering group could be something like this:

*First meeting:*

* general discussion on the work and targets of the group;
* present state of own company and of competitors – presentation of the analysis by the project consultant, discussion, conclusions;
* start of stakeholder assessment: identifying the relevant stakeholders.

*Second meeting:*

* completing the stakeholder assessment: stakeholders' expectations/requirements, our actions, performance indicators of the actions, our expectations from the stakeholders, indicators for measuring results of cooperation;
* part of the discussed issues can be used in defining the CR vision.

*Third meeting:*

* risk assessment;
* SWOT analysis (strengths, weaknesses, opportunities and threats);
* first part of the materiality assessment of performance indicators, at the same time as evaluation of IT systems as to their capability of collecting the required data.

*Fourth meeting:*

* completing the materiality assessment.

*Fifth meeting:*

* elaborating the managing principles guiding corporate responsibility (the members have drafted suggestions together with the recorder of the group);
* first action plan for CR.

### 2.2.3 Timing of the Steering Group's Work

For each meeting of the steering group, it is recommended to allocate three to four hours of working time, especially for the stakeholder assessment, which usually covers almost all relevant CR issues, as well as for the materiality assessment, which always raises a very lively discussion.

If meetings are held once a month, the steering group can complete the CR management model in less than six months. If the work has been started at the beginning of the year and completed before summer, the autumn season can be used for the arrangements for collecting new data. As the indicators of economic responsibility and labour practices usually exist already, the new indicators are usually needed in the areas of supply chain and environmental responsibility.

*If meetings are held once a month, the steering group can complete the CR management model in less than six months.*

Comprehensive collecting of data should be possible from the beginning of the next year, which would then make reporting on that year possible. Before that, it is useful to practise reporting on the start year already, even though the results will not be published yet. As I will later suggest, it is better to start public reporting with incomplete information than to wait until everything is ready and perfect – openly showing imperfection and a will to improve creates trust in readers.

If the company has possibilities and interest in using *a consultant* who has enough practical experience of leading such a development project, such a consultant could support the chair and the recorder in guiding the steering group's work. I think such cooperation will ensure that the steering group works systematically, that the work is efficient, that any problems arising can be avoided and that the targets set can be reached on schedule.

### 2.2.4 The CR Organization After the Development Project Phase

As soon as the development project has been completed and the CR management principles and programmes have been integrated into everyday management, the steering group shoud continue its work as part of the annual planning and reporting. Only when responsibility is no more regarded as a separate process, but clearly integrated in all operations, can the steering group's tasks be closed down and responsibility issues managed permanently on the management board's agenda.

In the same way as the steering group may be needed for a relatively long time, it is also important to make a single person responsible for developing, coordinating and conducting CR work. It depends on the size and sector of the company as to whether this job is full-time, or whether some other tasks are combined with it, such as quality, environmental or communications tasks. Hopefully, the days are far behind us when first the environmental responsibilities and later CR development as a whole were regarded as 'additional work' that had to be carried out 'along with one's own work'. Typical titles for this job are CR specialist, CR manager, CR development manager and so on.

In big companies this function is so extensive and important that the major person in charge will be a director, who will manage a CR team. It depends again on the size and sector of the company, whether there are other CR specialists or environmental and communications specialists in the team. Potential director titles include: Responsibility Director; Director of Corporate Responsibility; Director of Sustainability, Vice President, Sustainability; Head of Corporate Responsibility (I had that title); Chief Responsibility Officer (CRO); Chief Sustainability Officer; or also Chief Compliance Officer if the work consists more of controlling how the company complies with its principles, management models and requirements. Quality management systems, as well as health and safety issues and environmental issues, are often combined with CR tasks, and the title could then be Director or Vice President, EHS or EHSQ and Sustainability.

In order to give CR issues enough weight in the company, the CR Director should be subordinate to a member of the management board. As corporate responsibility is strongly associated with corporate strategy, management development and risk management, the appropriate person on the management board is the one responsible for those issues. They will then get to chair the CR steering group. In SMEs, there is usually also a suitable person in the management team, and if the CR manager also takes charge of environmental and work safety issues, he/she might as well be a member of the management team. In these companies – and why not even bigger ones – CR issues can also be reported directly to the Managing Director.

Those who want to compare what titles other companies are using can try to search for the titles on company websites. The problem is that it is difficult to find CR people in charge or CR organizations on the websites, just as it is difficult to find any other people in charge. For some reason, companies want to hide all important people – maybe because they do not want anybody to contact them.

The CR steering group and the CR manager/director make proposals on management principles, operating models and programmes and reporting, as concerns CR, to the management board to decide, through the group member who belongs to the board. The board of directors of the company will decide mainly on the general business principles (Code of Conduct) and governance and risk management principles and they should be notified of other CR issues such as the annual CR report. There are, of course, no obstacles to taking the other management principles guiding CR to the board of directors – this would give them more weight both inside the company as well as outside. As soon as the CR issues become clearly integrated in all planning and operations, they will be part of normal annual and long-term planning, risk assessment, strategy process and so on. In the future, the CR report will be part of the report by the board of directors, at least in big companies.

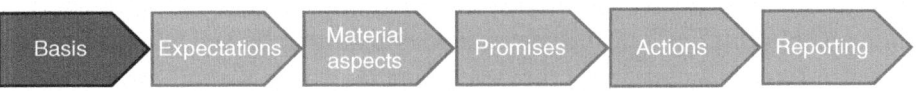

## 2.3 Overall Basis for CR Management

Before starting to define the exact content of corporate responsibility with the help of materiality assessment and management principles, let us view the basis for management in general – corporate values, vision and strategy.

### 2.3.1 Corporate Values

Corporate values are said to prevail in the way of working in every company, even if the values have not been defined. Values of individuals are a mixture of knowledge and emotions. Knowledge gives the direction, emotions help to get there. Corporate values are a combination of individual values, corporate strategy, operating principles and goals. Corporate values often seem to represent the goals of the company's management rather than the motives and efforts of the staff.

In Finland, the Central Chamber of Commerce used to order surveys on corporate culture, targeting both management and employees. The latest survey is as old as from the year 2009 – maybe the results did not encourage continuation. According to the survey, the management and the employees experienced the values very differently, and the employees were not as familiar with the values as the management was. The employees thought the values should be revised, as the existing ones were unclear and implausible. The interviewed workers said that the values had been recognized only in talk, not in deed. The business executives were also quite sceptical about whether the values were observed in the companies' operations. The outsiders gave a much more severe critique – most values were nothing but empty words, and they had been written down only because they looked good – in the companies' operations they are rarely seen.

Having searched for corporate values on the websites of the big companies, I have noticed that companies using values in their management are nowadays in the minority, and among SMEs it is all the more difficult to find values.

### 2.3.1.1   How Should Values Be Defined?

There is no universal recommendation for defining values – every company is individual in this sense. If the values are defined carefully and taken seriously, they can serve as a useful tool for developing the company and management. Defining is not a simple process – the employees need to participate in defining and to engage in the result, and overall developments in society have to be taken into account, too. Some advice from value experts:

> The importance of values and ethics is increasing. Experienced top managers are in a situation, where they have to develop their know-how in areas that have not been part of the managers' repertoire before. More and more managers link the company's success with social development and give attention to social issues and environmental challenges, which were previously the headache of political leaders and NGO activists.

> Tapio Aaltonen, a Finnish consultant.

> Values guide the choices made in companies. They are used especially in making difficult choices that cannot be solved acting like before. The companies should regard values as management tools, when better financial results are sought with a committed staff in a fast changing world.

> It is possible to act in accordance with the values, but it is never possible to implement them completely. Values are tools for orientation – they are like stars in the sky. The stars guide the travellers, but they can never reach the stars.

Martti Puohiniemi, A Finnish value researcher and consultant.

Companies need employees with many different thoughts. If the discussion culture of the company is healthy, different opinions can be very useful. An innovative employee can bring new thoughts and ideas to a conservative company. Value conflicts raise plenty of discussion and confrontation. Employees get exhausted if the employer's values are unfamiliar to him/her and there is no flexibility in adapting them. For example, if the company only wants to maximize profits, the employees will certainly become distressed.

Journalist Laura Honkasalo interviewing Martti Puohiniemi in a Finnish magazine.

### 2.3.1.2   Values Are Promises That Need to Be Measured

As concerns managing corporate responsibility, values should always be regarded as *promises*: these values are the basis of our operations, these efforts are important in our work, these are principles we respect. And if values are public promises, then it is necessary to follow and measure their realization, and these results should be included in the CR reporting like other indicators of responsibility. The well-known principle matches with values also: 'if you don't measure, you don't know the present state and cannot set targets, hence you cannot manage'.

Here are some examples of values found on corporate websites. The usual amount of values is from three to five, typically four. I have grouped them according to the subject area:

*Values linked with economy*: profitability, profitable growth, best result as target, efficiency, we are the best in our sector, continuous development, quality, high quality, innovativeness, regeneration, target-orientation, development...

*Values linked with customers:* honesty, sincerity, communality, valuation and trust, satisfied customers, we exceed our customers' expectations, we respond to our customers' needs, customer as starting point of operations, customer-orientation, succeeding with the customers...

*Values linked with employees:* work, joy of working, know-how, courage, professional, qualified and healthy employees, we create a good working environment, looking after employees, mutual trust and valuation, working together, succeeding together, constructive cooperation, ability to cooperate, team work, commitment, entrepreneurship...

*Values linked with corporate responsibility*: (some of the earlier mentioned values belong here also) responsibility, taking responsibility, taking responsibility for society, respecting the environment, reliability and safety, safety and responsibility, sustainable growth and development...

Each of you can evaluate which values you think are target values set by management, which are based on individual thoughts and motives, which are nothing but empty words and which are probably no values at all, in the proper meaning of that word.

It is easier to use indicators to measure the realization of target values than it is with individual values. One can find performance indicators for profitability, high quality, regeneration, satisfied customers, healthy employees, good working community and so on. And it is more difficult to measure and verify values such as honesty, sincerity, courage, team work, succeeding together, entrepreneurship and so on.

> *It is easier to use indicators to measure the realization of target values than it is with individual values.*

An example of values that are different from those typically used. The Moomin World Team Park's values are: family-centred, non-violence, friendliness, environmental awareness, good manners, open-mindedness and safety.

### 2.3.1.3 Summary of Values as Basis for Managing Corporate Responsibility

- If a company uses values as basis for management, at least one of them should be linked with corporate responsibility, to keep the CR efforts credible;
- As it is the employees' task to make the values come true, it is important that they can participate in defining the values;
- When defining the values, one must take into account that the realization of values must be measurable and that the stakeholders must be informed about the results. (though the GRI Guidelines do not take a stand on this issue).
- It is important to ask the employees regularly, how well the values are known, how important they are found, how well they are observed, and if not, why.

## 2.3.2 Vision of Corporate Responsibility

Corporate vision is the cornerstone of everyday management and it serves as the starting point for all planning. The vision gives all employees a picture of the future, of the target position where the company wants to be in five or ten years' time. The vision should appeal to thinking as well as to emotions. Without vision the work has no meaning, direction or indication of how the business and development work should be prioritized.

After having defined the vision, it is time to consider how it will be carried out, that is, to create the strategy for how to reach the target position.

The description of vision usually includes, among other things, the assumption in which markets and with which products the company plans to operate and compete in the next few years. The vision may also include rough targets for turnover and profits. According to research on the subject, many very successful companies have a clear and strong vision. The vision must be realistic but also target-oriented, and it should be communicated to the employees so that they understand the vision is the common will of everybody in the company. It is also a summary of the company's efforts, meant for outsiders.

The visions that companies publish are usually very short and concise. Typical outlooks for the future are 'in the year this and that we will be our country's best, biggest, most profitable, leading in our sector, leading in the global market, trailblazer...' Corporate responsibility is very seldom mentioned in corporate visions; if it is, then it is expressed as 'we are the best and most responsible company in our sector' or 'our trailblazer status is based on the principles of sustainable development'.

As corporate responsibility is a relatively new area of management to most companies, the steering group should define a separate vision for corporate responsibility, predicting what will happen in this area in the next five or ten years. The content of CR vision can be analysed either according to CR subjects (raw materials, energy, water, labour rights etc.) or to stakeholders – stakeholder assessment gives good information about their expectations and requirements. Personally, I like analysis according to stakeholders, as stakeholder interaction is a crucial part of the whole issue.

CR vision should be re-examined and, if necessary, revised every two years or so, and it should be presented to the management board and, why not, also to the board of directors.

**Vision, Strategy and Social Responsibility**

Finnair's vision extends to the year 2020:

Finnair reviewed its vision for 2020. We want to be number one airline in the Nordic countries and be the most desired option in Asian traffic. In transit traffic between Asia and Europe Finnair wants to be among the three largest operators. Finnair aims to become the airline of choice for quality and environmentally conscious air travellers in intercontinental travel in the Northern Hemisphere.

Via Helsinki means the shortest possible route between Europe and Asia: the most direct route between Europe and Asia runs via Helsinki Airport. The route is also the ecologically most sensible way of traveling to Asia. A flight from Berlin via Helsinki to Tokyo produces 84 kilos less carbon dioxide emissions per passenger than a flight via Frankfurt. When flying via Helsinki to Asia, passengers are travelling all the time in the right direction.

Moreover, a stopover in the right place reduces emissions, because fuel is not consumed carrying the extra fuel necessary for a direct flight.

Finnair's effective Asia strategy has great impact on both the company and the whole of society. The impact of Asian business on employment is remarkable. Finnair is reporting a reverse China phenomenon: jobs are not flowing from Finland to China, but in the opposite direction.

Around 95 per cent of an airline's emissions arise from engine emissions during flying. The biggest environmental act that an airline can make, therefore, is to fly with modern, low-emission aircraft. Finnair's fleet in Europe is the most modern in the world and the modernization of the long-haul fleet is just about to finish. In 2017 the company will have a long-haul fleet of over 20 aircraft, the core of which will consist of 15 new Airbus A350XWB aircraft.

Every new generation of aircraft produces on average 20 per cent less emissions than its predecessor. Many other airlines, due to financial difficulties, have not invested in new fleet.

The cornerstones of Finnair's growth strategy are Asia's growing market, the best flight connections and cost-competitiveness. Our success factors are quality, freshness and creativity.

http://www.finnairgroup.com/responsibility/responsibility_1_4.html

### 2.3.2.1  Weak Signals in Outlining Visions

CR visions, as well as visions generally, benefit from the skill of identifying weak signals and strengthening them before competitors, which often makes it possible to become trailblazers.

Weak signals can be divided into two groups:

1) So-called early information (like foreknowledge of scientific research results), which is not yet concretized
2) First symptoms of change (as before flu one feels tired, then the throat becomes sore, then come the sniffles).

There are plenty of weak signals around us, we just have to identify them. It is of course easiest to find them in our own area of work. The Internet gives us excellent opportunities for searching for weak signals. Websites of companies and scientific communities are particularly useful, as well as participating in discussion groups, meeting students, listening to stories told 'among the masses'.

If the piece of information you have found does not surprise or shock you, if it does not question your way of thinking or if it is familiar or self-evident to you, it is not a real weak signal, and you should continue searching.

Discussion on weak signals is definitely interesting to the CR steering group. Anybody can find some weak signals after a short consideration.

*If the information you have found does not surprise or shock you, if it does not question your way of thinking, it is not a real weak signal.*

### 2.3.2.2 The Finnish Strategy for Natural Resources Used Weak Signals and Mini-Scenarios

The work for the Finnish Strategy for Natural Resources was coordinated in 2009 by SITRA, a public fund with the task of promoting Finland's stable and balanced development, economic growth and international competitiveness and cooperation. SITRA's tasks are defined by law and it reports to the Finnish Parliament. Sustainable well-being is at the core of SITRA's operations.

The strategy was later taken to the government programme of Prime Minister Jyrki Katainen and it was awarded first prize in the national competition of the 2010 European Business Reward for the Environment.

As part of its work, SITRA combined plenty of incidents and weak signals into a mini-scenario of five subjects that sounded pretty radical:

1) Metropolitan Finland moves to Lapland
2) From paper and board to suits
3) Solar power from Sahara
4) Utopia of natural resources
5) Finland as Europe's food supplier.

Seven years have passed since this project, and some parts of the scenarios have started to come true.

## 2.3.3  Corporate Responsibility in Corporate Strategy

There are still many people, especially in SMEs, who dislike the concept 'strategy' and regard it as mere theory and concerning only big companies.

I think strategy suits small companies and big companies and other organizations alike. Strategy is a long-term plan which aims at finding competitive advantage in the market and building a basis for future success. In order to perceive the path to the future, one must take into account the needs and requirements of the operational environment (markets, technology, legislation, competition and so on), understand their effects on future targets and develop the company's resources and procedures for responding to the changes and achieving the goals.

Two Finnish experts on strategy, a retired CEO **Lasse Kurkilahti** and **Professor Toivo Äijö** analysed the strategies of 65 Finnish companies in 2014, based on publicly available material. Their report was published in Talouselämä magazine, number 35/2014. At the beginning of their report, they cite **Professor Richard Rumelt** of UCLA: 'Business executives churn out punchlines and highflown goals and call that their strategy. Boards of directors approve 'strategies' that are mainly wishful thinking. One must require more. The most common mistake is to mix up goals and strategy'.

Kurkilahti and Äijö concentrated on two questions in their analysis: how clearly and sharply the strategy has been defined – especially the company's ability to stand out from their competitors; and how well the realization of the strategy has been ensured.

They had difficulties in finding and analyzing strategic information. Only about one third of the companies had any kind of a strategy definition and only 23 per cent had a well-defined strategy. Only 17 per cent of the studied companies showed clear factors for standing out from the competitors. Strategic goals were missing in over half of the companies, and less than a quarter had defined them well.

I have made the same kind of observations when searching for good company cases where corporate responsibility is included in the strategy.

In listed companies, strategy is the guideline for management, but it is also an important part of public information issued for the investors, who then make conclusions on the company's future plans and development of shareholder value. Unlisted companies, except some big ones, seldom introduce their strategy publicly. Many of them may have defined the strategy but do not want to publish it – maybe due to competition reasons, as they can inform the potential investors in private. Whenever corporate responsibility has been incorporated into the strategy, it is worth noting. Openness and transparency of operations are core elements of corporate responsibility, and strategy gives an excellent opportunity to highlight the importance of responsibility to the stakeholders.

Kurkilahti and Äijö hoped that the companies would at least give the following information to the owners, investors and customers:

* Introduction to the strategy: diagnosis of the company's standing, possibilities and challenges. Vision, mission, values and concrete, measurable goals.
* Definition of strategy, which has to be unique, clear and sharp. The core issue is how the company stands out from its competitors. The definition has to include at least the business concept (what, to whom, how), the basis for success (competitive advantage and core competence) and actions for making the strategy come true.
* Ensuring the realization of the strategy: results and actions needed for them, following the satisfaction of customers and employees, following the work of the Board of Directors.

Corporate responsibility seldom gets to the top of the strategy list. The Body Shop may have been one of the first companies whose brand and operations have rested visibly on responsibility. Most pharmaceutical companies can claim that their operations are based on responsibility, likewise the energy companies whose operations – if they work with renewable energy – have direct effects on climate change. Food production is nowadays a strictly regulated sector, and consumers are so interested in the origin, production methods and health effects of food, that corporate responsibility has become a key competitive weapon for the food industry.

*Corporate responsibility seldom gets to the top of the strategy list.*

In my opinion, corporate responsibility leads to better results when it has been incorporated into the strategy, not necessarily as number one, but at least among the five most important topics. This would mean that corporate responsibility is clearly at the top of management's agenda and would not rely only on the know-how and enthusiasm of middle managers and experts. But corporate responsibility should not be incorporated into the strategy just for corporate image or other such reasons, if it does not naturally suit the strategy. CR cannot be among the competitive weapons in all sectors and all companies, though it should neither be totally neglected.

It is necessary to work in many areas of corporate responsibility regardless of the strategy. The fundamental issues have to be in order, even if the customers and investors did not require any actions. At the same time, one has to make sure that the strategy is not in conflict with the CR principles and goals. For example, if the company announced major plans to start producing peat pellets, and at the same time aimed at continuous reduction of its greenhouse gas emissions, the situation would clearly be conflicting.

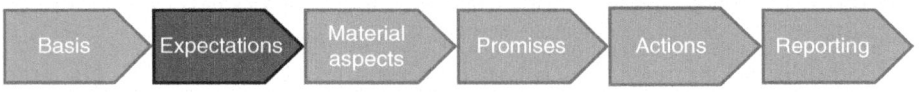

## 2.4 Stakeholder Assessment

One of the fundamental issues in managing corporate responsibility is knowing the stakeholders' expectations. This means that stakeholder assessment is a necessary starting point for analyzing the current CR status of own operations. The assessment consists of the following parts:

• Identifying the stakeholders
• Examining the requirements/expectations of each stakeholder group
• Own actions (present and future) for responding to the requirements/ expectations
• Our expectations of the stakeholders
• Measures of success in the stakeholder engagement.

As stakeholder assessment covers nearly all issues of corporate responsibility – both the present state and the need for future development – it pays to use plenty of time for it.

### 2.4.1 Identifying the Key Stakeholders

Stakeholders are defined as entities or individuals that can be expected to be significantly affected by the organization's activities, products and services; and whose actions can be expected to affect the ability of the organization to successfully implement its strategies and achieve its objectives. There are usually many stakeholder groups, but some of them are key groups in which the company should invest most. Typical internal stakeholder groups are owners, employees and managers/directors, and typical external groups are customers, suppliers, partners, NGOs, trade unions, authorities, media and competitors. It is often useful to also recognize sub-groups; for example, customers can be divided into consumer customers, business customers, domestic customers and foreign customers. Or the authorities can be divided into tax, environmental permit, labour protection and labour force authorities.

The importance of each stakeholder group can be described by giving them weighting on a 1–10 scale, and presenting them in the assessment results in the order of importance (see fig. 2.1).

In the publicly presented assessment it is better to leave the weighting out for discretionary reasons.

## 2.4.2 Examining the Stakeholders' Expectations and Requirements

The more the company representatives deal with the stakeholder representatives, the better the stakeholders' expectations and requirements are known in the company. If the contact with stakeholders is not adequate enough, there is a danger that assessing the expectations and requirements relies on

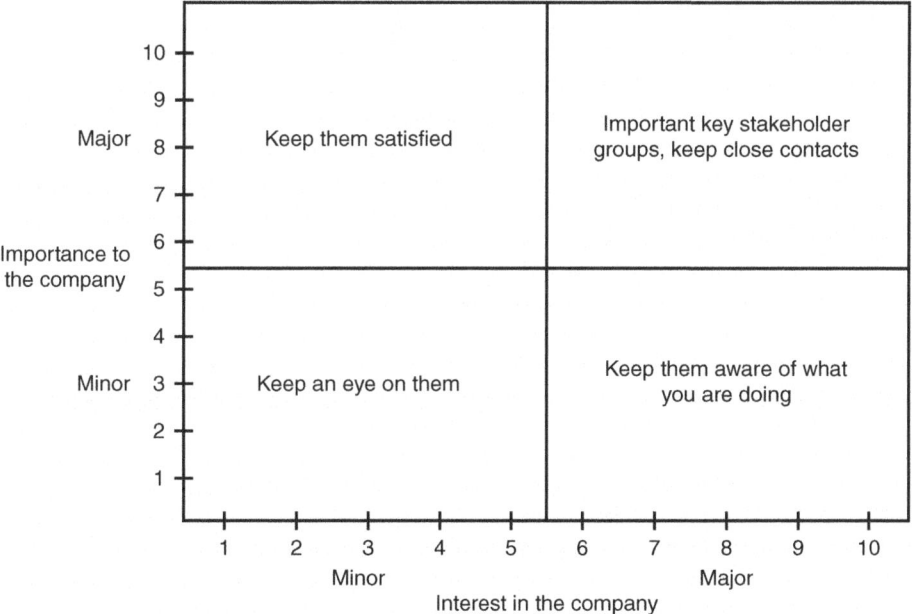

**Fig. 2.1** Assessing the importance of stakeholders

imagination, and the assessment can be incorrect and misleading. Therefore, it is necessary to obtain information directly from the stakeholders.

Information about *customers* is collected by different customer surveys, in which one can add questions about corporate responsibility, if such questions have not yet been used.

The surveys targeted at *suppliers of goods and services* can deal with typical corporate responsibility issues arising in the cooperation.

The opinions of *employees* on the realization and importance of corporate responsibility can be studied in connection with job satisfaction or other similar surveys.

In SMEs, it is easy to make the opinions and expectations of *owners* clear, and the subject should be taken up on the board of directors' agenda. In bigger companies it is useful to make an inquiry as to the owners, as well as to *investors* if the company is listed.

If environmental and other NGOs are important stakeholders, their leading figures should be interviewed personally.

## 2.4.3 Company's Own Actions in Response to the Expectations and Requirements

In this part of the assessment, all current actions as well as those that have not yet been started but are found necessary, should be incorporated into the future action plan. If the steering group's work is still at an early stage, this part as well as the stakeholder assessment as a whole can and should be updated later on.

Corporate management often tends to take a very positive attitude to their own behaviour, especially when presenting it publicly. This enhances the importance of listening to the stakeholder representatives, to make sure that the future action plan is the right choice.

## 2.4.4 Indicators for Monitoring the Success of the Actions

I return to measuring the results of corporate responsibility later in 2.8, as well as under each performance indicator. The stakeholder assessments published by companies usually end up by introducing own actions, without saying with which indicators the results are monitored. It is, however, already useful at this stage to tentatively start thinking about the indicators and, when needed, to specify the assessment as soon as the indicators for reporting have finally been chosen.

## 2.4.5  Our Expectations of the Stakeholders

The stakeholder assessment usually covers only the stakeholders' expectations and requirements of the company. However, the stakeholder relations are interactive relations, including inputs as well as outputs from both parties. It is useful to also think about what the company gets – and sometimes can even require – from its stakeholders. By investing in employees' welfare, the counterpart is better commitment and better labour productivity. From the owners and investors, the company can get funds for projects that are responsible, protect reputation and save costs. From the environmental NGOs, the company can get expertise, and so on.

## 2.4.6  Indicators for Measuring Success of Stakeholder Cooperation

It is possible to measure the results of the company's own actions. Measuring the benefits of stakeholder cooperation is not that easy.

If the company finances a child labour project organized by UNICEF in India, in the neighbourhood of the factories where the company purchases clothes for retail sale, the counterpart is UNICEF India's annual report relating how many children the project managed to get to school instead of going to work. If the company donates money to UNICEF's general campaign for paying for the girls' school in Nepal, it is not possible to measure the counterpart, to allocate the results to the company in question, though the purpose of the donation is good. If a company sells Rose Ribbon products and pays out part of the earnings to the Cancer Foundation to be used for research on breast cancer, the company gets more sales and a better reputation. If a company donates money to the local sports club's junior team, it is not possible to measure the results of such cooperation. Or if a company sponsors the ice hockey world championships as one of the 'platinum partners', it is not possible to measure the benefits, even though the company's logo is visible on every possible occasion.

Successful stakeholder cooperation is an interactive relationship, where it is possible to get measurable outputs from measurable inputs. Donations and other charity cannot be regarded as proper stakeholder cooperation if they do not generate measurable outputs. Charity is important, though, as societies do not seem to run without it, even if all welfare should be paid for with high taxes.

*Stakeholder cooperation is an interactive relationship, where it is possible to get measurable outputs from measurable inputs.*

**Table 2.1** Stakeholder assessment

| Stakeholder group | Expectations of the stakeholders | Our actions | Indicators for measuring our success | Our expectations to stakeholders | Indicators for measuring success of cooperation |
|---|---|---|---|---|---|
| Employees | Permanent job, adequate compensation, good management | Ensuring profitability, welfare program, training managers and employees | Productivity of work, job satisfaction surveys, investments in welfare at work and training | Commitment, quality, productivity, entrepreneur-ship | Level of commitment, loss, productivity, job satisfaction, employee turnover |
| Customers | Long-lasting, safe products, low environmental impacts | Product development, investing in recycling, environmental declaration of products | Development of sales, recycling rate of materials, $CO_2$ and other emissions, customer satisfaction | Feedback | Amounts and types of feedback |

Stakeholder assessment is a cross-section of the mutual dependencies and cooperation between companies and their diverse stakeholders. Assessment is an important part of developing responsible management, but it should not remain as a separate action – stakeholder contacts have to be maintained continuously and regularly.

The results of the assessment discussions can be written down in a table like this model (Table 2.1).

## 2.5    Risk Assessment

Corporate responsibility issues have a clear connection to the company's risk management, especially to reputation risks. Bad results, failures and breaches will get much more publicity than responsible, irreproachable operations, and widely published negative news affect the company's reputation as well as the sales and the share value. In the world of the Internet, the word spreads fast as lightning all around the world.

The saying, 'it took us 15 years to build our good reputation, and we lost it in 15 minutes' has been depressingly true for many companies. There are plenty of examples of irresponsibility causing major damage, like those briefly described below.

**Risks that Have Actualized – Irresponsible Actions Have Remarkable Financial Impacts**

- Top managers of a big retail corporation falsified their financial statement to show better results, in order to raise the value of their options and bonuses. When the betrayal was revealed, the share value of the corporation decreased by 80 per cent and has never recovered. The managers were sentenced to prison.
- Major deceits were found in the financial management of a major American energy corporation and of their auditor company. Neither of the two survived.
- A giant IT company did not comply with EU regulations in their dominant market position. The EU Commission punished them by charging them fines of 561 million euros.
- Some Finnish companies had made a price agreement and illegally over-priced the contracts they made with municipalities. The Market Court decided to charge them fines of over 80 million euros, of which the leading company of the cartel had to pay 68 million euros.
- A certification body had a 75 per cent market share of marine and ship vetting services. One of the auditors took bribes and got caught. The market share fell to 25 per cent.
- A retailer belonging to a nationwide retail chain fired his shop steward illegally. The trade union representing the shop steward announced a consumer boycott of the store. Over 150 negative articles were published in newspapers, not only about the store but also about the chain and its parent company.
- A Finnish mining company was guilty of serious environmental omissions and violations. The company lost its reputation totally, the share price fell close to zero and the company went bankrupt.
- There have been many severe accidents in the clothing industry of Bangladesh – collapses of buildings, fires – and hundreds of workers have died. Although the main reason for the accidents has been the bribing of building inspectors – 'actually I got an official permission for four floors, but I built nine, I am sure the foundation is strong enough, though the soil feels soft' – the reputation of the clothing industry in Bangladesh as well as the reputation of the retailers who buy from there has suffered severely.
- A Swedish textile company founded in 1870 had in 1998 bought an Estonian weaving factory founded in 1857. In 2007, there were plenty of children working on the cotton fields in Uzbekistan as in every autumn, and the Estonian factory was discovered to be using cotton from Uzbekistan. The Finnish, Swedish and British clothing industry and retailers stopped buying from the Estonian factory, which had to lay off half of its 2,400 workers in 2009 and went bankrupt in 2010. The Swedish parent company with 600 workers went bankrupt a few months later. Fortunately, the factories both in Sweden and Estonia found new owners and some of the jobs were retrieved.

In big companies – and hopefully also in smaller ones – crucial risks are recognized, assessed, controlled, monitored and reported systematically as part of business operations. Risks can be grouped into strategic, operational and financial risks. They are connected to incidents or conditions that can complicate or prevent goals being met, or that make the company leave some business opportunities unused. Risk assessments should include more consideration of reputation risks. So far, they seem to concentrate more on the traditional business risks.

*So far, risk assessments seem to concentrate more on traditional business risks than on reputation risks.*

Risk management is conducted by risk management policy, in which the goals, principles, procedures, organizing and responsibilities of risk management are defined. There is also an international risk management standard ISO 31000.

A good example of a risk management system and principles in a big corporation can be found at Kesko Group's website:http://www.kesko.fi/en/investor/corporate-governance/risk-management-and-audit/

Risk management principles at Kesko Group:

- We set our objectives taking account of related business opportunities and risks. We take calculated and assessed risks within the limits set in strategy selections in, for example, expanding business operations, strengthening market position and creating new business.
- When assessing risks, we consider the impacts on people, the environment and reputation in addition to financial impacts.
- We avoid or reduce operational and damage/loss risks.
- We ensure a safe shopping environment and product safety for our customers.
- We create a safe working environment for our employees.
- We minimize the opportunities for crime or malpractice.
- We secure critical operations and the resources needed by them in order to ensure continuity.
- We have crisis management, continuity and recovery plans, plan implementation testing and sufficient insurance cover in place to prevent the realization of risks.
- We maintain risk management costs and resources in proportion to the obtainable benefits.

- We provide information on risks and risk management to stakeholders in accordance with Kesko's corporate governance principles.

As all risks cannot or need not be managed, the risks should be prioritized according to their relevance. Weighting can be given for each risk on the probability of realization on a scale of 1–10 and on the severity of realization also on a scale of 1–10. If the probability gets 3 as weighting and severity gets 9, the total weight is 3x9 = 27. If the probability is 6, but severity is 3, the total weighting is 18. The risks of corporate responsibility can be grouped into economic, social, environmental and other responsibilities.

The risks can be documented in a table like this model in Table 2.2.

**Table 2.2** Risk assessment on corporate responsibility

| Economic responsibility | | | | | |
|---|---|---|---|---|---|
| Object of risk | Description of actualization | Impact on sales | Impact on profit | Impact on share | Other impact |
| | | | | | |
| | | | | | |
| | | | | | |

| Environmental responsibility | | | | | |
|---|---|---|---|---|---|
| Object of risk | Description of actualization | Impact on sales | Impact on profit | Impact on share | Other impact |
| | | | | | |
| | | | | | |
| | | | | | |

Similar tables for Social responsibility and Other responsibility
(in column "weight of risks, x/y", x = the probability of the actualization in scale 1–10, and y = the seriousness of the actualization in scale 1–10)

**Table 2.3** SWOT analysis

| Strengths | Weaknesses |
|---|---|
| • Undisputed support of the management, corporate responsibility as part of the strategy | • Technical preparedness to add the use of recycling material is insufficient |
| • Key persons in production and sales enthusiastic about the new emphasis of responsibility | |
| **Opportunities** | **Threats** |
| • Demand for products made of recycled raw materials is growing fast | • Competition lowers prices and reduces profitability |
| • It is possible to get plenty of information from the 'Resource Wisdom' initiative (a Finnish initiative) | • Domestic supply of recycled raw material is limited |
| • Cooperation with other companies in the region – 'Industrial symbiosis' | |

## 2.6   SWOT Analysis

Before starting to think about the essential issues of corporate responsibility and to define the management principles guiding responsibility, it is useful to carry out a SWOT analysis, to discuss which are our internal strengths and weaknesses and external opportunities and threats with respect to the content and results of our corporate responsibility.

I have made a SWOT analysis (see Table 2.3), imagining that the analysis would be made in a company that considers the need to increase their use of recycled material (of course there are many other CR subjects in this company).

The results of SWOT analysis are associated with many parts of a CR management model, such as stakeholder cooperation, development of management principles, assessment of material performance indicators and action plan.

## 2.7   Evaluation of Own Present State and Comparison with Competitors

Corporate responsibility is nowadays a competitive weapon in many sectors. Therefore, when developing own operations, it is also useful to follow the competitors' actions, first by a thorough evaluation of their present state, later at regular intervals. The comparison should include the company regarded the best in the sector, either in the home country or internationally.

The steering group can choose at which stage this comparison is carried out. When consulting the steering group, I have always placed this procedure at the beginning of the project, before the systematic development work has been started. On the other hand, the stakeholder assessment tends to throw up a lot of thoughts and ideas and makes it possible to get more material for the comparison.

Sometimes, companies of the same sector may have a very open exchange of experiences. Yet, the comparison with competitors should not be based on competitor interviews or company visits. It is enough to use publicly available material: annual reports, CR reports, web pages – that is, the material all other outsiders rely on when determining their conception of the company.

Here is a list of issues taken into the comparison between our own company, the major competitors and the best practice in the sector:

1) Issues describing the management of corporate responsibility

- values, CR vision, CR in the corporate strategy
- stakeholder assessment
- management principles guiding CR
- standards used in managing CR
- CR organization (who develops and coordinates, role of management team, role of board of directors), contact details of persons in charge

2) Action plan for corporate responsibility
3) Performance indicators and reporting (can later be compared with own materiality assessment)

- economic responsibility
- environmental responsibility
- social responsibility (own employees)
- responsibility of supply chain, ways of control
- product safety and healthiness
- relations with society

4) Summary and conclusions

Big companies that have already been reporting for some time can offer a large part of the information sought. As concerns smaller companies, such information, especially the management principles, are often hard to find, because these companies lack the systematics of CR, even though they might have many separate achievements. The evaluation helps with *finding holes in the competitors' operations and gives ideas of how to take such holes into account in developing own work and competitive weapons.*

In the competitor comparison, as later in finishing the report texts, objective, neutral opinion on the own company and on the competitor companies is valuable. If a consultant has been engaged in the development project, the evaluation of own present state and comparison with competitors is part of their work. In smaller size projects, university or college students can be used to collect this type of material.

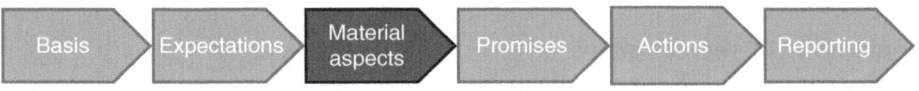

## 2.8  Identifying Material Aspects of Own Responsibility

Before the development project of corporate responsibility can be started, it is necessary to define the boundaries of the project and decide which are the most relevant aspects and how the results should be measured. After this, it is time to define the management principles – promises for different areas of CR – to draw up the action plan for the material subjects and finally to report on the results of the action plan.

The *materiality assessment* has a central role in developing corporate responsibility and reporting, and it should be carried out thoroughly. As I do not see any other sensible scheme for reporting than the GRI Guidelines, I prefer to take GRI indicators as the check-list of materiality assessment. In addition to indicators, GRI includes a thorough list of issues relevant in managing CR – a much more thorough list than I offer in this book. I have noticed that some companies carry out their materiality assessment by concentrating on broader issues such as energy, materials and welfare at work, but I go through the whole GRI list and use the indicator titles and codes in the assessment.

GRI has existed since the year 2000 and has become so common all over the world that it can be regarded as the globally accepted standard for CR reporting – and there is no seriously taken alternative for GRI. Of course GRI has met with critique – I also criticize GRI in many respects – but at least part of the critique comes from the circles that oppose CR reporting in any aspect. GRI reporting offers stakeholders fact-based, comparable information about how responsibly companies have earned their profits.

As the stakeholders' interest in corporate responsibility is predicted to increase 'from here to eternity', it makes sense to take all possible benefits from the best available CR management model and reporting guidelines and trust that the guidelines will improve on every revision round. And immediately some critique: in my opinion, the latest GRI G4 version is not in every way better than the previous G3 version, at least not easier, but I will return to this matter.

In this chapter, I introduce the different sectors of corporate responsibility by using GRI's indicator list as my guideline. As there are plenty of indicators – don't worry, you will not need all of them – I will present them in Chapters 3 to 8. I will refer to the GRI Guidelines by using the code of each indicator (for example, EN1 = Use of materials) as they are now – I will comment on the new GRI Standards in 12.2.2. I do not go deep into the counting methods or collecting of data. I comment on the most common subjects, not all of them, and present my experiences and give hints for what is worth doing. Some counting instructions fit in when they suit the subject. I will not return to the content of indicators in Chapter 12, when dealing with reporting.

It is important for the CR steering group – especially for the chair and secretary – to get thoroughly acquainted with the GRI Guidelines (but see my confession below), before the group starts to carry out materiality assessment and definitions. The group should not get depressed about the fact that the GRI recommendations are extensive and contain a huge number of indicators. Not every indicator applies to all companies, and the group should be able to give a sigh of relief after having waded through the guidelines: 'actually there are not as many indicators for us as it seemed at the beginning'. The group will certainly discuss all subjects at least briefly, as they are very interesting, but usually small companies can manage with 10–15 indicators and middle-sized companies perhaps with 20–25 indicators for developing CR actions and reporting on them. Only larger companies need to adopt most of the GRI indicators.

I must confess that I have never read all the instructions that GRI has so diligently produced, yet still I have been able to produce reports that have been awarded many times over the years. When the amount of information becomes too big to handle, it is best to concentrate on the absolutely necessary parts and hop over everything else. I have always concentrated on the indicators and on some management aspects, but never too much on complicated definitions and theories.

## 2.8.1  Materiality Assessment, Defining the Boundaries

Materiality of aspects is important for developing the strategy, business operations and risk management, at least as much as for CR reporting. Materiality assessment can be used to examine the opportunities and risks. It brings external opinions into evaluating the company's performance, something that is not natural in the internal planning, decision-making and risk management processes.

In order to avoid losing resources by handling every possible, often small question, the wide area of corporate responsibility, covering all of the company's operations, should be defined so that the work is directed to the most material aspects. Material assessment is carried out in the CR steering group and revised about every two years. At the same, *the value chain is defined*: how far do our CR actions and reporting extend – for example, do we extend our responsibility to the production of all raw materials that we use in our products, do we participate in the recycling or disposal of our products after they have been used, or is some part of our company outside of our basic work and value chain.

The value chain concept was for the first time presented by Michael Porter in 1985 in his book, *Competitive Advantage: Creating and Sustaining Superior Performance* (New York, NY: The Free Press). Today, it is typical that companies work in networks. For example in the car industry close to 75 per cent of a car's costs are due to other parts of the network than the car manufacturer – suppliers of components, logistics etc. In hospitals, 15 per cent of the costs are directed at the patient's nursing, and the other costs consist of finances, administration, equipment, buildings etc.

### 2.8.1.1  Defining the Boundaries

According to the GRI definition of boundary, the following should be included:

- all actors that have significant impacts on sustainability (real and probable);
- that are under the decision-making powers of the reporting company;
- whose finances, operations and practices the company can significantly affect.

As concerns aspect boundaries, there are always aspects that are not material in all entities of the company or in the whole value chain. For example, child labour is material in the entities that purchase from developing countries, or greenhouse gas emissions are material throughout the value chain, in every entity and from suppliers to consumers.

Typically, companies report only about their own operations, and too often they define the collection of data to cover only their home country, while the data from their other countries of operations is imperfect or totally missing. The goal must be to include all operations under own decision-making power in the CR management, operations and reporting. The own decision-making power means having over 50 per cent of ownership and votes. The power is dominant when the ownership in between 20 and 50 per cent, and significant when the ownership is less than 20 per cent. The companies in the supply chain or parties connected to the use of the company's products/services are considered to be indirectly affected. In my opinion, the share of ownership is not always decisive as the company may have significant impacts on the ways their contract suppliers or transport partners operate, though there is no ownership included.

*Too often companies define the collection of data to cover only their home country.*

If CR reporting is included in the annual report or the board of director's report, according to the EU the coverage has to be the same as in the financial statement report.

It is still very rare that the external operators in the value chain – for instance suppliers or subcontractors – would be kept under strict control or their actions would be reported, even though their impacts would be significant and it would be possible to have an influence on how they work. Cooperation with such operators is often left at a descriptive stage: 'we require that our suppliers of goods and services follow the same principles as we do'. The more the companies act as partners, the better possibilities there are to expand the coverage of CR efforts and reporting. For example many transport and waste management companies can nowadays produce data on the environmental impacts their services cause to the clients.

Stockmann Group (department and fashion stores) presented their fashion value chain in their CR Report in 2013 on page 11:http://www.stock manngroup.com/documents/10157/17245/CSR±2013±ENG.pdf

## 2.8.2  The Order of Importance of Performance Indicators

GRI recommendations give quite bureaucratic instructions for defining material aspects and stakeholder engagement. I think the assessment of material aspects and their performance indicators belong not only to the company's own experts but also in the stakeholder engagement process (GRI G4–27: *Key topics and concerns that have been raised through stakeholder engagement*).

Own positions and stakeholder positions can be entered into a table (see Table 2.4), where all GRI indicators are addressed by evaluating which stakeholders are interested in them and by giving weighting to them both from the company's and the stakeholders' standpoint. In order to see the difference in importance, it is useful to give weighting to indicators on a 1–10

**Table 2.4** Materiality assessment of performance indicators

| Indicator | 2017 | 2018 | Stakeholders interested in the indicator | Value to stake-holders | Value to us |
|---|---|---|---|---|---|
| **Economic responsibility** | | | | | |
| *Financial results* | | | | | |
| EC1a Economic value generated to stakeholders | | | | | |
| EC1b Economic value generated by countries | | | | | |
| EC2 Financial opportunities due to climate change | | | | | |
| EC3 Coverage of benefit plan obligations | | | | | |
| EC4 Financial assistance from government | | | | | |
| *Market position* | | | | | |
| EC5 Standard entry level wage compared to minimum wage | | | | | |
| EC6 Proportion of senior management hired from local community | | | | | |
| *Indirect economic impacts* | | | | | |
| EC7 Investments in local infrastructure | | | | | |

The value of the indicators to our stakeholders / to us: 1 = very unimportant, 10 = very important

2017/2018: x = included in reporting, y = not yet in reporting, 0 = not a material indicator

And so on, all GRI indicators should be assessed in this table, and then at the end, all material indicators can be emphasized, for instance by highlighting those rows in yellow.

scale, and then choose as material aspects/indicators those that get the weighting of 6 or higher from either the company or the stakeholders (or from both). When reporting becomes actual, the material indicators should be shown in an illustrative matrix, to which I will return in Chapter 9.

The company experts' own evaluations of the weighting for the aspects are naturally subjective, but they have so much experience of most of the issues that the evaluations will be quite realistic.

The stakeholders' evaluations are too often imagined in the CR steering group. It is important to collect information and opinions directly from the stakeholders. This can be done by adding appropriate questions to the job satisfaction surveys and to customer, supplier and investor surveys, by participating in the general or sectoral surveys on reputation and corporate image, and by carrying out specially targeted surveys on the importance of CR aspects.

### 2.8.3 Essential Issues in Materiality Assessment

There are other essential issues behind the materiality assessment than just searching for the material aspects and indicators for the development programme, follow-up of results and reporting. I cite here – with some adaptations – the blog 'Why the Materiality Matrix is useless' published 28 December 2014 by **Elaine Cohen**, founder and Managing Director of the consultant company BeyondBusiness (http://www.b-yond.biz). The blog can be found here: http://csr-reporting.blogspot.fi/2014/12/why-materiality-matrix-is-useless.html?showComment=1420660334832

As you can figure from the name of the blog, Elaine Cohen does not like presenting materiality in a matrix; she prefers making a list. She points out that when dealing with materiality, the following issues should be treated:

Material impacts are:

- The way our business activities affect the lives of our stakeholders and our long-term business viability
- The basis for creating a sustainable business strategy with relevant targets
- Defined as the result of an analytical process that engages internal and external stakeholders about what affects them and how
- The basis for creating sustainability communications including reporting
- Specific to a business, a sector, a geography, an issue
- A catalyst for planning and action
- Connected to a business's core social mission

And on the other hand, Cohen reminds us that the following – often very human – arguments do not belong to materiality assessment:

These are things that material impacts are NOT (or not only):

- What's going to help us make more profit
- What our stakeholders mention in passing
- How we perform
- What we think is politically correct
- What everybody else is saying
- What's easiest to report
- What shows us up best
- What's in fashion
- What the lawyers tell us to say
- What we've always said
- What the assurers can count
- Things we have data for
- A way to appear as though we have written a G4 Sustainability Report

# 3

# Economic Responsibility

Economic performance has always been measured in business, and it has some material aspects that are important when developing the basis for corporate responsibility.

In financial reporting, the company concentrates on describing the financial statement and the business results from the owners' point of view. The corporate value is mainly comprised of the economic result.

In listed companies the relationship between corporate value and corporate responsibility may sometimes seem odd – when hundreds of employees are laid off, the share price usually goes up, sometimes even by over 10 per cent. There is of course a clear logic in this: the company cannot employ people nor buy raw materials just for the sake of being responsible if the demand for the company's products has dropped.

In describing the economic part of corporate responsibility, the question is, what kind of direct and indirect effects the company's actions have on other stakeholders, in addition to the owners. For example, if violations of labour rights are found in the company's supply chain and these violations become public, the customers may regard the company as irresponsible, which will then lead to decreasing sales and diminishing profit. The company then has to lay off employees, the owner dividends are at risk of decreasing, and the share value can go down.

© The Author(s) 2017                                                                 **69**
J. Kuisma, *Managing Corporate Responsibility in the Real World,*
DOI 10.1007/978-3-319-54078-8_3

Respectively, we have to remember that the economic success of a company is the cornerstone of successful corporate responsibility. Companies operating under loss will definitely be much more interested in turning profitable than in the finesses of becoming more responsible. And on the other hand, many CR actions indisputably improve financial results. I will go through them in the environmental and HR sections.

My strong opinion is that *systematic implementing of corporate responsibility will always improve profitability, as the savings will always outweigh the costs.* It is difficult to show that the increase in sales or the rise in share price is due to CR actions, but the impacts of irresponsible actions will become evident much faster and more clearly.

*Systematic implementing of corporate responsibility will always improve profitability, as the savings will always outweigh the costs.*

The minimum information on economic responsibility, which in the GRI recommendations is part of the background information of the company is, in my opinion:

- disclosing the company's main owners (G4-7 and G4-9)
- turnover (G4-9)
- profit before taxes (part of EC1)
- amount of employees (at the end of the year or the average during the year) (G4-10)
- paid taxes, salaries and additional personnel costs (part of EC1).

The data for the economic indicators is normally available in the company's bookkeeping, final accounts and the information systems serving financial administration, such as the purchase ledger. If the company does not disclose its financial results in public, the threshold of handling the issue in the CR report may be high. A smooth way of proceeding would be to increase the amount of public financial information first – as concerns many SMEs, today even finding out who their owners are can be extremely difficult.

## 3.1  Economic Value Generated and Distributed to Stakeholders (EC1)

The basic GRI indicator for describing the company's economic impacts to stakeholders is EC1 (Direct economic value generated and distributed). This indicator shows how the company's revenues are divided between different stakeholders (owners, personnel, investors/financiers, suppliers of goods and services, public sector, social security/pension insurance, common-good organizations) and how much is left in the company for investments and other development. When needed, the data can be allocated to countries, regions, etc. (see more of this in 3.4).

Although the data of this indicator can usually be found in the financial statement (whenever the company publishes financial information to this extent), disclosing such figures side-by-side brings possibilities for interesting comparisons, especially when the economy is fluctuating. For example, it is possible to compare how the stakes of owners, personnel, tax authority and common-good organizations have developed during recessions as well as upturns.

The *tax footprint* is a broader concept than the tax authority's stake in this indicator. No exact definition has been given for the tax footprint, but the purpose is to disclose all taxes that the company has paid and forwarded to society. The forerunners have published this kind of information:

• direct taxes paid by the company (income taxes, real estate taxes)
• taxes and tax-like payments forwarded by the company (such as VAT, excise tax, automobile tax, withholdings from salaries, customs duties)

The tax footprint should be specified by countries of operation.

Support of common-good organizations is in some cases very interesting, though there is no separate GRI indicator for this. I normally also count sponsoring in this support, though it is usually directed at individuals.

Each company can specify this support in their own way, such as dividing it into the following groups: education and research, healthcare, sports, culture, environmental and other NGOs, youth work. It does not make sense to specify small sums, but the larger the sums, the better they show what issues the company regards as important in their donations and sponsoring. In this connection, it would be interesting to see whether and how the companies participate in development aid projects. In particular, the companies that have operations in developing countries, or buy products and services from them, have benefitted from the low cost level in those countries. Having seen the total sum spent on common good, report readers can compare it with the company's turnover or profit if they wish to do so – so why not disclose this percentage voluntarily? What if companies donated 0.7 per cent of their profits to development aid? (A well-known figure taken from the government's budget, though still much disputed and seldom realized.) In some companies, it could be possible to get such a decision from the top management, but what about the owners?

*What if the companies donated 0.7 per cent of their profits to development aid?*

In the US, charity plays a significant role both among companies and among citizens. Sometimes, it seems that money is collected there for almost any purpose, often for activities that in Finland are financed fully through taxation. The latest US initiative – from December 2014 – is the 'Pledge 1%' movement, organized by a couple of foundations. Pledge 1% suggests that companies would donate 1 per cent of their financial capital, 1 per cent of their products (I wonder how the paper machine manufacturers could arrange that) and 1 per cent of their employees' working time (as voluntary work) to charity (www.pledge1percent.org).

## 3.2   Financial Implications and Other Risks and Opportunities Due to Climate Change (EC2)

Climate change is a very serious issue, which will in the long run cause huge costs and changes in behaviour for citizens, companies, as well as society as a whole. At the same time, it will introduce new opportunities for business, the growing cleantech sector being a good example of this. In risk assessment the impacts of climate change will definitely be analyzed as a separate entity, but the financial dimensions of the opportunities are seldom put forth – maybe such sales and profit estimates are regarded as commercial secrets (more on this subject in Chapter 4).

## 3.3   Standard Entry Level Wage by Gender Compared to Local Minimum Wage (EC5)

GRI wants companies to disclose their pay policies, especially in those low wage countries where they have minimum wage legislation. When a company has plenty of workers close to the minimum wage level, it should disclose the entry level wage in relation to minimum wage and also specify it by gender. The purpose is to let stakeholders evaluate how the company invests in the economic welfare and commitment of its workers and how competitive the remuneration is in the labour market in question.

In many countries, the minimum wages have fallen behind cost development due to high inflation rate, and minimum wage cannot therefore be regarded as a 'living wage', a wage that is sufficient for living. I return to remuneration in Chapter 6 and in 5.7.

GRI does not suggest comparing entry wages with the lowest wages in generally binding collective agreements, as such agreements are rare in the world compared with minimum wage laws. It would also be more difficult to compare entry wages with lowest collective agreement wages than with unambiguous minimum wages. Nothing prevents the company from making such comparisons if the aspect is seen as material.

## 3.4  Proportion of Spending on Local Suppliers at Significant Locations of Operation (EC9)

The purpose of this indicator is to get information on how much the company buys products, components and services from the countries where it has significant locations of operation. That is, how much does the parent company based in Finland buy from Finland itself, or from its subsidiary companies in Sweden or Poland. The starting point has been the fear of the poorer countries that foreign companies located in them will not buy products and services from those countries but import most of them from abroad, thus leaving fewer economic benefits to the location countries than they had wished for. A good (or actually sad) example of this is the expansion of big Western European retail chains to the former Eastern Europe, preferring to use Western European products in their ranges rather than those produced in Eastern Europe.

Table 3.1 describes Kesko's purchases divided by country of operations.

Production is today built so much on networks that the purchases directed to the suppliers in the countries of operation do not directly represent responsible sourcing, even though favouring domestic production is still very much in the public eye, in spite of the EU principle of free movement of goods. All goods – like fruit – are not produced everywhere, and goods are not always produced in the country where they are bought.

Anyway, division of purchases is an interesting subject. If there is plenty of supply for the company in the own country, but the purchasing is directed to other countries, the stakeholders may ask why the share of imports is so high.

**Table 3.1** Kesko's purchases by operating country in 2015

| | Suppliers of goods and services in operating country | Purchases from suppliers of goods | | Suppliers of goods and services in other operating countries | Purchases from suppliers of goods | |
|---|---|---|---|---|---|---|
| | number | € million | % | number | € million | % |
| Finland | 9,561 | 4,930 | 80.8% | 2,088 | 1,174 | 19.2% |
| Sweden | 1,049 | 114 | 82.7% | 156 | 24 | 17.3% |
| Norway | 817 | 374 | 97.6% | 41 | 9 | 2.4% |
| Estonia | 882 | 56 | 55.5% | 299 | 45 | 44.5% |
| Latvia | 611 | 24 | 34.3% | 333 | 46 | 65.7% |
| Lithuania | 892 | 78 | 30.8% | 1,195 | 176 | 69.2% |
| Russia | 1,892 | 229 | 95.5% | 60 | 11 | 4.5% |
| Belarus | 1,003 | 51 | 62.3% | 244 | 31 | 37.7% |
| **Total** | **16,707** | **5,857** | **79.4%** | **4,416** | **1,516** | **20.6%** |

If part of the purchases are made in countries outside of the EU, the buyers may face risks linked to labour rights, and the stakeholders may want to know how these risks are controlled. And if there are plenty of locations and employees all around the country but the purchases are split to many regions, the regional figures also get interesting – how much money is used in purchases, wages, taxes by region.

My suggestion on this subject is that *purchases of all significant countries of operations are divided into purchases from each 'home country', from other EU countries and from outside of the EU.* The purchase ledger can produce such statistics if it can put the suppliers = invoicing companies field into postal code order.

Statistics become a bit difficult, because the invoicing company is not always the manufacturer. Some of the invoicing companies may be import companies that sell products from all over the world. Part of those companies are sales offices – for example, a sales office of a Japanese company located in Belgium, which means that the purchase ledger will classify purchases from it as purchases from the EU.

This statistical misconception will decrease slightly if the largest of such invoicing companies are examined separately and it is decided in which group the purchases from them actually belong. The imports that cannot clearly be sorted out can be left as estimates – for example, at Kesko the purchase ledger showed that the purchases from Finland were 72 per cent of the total, but we estimated that the import companies' share of that was approximately 10 per cent.

If the scale of operations is large enough, and dividing the economic benefits by region seems sensible (at least the regional newspapers are very interested in such information), the useful data would consist of salaries, taxes, purchases of goods and services and investments by region. Here also the purchases are compiled by the purchase ledger, and the problem of invoicing is the same as with imports – the headquarters and invoicing unit of the supplier company are usually in the capital area and the production units may be somewhere else. It does not make sense to go deeper into this issue, the explanation that this is the fact should be satisfactory.

The other indicators of economic responsibility are seldom taken among the material aspects/indicators, and I do not elaborate on them here, but just mention the titles:

- EC3 Coverage of the organization's defined benefit plan obligations
- EC4 Financial assistance received from government
- EC6 Proportion of senior management hired from the local community
- EC7 Development and impact of infrastructure investments and services supported
- EC8 Significant indirect economic impacts

Bribery and corruption are, to my mind, part of economic responsibility, but GRI handles them among the company's impacts on society – I come back to these issues in this connection.

# 4

# Environmental Responsibility

As concerns environmental responsibility, most companies will identify material aspects/indicators: use of materials, energy and water, emissions, waste, transport, environmental quality of the products. The data collection and statistics needed for environmental indicators are often insufficient compared to financial and human resources data, which means that the data collection has to be organized from the beginning. Part of the data can nowadays be obtained from service suppliers such as transport and waste management companies.

Environmental responsibility is based on *environmental policy* and *environmental management systems.* Whenever the management system is found important (the business customer may require it from SMEs also), the best choice is to build it in accordance with the *ISO 14001 standard.* The *European Eco-Management and Audit Scheme (EMAS)* is another choice but it is not used as widely as ISO 14001. Applying ISO 14001 does not guarantee good results, but it instructs which actions are needed and how the environmental affairs should be managed systematically. Some companies claim they have organized their environmental management system in accordance with ISO 14001, but the 'in accordance' has not been certified by

© The Author(s) 2017
J. Kuisma, *Managing Corporate Responsibility in the Real World*,
DOI 10.1007/978-3-319-54078-8_4

a third party. In my opinion, such a claim has no value – stakeholders believe only in certification.

The core principle of sustainable development is that we consume as little non-renewable natural resources as possible, and renewable resources only as much as can be replaced when the regeneration is faster than the use. This approach has been common, for example, in sustainable forestry, use of materials and energy, and protection of biodiversity.

I will go through the essential aspects/indicators of environmental responsibility and comment on their importance and the collection of data based on my experiences. The exact information about the indicators and reporting instructions are found in the GRI Implementation Manual.

## 4.1    Materials used (EN1), Share of Recycled Materials (EN2)

It is commonly known that on a global level all renewable natural resources for each year are spent by the end of the summer, and the rest of the year we live at the expense of future generations. This happens especially in developed countries, but China and India are getting closer fast, and after them other developing countries that are eager to raise their standard of living.

This just cannot go on. We need a remarkable improvement of material efficiency. In 1.4, I addressed energy and material efficiency and recalled the long ago published theories Factor Four and Factor Ten. According to Factor Four, if we want to prevent the threat that materials diminish and totally run out, we have to be able to produce the current amount of products with no more than a quarter of the current materials, or if we want to double the production, with half of the current materials. This would mean a remarkable increase in recycling, intensification of loss control and a need for new radical production and product innovations.

The indicator 'Materials used' has been in the GRI recommendations from the beginning, and I find it an essential indicator of environmental performance. Nowadays, GRI recommends breakdown of use into renewable and non-renewable materials, which should be self-evident. The share of recycled materials is now required in almost any branch of industry, and the importance of this issue is growing fast, though recycling of raw materials is not always the best solution in countries with small populations if the final products are used elsewhere.

### 4.1.1 Reporting on Materials Used is Still Small-Scale

Compared to the need, the reporting on renewable and non-renewable materials used is still small-scale. Partly, this is due to the fact that statistics for material purchases are compiled in euros, and seldom according to weight or allocated into material groups. Those responsible for production may be able to plan such data collection combined with receiving incoming materials. Those who work with loss calculations certainly know this subject already. By improving material efficiency and the recycling rate, and by introducing new material innovations, it is possible to save costs as well as reduce environmental impact, which means that GRI indicators and costs should here be examined side-by-side.

The GRI recommendation suggests that the materials are divided into renewable and non-renewable materials, as well as into the following material groups:

- Raw materials (that is, natural resources used for conversion to products or services such as ores, minerals, wood)
- Associated process materials (that is, materials that are needed for the manufacturing process but are not part of the final product, such as lubricants for manufacturing machinery)
- Semi-manufactured goods or parts, including all forms of materials and components other than raw materials that are part of the final product
- Materials for packaging purposes, which includes paper, cardboard and plastics

The Finnish Motiva Group is an expert company promoting efficient and sustainable use of energy and materials. Its services are utilized by the public administration, businesses, communities and consumers. Motiva operates as an affiliated government agency. Motiva has experienced that there is savings potential in every company as concerns material efficiency. The potential varies between 1 and 6 per cent of turnover or between 5 and 20 per cent of material costs. If a company uses a consultant accredited by Motiva for carrying out a material efficiency survey, it is possible to get a 40 per cent subsidy from the Ministry of Labour and Industry. Motiva also offers a material efficiency test for SMEs on their website.

### 4.1.2 Chemicals Should Be Included

The amounts of chemicals, fertilizers and pesticides used are seldom reported, even though their environmental impacts are very big. When chemicals are reported, only their total amount is disclosed, not specifying the chemicals used. Normally, verbal promises are given that the chemical contents of products are monitored and tested, and that the chemicals used in production are bought from European manufacturers and importers who are obliged to register the chemicals with the European Chemicals Agency (ECHA) in line with the EU REACH regulation. The suppliers are allowed to use only chemicals approved by the EU, and the suppliers are often given a list of totally forbidden chemicals and of those that may be used only in a limited way. It is very rare to act the other way around by giving a list of chemicals that have to be used.

*The amounts of chemicals, fertilizers and pesticides used are seldom reported, even though their environmental impacts are very big.*

A responsible company acts transparently. The amount of chemicals used could be proportioned with the production, i.e. x tons of chemicals used per produced ton of products. The next step could be to divide the use of chemicals according to the purpose. The company could then describe their production processes and explain which chemicals are used in each phase, why they are needed and in what quantities.

## 4.2  Use of Energy, Energy Efficiency, Greenhouse Gas Emissions (EN3EN7, EN15–19)

Almost every company classifies use of energy and greenhouse gases generated in energy production as their material environmental impacts, even though the use is not considerable. As production and use of energy are in any case crucial topics of corporate responsibility, it is important that all companies take these topics seriously, particularly as improving energy efficiency not only restrains climate change but also brings forth cost savings.

It's easy for individuals to save energy, whereas changing the structure of energy production from using non-renewable sources to renewable sources is a process that takes time and cannot be reached on scientific grounds alone. There is a political struggle for power on such a big issue, at a national as well as a global level, and money has a major effect on the solutions.

In his interview, Professor **Peter Lund** would like to see companies promote a shifting to renewable energy.

### Peter Lund: Companies Have to Set an Example of Switching Over to Renewable Energy

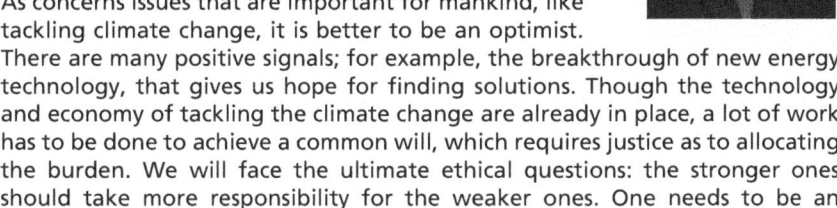

Peter Lund is a professor at the Department of Applied Physics of Aalto University, Finland.

**Are you an optimist or pessimist as concerns keeping climate change within moderate limits?**
As concerns issues that are important for mankind, like tackling climate change, it is better to be an optimist. There are many positive signals; for example, the breakthrough of new energy technology, that gives us hope for finding solutions. Though the technology and economy of tackling the climate change are already in place, a lot of work has to be done to achieve a common will, which requires justice as to allocating the burden. We will face the ultimate ethical questions: the stronger ones should take more responsibility for the weaker ones. One needs to be an optimist, even in facing this challenge.

**Do you believe that the Paris Agreement was a crucial turning point in tackling climate change?**
The Paris Agreement in December 2015 was a remarkable mental step forward in tackling climate change. Although the emission cutbacks promised in Paris are still far from the goal, and plenty of concrete actions are still needed, the conference has clearly affected our way of thinking. The discussion on climate has turned towards substance issues and the means of turning towards a carbon neutral society. We must not lose the optimism reached in Paris, but we must quickly move from words to deeds. Companies can have plenty of influence here by showing the way in practice.

**Energy seems to be a political issue, sometimes even more than a scientific issue. It is difficult to find out which kind of power production we should favour – those now familiar or those at their first steps – to protect our future. What do you suggest?**
As a matter of fact, the reason for climate change is the economy, which stands on an unsustainable footing. When searching for solutions, we should make the economy sustainable as well. The climate will not be saved without energy revolution. The economy will not be saved without innovation revolution. Combining these will succeed by investing in new energy technology and innovations. Renewable energy sources and improving energy efficiency are focal points of this development. It has been estimated that three quarters of the needed reductions of $CO_2$ emissions can be reached with these, half of them with improved energy efficiency only. Already now, more than half of the investments in the energy production in the world are based on renewable energy. At the same time, millions of new jobs and sustainable economic growth are created.

**What should companies do to slow down climate change?**
Many companies see that tackling climate change will give them new business opportunities and possibilities for showing true responsibility. Global

companies like the Swedish IKEA and H&M are transferring their energy use into renewable energy only. Many SMEs implement the Green Office principle and save resources, energy and money. The example given by the companies is important to the whole of society.

**And what should ordinary people and SMEs do, who underestimate their own influence?**
Big rivers start from little streams. The changes start from brave individuals, from the small everyday deeds. As soon as there are many individuals who act towards the same goal, a big swing will take place. Many innovations in clean technology have been born in small companies. Don't forget the influence of social media and require deeds from the politicians!

Energy consumption is classified in many ways: into self-produced energy and purchased energy, into types of energy (electricity, heating, fuels) and into renewable and non-renewable energy, of which nuclear power is taken separately as a category of its own. GRI uses the joule as the unit of measure, but kilowatt-hours seem to be still widely in use. In addition to monitoring total consumption, it is important to follow the energy intensity: proportion the energy use to the company's turnover, amount of employees, surface of premises, tons or pieces produced, whichever of these is the most characteristic data for the company.

Developing consumption statistics for electricity is not too difficult; even when an efficient metering system does not exist, the bills show how much has been consumed and how much it has cost.

Monitoring the use of heating is more difficult, if the company has business locations in malls or office buildings, and the monthly dues paid also cover heating costs. In such cases it would be necessary to cooperate with the estate managers and try to sort out the company's share of the real estate's surface and of the heating consumed.

### 4.2.1  Energy Companies Are Too Slow in Counting Their Environmental Profile

The breakdown of renewable and non-renewable energy sources requires receiving the data from the energy company that has sold the electricity or heating. Many energy companies can already keep to their reporting clients' schedule and publish their environmental profiles early enough at the beginning of the year, but many energy companies are only able to disclose this profile (data on the origin of electricity and heating) as late as in spring or even later. This means that the reporting company has to use data on energy production from the previous year. Changes from one year to another can be significant, especially when a large amount of electricity is delivered through, for example, the Nordic Electricity Exchange (there may be similar arrangements between other countries) and the share of hydropower can vary considerably between years, due to the amount of rain and other weather conditions. It can then happen that using the year-old data means that the emissions of purchased energy are marked down as exceptionally low, because 'there was plenty of water that year, and the share of hydropower was high', but when the correct data on the reporting year finally arrived, the year was actually bad as concerns water resources, and hydropower was replaced by fossil fuels and nuclear power.

Reporting with old and incorrect data is inconvenient. I have suggested that the energy companies should use the time span of 1 October to 30 September instead of the calendar year, when they publish their environmental profiles. This would help their company clients to get the correct profile into their reporting.

## 4.2.2 It Makes Sense to Calculate Your Own Emissions

There are standards available for calculating greenhouse gas emissions, for example Greenhouse Gas (GHG) Protocol (http://www.ghgprotocol.org/) developed by the World Resources Institute (WRI) and the World Business Council for Sustainable Development (WBCSD), and these are mainly used by big companies. ISO standard series (www.iso.org) includes the ISO 14064 standard for the same purpose. The Carbon Disclosure Project (CDP) (www.cdp.net) is an independent non-profit organization whose mission is to collect company specific data on greenhouse gas emissions, prevention of climate change and adaptation to climate change.

SMEs' calculating of greenhouse gas emissions is generally limited to emissions that arise in the production of purchased electricity and heating, for which the figures can be gained from the energy companies, and to transport of goods, other materials and members of the workforce. In Finland, LIPASTO is a calculation system for traffic exhaust emissions and energy use. The system is developed by VTT Technical Research Centre of Finland Ltd. (http://lipasto.vtt.fi/en/index.htm) Similar systems and instructions are found in other countries too, for example in the Netherlands (https://www.rijksoverheid.nl/) and the UK (https://www.gov.uk/government/policies/transport-emissions), and plenty of general instructions are offered on the Internet: (http://www.cefic.org/) and (http://www.cofret-project.eu/Library-Info/Calculation-Tools/).

As climate change is a material aspect to both small and big companies, I recommend that at least one expert in the company becomes familiar with the calculation of emissions – it will then be part of the company's basic know-how from here to eternity. The subject is too wide for an in-depth handling in this book – I will return to it in 4.7.

### 4.2.3   How Carbon-Free Is the So-Called 'Carbon-Free Electricity'

A new theme in calculating the energy emissions is the so-called 'carbon-free electricity'. It is true that one can get carbon-free electricity by using renewable energy sources in production, but this takes into account only the production phase, not the whole life cycle, which includes construction of the power plants in question. It is the same with nuclear power: the electricity produced is carbon-free, but the $CO_2$ emissions from the construction of nuclear power plants have been huge. Uranium has been extracted to produce the energy, and there will be nuclear waste at the other end of the life cycle.

In Germany, it is typical to calculate the emissions of nuclear power over the whole life cycle. GRI's instructions for calculations do not require the life cycle approach, and it should of course be adapted to all forms of energy – and this would be really difficult. I have found one calculation of the life cycle calculation for nuclear power plants by Professor Benjamin K. Sovacool of the Danish University of Aarhus (http://www.sciencedirect.com/science/article/pii/S0301421508001997).
He has put together 103 life cycle studies of nuclear power plants and has received a mean value of 66 g $CO_2$e/kWh, though the range of emissions was as large as from 1.4 grams to 288 grams. For comparison, the average $CO_2$ emission of purchased electricity was 209 grams per kWh in Finland in 2015 (without the life cycle approach).

Many companies claim that as they have bought carbon-free electricity, their emissions from the purchased electricity are zero. Unfortunately, the issue is not as simple as that. The emissions arise in the production of the power plant, and one customer deciding to buy carbon-free electricity does not change the structure of production, Only when the carbon-free purchases exceed the volume of the carbon-free production, does the electricity company have to increase the use of renewable energy sources in their energy production, and the total emissions will then decrease at the national level. It is of course possible that the electricity company has already increased the use of renewable sources, or that it concentrates totally on renewable energy (I buy energy from a company that has only hydropower and wind power – if they get many more clients, they will invest in a new wind power plant.) And the issue gets more complicated if the supplying electricity company buys part of the electricity through the Nordic Electricity Exchange or imports it from a neighbouring country.

GHG Protocol and Carbon Disclosure Project accept green (carbon-free) electricity under certain conditions. The Hotel Carbon Measurement Initiative (HCMI) does not take green electricity into account but uses national average emission coefficient as its basis:

https://www.wttc.org/mission/tourism-for-tomorrow/hotel-carbon-measurement-initiative/http://www.ecompter.co.uk/benefits-hotels/

## 4.2.4 Environmental Label for Electricity

It is also possible to buy 'certified' eco-labelled electricity, which includes a guarantee of origin of feeding green electricity into the electrical grid and guarantees, by investments to a climate fund, that part of the electricity sales will be used for producing new renewable energy. The EcoEnergy label was originally introduced by the Finnish Association for Nature Conservation. It is administered by 42 environmental organizations in 34 countries – the Finnish Association runs the secretariat. You can find the members and the EcoEnergy suppliers at their website http://www.ekoenergy.org/

## 4.2.5  Carbon Compensations

All over the world there are plenty of so-called carbon funds, which finance projects aimed at decreasing greenhouse gas emissions in developing countries. Examples of such projects can be found on the website of BASE (Basel Agency for Sustainable Energy), which is a UNEP Collaborative Centre based in Basel, Switzerland: http://energy-base.org. Have a look also at the website of the World Bank's Carbon Finance Unit: https://wbcarbonfinance.org/Router.cfm?Page=Funds.

Many companies have compensated for their own $CO_2$ emissions by paying a corresponding sum to one of the carbon funds and then disclosing in their own reporting what kind of projects this fund finances and what are the results accomplished. Responsible funds let third party auditors inspect their projects to make sure that the money is used properly and the reported results are truthful.

Climate change is a global problem and it is possible and useful to prevent it by participating in projects anywhere in the world. It is important that the project is proved to be accountable and cannot be used for greenwash (and who would want to pay for such a greenwash project!) The company paying the compensation cannot, however, claim in their own reporting that they are a carbon neutral company. The compensation does not reduce the company's own emissions, but the emissions are diminishing in the project that the company has financed in another country far away. The correct way is to report own emissions and emissions diminished elsewhere beside each other, which will show that the company has taken global responsibility by controlling the global emissions with its own though very small input. I return to compensations in 4.7.

*Tradable emission permits* mean arrangements whereby the plants that put out harmful emissions are obliged to own a certain amount of *emission permits* per unit of their emissions, and the plants/companies can trade these permits between each other. Emission trading aims at restricting harmful emissions in a cost-effective way. The permits are granted by emission trading authorities, in Finland the Energy Authority. In addition to $CO_2$ emissions, the internal emission trading in the EU also consists of some emissions from aluminium production and the chemical industry. A company participating in the EU emissions trading scheme can also apply for the permits given out free of charge. More information about the EU scheme from here: http://ec.europa.eu/clima/policies/ets/index_en.htm

Emission trading requires much longer text and debate, but there are better experts for this purpose. As I am more or less a layman on this subject, I have never learned to understand how trading the emission permits would decrease the total amount of $CO_2$ emissions. I understand that if the emission permits raise the costs of the company, they try to reduce the emissions. But if a company reducing the emissions can sell emission permits to another company for money, isn't that called a zero-sum game? Anyway, the word 'emission permit' sounds very positive in the midst of climate change development. I hope I am incorrect and emission trading will bring good results.

## 4.2.6  Reducing Emissions

When reducing emissions, it is important to improve energy efficiency and reduce the use of energy in every possible way. When I addressed energy efficiency in 1.4.2, I took up the old Factor Four theory: if production will presumably double from the present into some unspecified future, it has to be accomplished with half of the raw materials and energy used today, in order to put sustainable development into effect. Factor Four, like the much stricter Factor Ten, seems to have disappeared, at least from the energy-political discussions, as the demand for energy is estimated to be increasing continuously even in developed, high-technology countries.

Reducing food wastage reduces both $CO_2$ emissions and use of water. According to the survey, 'Food Wastage Footprint: Impacts on Natural Resources' by the FAO (Food and Agriculture Organization of the UN), more than one third of the world's food production will get wasted – approximately 1.3 billion tons. The amount of water used for its production equals the annual flow of the river Volga in Russia, and the energy used for the production leads to 3.3 billion tons of $CO_2$ emissions. If that food wastage was a country, it would rank third in the emission statistics after China and the US:http://www.fao.org/news/story/en/item/196220/icode/ http://uk.businessinsider.com/these-6-countries-are-responsible-for-60-of-co2-emissions-2014-12?r=US&IR=T

Researchers estimate that one third of existing oil reserves, one half of gas reserves and over 80 per cent of coal reserves should be left in the soil instead of using them, in order to keep global warming under two degrees when proceeding towards the deadline year of 2050. Still, around 670 billion dollars were used in 2014 in the search for new fossil fuel reserves – the Arctic area has been one of the destinations, but we have heard that Alaska will now be preserved. The future looks quite alarming for China, Russia, the US, Saudi-Arabia and the Middle East countries, and many industrial companies and investors – there will be big changes ahead. Two articles on this subject (and many others) can be found here: https://blogs.ucl.ac.uk/future-energy/2015/03/12/leaving-fossil-fuels-in-the-ground-how-much-where-and-over-what-time-frame/; http://www.ucl.ac.uk/news/news-articles/0115/070115-fossil-fuels

*Around 670 billion dollars were used in 2014 in the search for new fossil fuel reserves.*

According to a survey report published by the WWF, The Natural Resources Defense Council and Oil Change International, the OECD countries have invested public money worth over 73 billion US dollars in foreign coal projects in the last eight years. The biggest investors have been Japan, South Korea and Germany. The reasoning for these investments has been the growing demand for energy in developing countries, but as a matter of fact, no money has been given to low-income countries, but mostly to export projects of own technology companies.

Oil Change International has studied the public investments of G20 countries thoroughly and found out that there were huge public subsidies for fossil fuels in 2013 and 2014:

- *National subsidies* delivered through direct spending and tax breaks of $70 billion
- Investments by majority *state-owned enterprises (SOEs)* that account for another $286 billion
- *Public finance* from majority government-owned banks and financial institutions that amounts to another $88 billion per year on average in 2013 and 2014.

The report can found here: https://www.odi.org/sites/odi.org.uk/files/odi-assets/publications-opinion-files/9958.pdf

It will be interesting to see whether the Climate Agreement signed in Paris by almost 170 countries will come true in practice. As China, the US and the European Union have ratified the agreement and it came into force in November 2016, we can have more positive expectations of the practical efforts; hopefully there will be no setbacks in the political circles. Of course, one setback could be the new president of the United States, who does not believe in climate change, and has said that the US commitment to the Paris Agreement will be cancelled. We will see – I still hope that the facts will win.

### 4.2.7  The Material on Climate Change is Endless on the Internet

As you have noticed, I regard climate change as a crucial subject for companies and mankind as a whole. It is possible to find as much material on climate change on the Internet as one wants to search for and study.

A very illustrative presentation about the origin and impacts of $CO_2$ emissions, is the video 'A single ton of $CO_2$ e', which lasts for 45 minutes: http://www.circularecology.com/what-is-1-tco2e-video.html#. VMNrkjgcSM8

Mr **Petteri Taalas**, former Director General of the Finnish Meteorological Institute, today Secretary-General of the World Meteorological Institute, is a globally respected expert whose presentations can be found on YouTube, like this one: https://www.youtube.com/watch?v=CvBMVOTiLSo

On YouTube, you can also find an illustrative animation film about the history of $CO_2$ emissions, called 'Time history of atmospheric $CO_2$': https://www.youtube.com/watch?v=UatUDnFmNTY and a video by NASA: 'Nasa video shows carbon dioxide pollutions path across planet': http://www.new republic.com/article/120310/nasa-video-shows-carbon-dioxide-pollutions-path-across-planet

And for those of you who want to lighten the gloomy mood – and maybe also get a bit frustrated – go to www.youtube.com and search for videos with the keywords 'Al Gore Climate Change'. Beside Al Gore's serious statements you will get 'news', interviews and discussions with various politicians and 'experts'. In many of these videos, Al Gore is called a liar and the speakers laugh at climate change, regarding it as an indifferent subject that does not really exist and on which human beings have no effect whatsoever.

## 4.3  Biodiversity Issues

These issues are not material in all countries nor all sectors. They may be part of the supply chain's environmental impacts, arising for example in disputes on palm oil production or logging of tropical wood. An environmental permit can include regulations for the protection and reconstitution of areas such as mines or sandpits, and the constructors of roads and suburbs know the power of protected animals like flying squirrels. There are exact instructions on biodiversity in the GRI Guidelines.

## 4.4    Use, Recycling, Reuse of Water EN8–10, Water Discharge EN22

In Finland, Sweden and Norway, we are used to the fact that water is abundantly available and that companies can use municipal water and waste-water services. The biggest proportion of water is taken from the water supply system, which makes it easy to get accurate data on the use of water, whereas very few companies have any data on the use of surface water, ground water or rainwater, more often on the recycling of water. Discharges to water systems are also rare in these countries, except in some special cases, as treatment of wastewater has been regulated under environmental legislation and in terms of environmental permits. The condition of the Baltic Sea unfortunately indicates that the runoffs from agriculture are still considerable.

In developing countries and in some European countries, there is a short-age of water and the municipal wastewater system is almost non-existent, which makes efficient use of water and responsible treatment of wastewater much more valuable than what we in the most developed countries have happened to think. Also reporting becomes more difficult – I have not succeeded in finding good cases.

Use of water has become a material issue in product development as well. We have already seen some examples of declaring the water footprint of products based on the ISO 14046 standard. Some companies and organiza-tions have developed a water footprint counter and placed it on their website, like the global chemicals company Kemira (headquarters in Finland), serving customers in water-intensive industries: www.waterfootprintkemira.com. More information on product-specific water footprint and counting can be found on the website of Water Footprint Network: www.waterfootprint.org/?page=files/productgallery

I return to this issue in 4.7.

## 4.5    Other Significant Air Emissions EN20 and EN21

Emissions of ozone-depleting substances (ODS) are not such a hot topic as they were some years ago, because the use of ODS is forbidden in most sectors in the EU and elsewhere and the ozone layer has started to recover.

Air pollutants, such as NOx, SOx, VOC and so on, arising in traffic and industrial processes, have significant environmental impacts as they cause deterioration of air quality, forest devastation and acidification. These emissions are partly regulated by environmental legislation, and companies that produce them have to report on them, as usually happens.

## 4.6    Handling of Waste and Hazardous Waste EN23 and EN25, Significant Spills EN24

A fundamental indicator of waste handling today is how much waste has been sent to recovery and to landfill, and how much hazardous waste has been handled. The recovered waste has to be categorized according to waste types and disposal method. Stakeholders find the categorization important, as they can then see what waste types are the most typical in the company's processes and what will happen to them afterwards. If there is no categorization given but only the percentage of recovered waste, for instance 92 per cent, reporting does not seem accountable, even if the figure is correct. GRI recommends the following disposal methods to be taken into the categorization:

- Reuse (e.g. reuse of drink bottles)
- Recycling (e.g. collecting aluminium drink cans for making new cans)
- Composting
- Recovery, including energy recovery (making products other than the collected ones)
- Incineration (mass burn, in many countries used for producing energy)
- Landfill
- Other (to be specified by the organization)

There are own instructions for handling and reporting of hazardous waste.

Though GRI does not require categorization of materials, I would recommend disclosing statistics on them also – many waste management companies can provide such data for their customers. Even though the high recovery rate is good as such, some stakeholders would like to know what the recovered waste consists of: the shares of cardboard, plastic, metal, glass and so on.

The EU waste policy places prevention of waste and reduction of harmfulness as its starting point. The waste hierarchy is described in Figure 4.1. Companies should start

*Companies should start by describing their efforts to prevent waste and only after this give information about their waste disposal.*

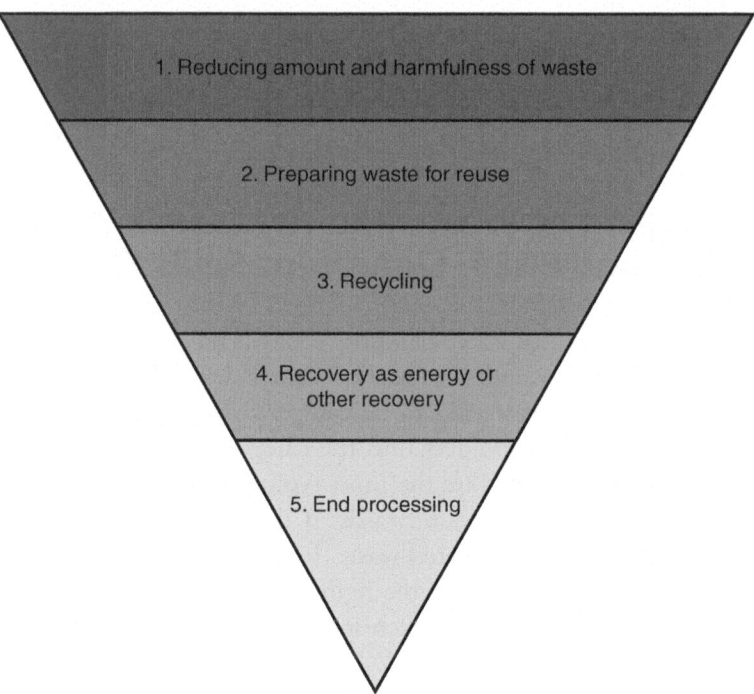

**Fig. 4.1**  The waste hierarchy

their reporting on waste management by describing their efforts to prevent waste and only after this give information about their waste disposal. Reducing the waste quantities and increasing the recovery will bring cost savings, which lead to possibilities of addressing the environmental performance and the financial performance side-by-side.

According to the latest waste law that came into force in Finland in 2012 (check your own country's legislation at your Ministry of Environment!), at least 50 per cent of community waste should have been recycled by the year 2016. If waste is created, the waste owner has to prepare it primarily for reuse and secondarily for recycling. If recycling is not possible, the waste has to be recovered in other ways, for example as energy. The waste can be placed in landfill or disposed of in other ways only if recovery is not possible. In the future, landfills will take in mainly topsoil, waste rock, ash and scum.

The waste owner is responsible for organizing waste management – this applies to waste from business, including community waste. By 2020, at least 70 per cent of demolition waste and rubbish should be recovered as material. The regulations on producer responsibility of packaging have also been tightened.

Of significant spills (oil, fuel, waste, chemical and other spills), locations, volumes and environmental impacts should be reported.

# 4.7  Environmental Impacts of Products and Services EN27–28

Responsible companies require that their suppliers of goods and services comply with the same environmental principles and similar environmental management that they themselves comply with. The basic starting point is usually an ISO 14001 certified environmental management system or the sector's own international standard, such as GlobalG.A.P. for imports of fruit and vegetables, FSC and PEFC in forestry. As concerns business relations, ISO 14001 is a good operating model, as the customers will then know what kind of a system the certificate holder applies to its operations. However, ISO 14001 does not include performance indicators, and thus it is not possible to evaluate how successful the environmental actions have been.

As the reporting develops, more and more companies can today offer essential indicators of environmental performance. However, their interpretation – whether the results are good or bad – has to be left to experts, who can look at the data on energy, emissions, waste and other indicators and analyze the order of the company's environmental impacts and the ways how the company has mitigated them. The indicators describing all CR actions are important, for example for responsible investors.

## 4.7.1  More Thorough Information for Professionals

The professional buyers of goods and services are, of course, interested in the total picture of the seller company's responsibility, but as their own purchasing principles and criteria become more exact, they want more information about the environmental impacts of goods and services offered to them – I return to the social impacts later. Consumers are much worse at determining companies' environmental responsibility based on the overall figures – it does not influence their purchasing decisions very much if the manufacturer of the product has used 285 GWh of energy and created 2,356 tons of waste. Therefore, product- and service-specific environmental indicators and labels are needed, which can in some cases be quite simple, but in most cases are not.

*Environmental declarations* have been available for quite a long time, for example in the construction sector. One of the forerunners is the Swedish/ Finnish SSAB/Ruukki. According to Ruukki:

> 'product life cycle environmental impacts have become an important driver in material and product choices especially in the construction sector. It is the product manufacturer's duty to offer this information. Ruukki's environmental product declarations offer specific environmental information on Ruukki's production, whereas many others only publish generic data about the industry. Ruukki's strategy is to develop *sustainable energy efficient products* and participate in *decreasing the global environmental impacts* of the construction industry. The declarations demonstrate the environmental benefits that can be gained by using Ruukki's steel products. Efficient manufacturing of steel reduces environmental impacts of buildings and decreases the total costs focused at the owner of the building'.

http://www1.ruukki.com/Construction/Environmental-product-declarations

## 4.7.2 Easy-to-Adopt Environmental Labels for Consumers

Consumers find it impossible to screen the enormous product and service selection to find the more environmentally-friendly choices. The legislator has to give the framework for the companies' environmental actions, and the raw material producers, industry and trade have to take care to respond to the environmental requirements, both by complying with the laws and regulations and by exceeding the compulsory requirements for competitive reasons. Unfortunately, consumers still put a lot of weight on price, and they have to be educated to make choices for the good of the environment. Product-specific (and service-specific) environmental labels make this work much easier.

To be efficient, environmental labels need to be neutrally granted, well-known and widely used. Too many labels on the same issue confuses both trade representatives and consumers. The Nordic Swan label is well-known and trusted, whereas the EU Flower has not achieved the same status. There are plenty of organic labels, as well as energy labels and who knows what. It is not possible to start introducing all possible labels here – each of you knows the labels in your own sector and can search for more exact information.

## 4.7.3 Results Through Product Development

The product and service assortment can be separated into groups, based on the environmental quality and placed on the Gauss curve (see Fig. 4.2) The best products, usually with environmental labels, are placed in group 1. In groups 2, 3 and 4 there are products that are neutral as concerns environmental quality, neither bad nor good, though the bigger the number of the group, the worse the products are regarded. Group 5 consists of those products (or services) that are the most harmful to the environment and should be totally excluded from the assortment.

The product development should aim at removing the products gradually to a better group and finally to group 1. Those who grant the labels want to give them only to the best products/services in the sector, limiting the size of that group, for example, to the best 10 per cent of the products and making the criteria stricter step by step. In some sectors, product development has been so successful that all products have finally complied with the label requirements (such as printing paper), and as the original competitive advantage of the label has been lost, the manufacturers have given up the label for cost reasons.

This can sometimes lead to tragicomic situations. When I was in charge of Kesko's CR reporting, I always insisted that the report was printed on environmentally labelled paper – the amount of paper needed was over one million sheets. The answer I got from the printers was that the Finnish paper mills have given up the Nordic Swan label. I did not find it sensible to write down on the last spread of the report the following text: 'The printing paper used for this report complies with the Nordic Swan label requirements, but it

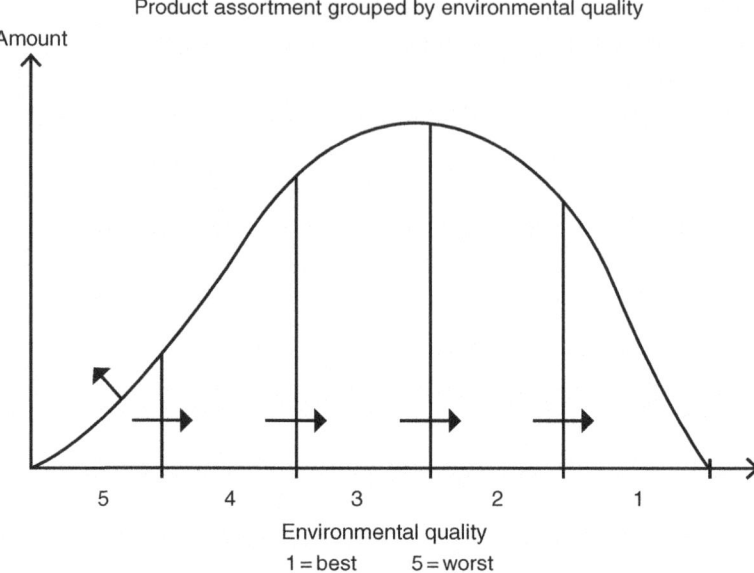

Fig. 4.2  Product assortment grouped by environmental quality

does not have the label'. We then bought Nordic Swan paper from Denmark.

Products with fewer environmental impacts are often more expensive than the average products, as their raw materials, production technology and smaller volume of production raise their prices. Consumers are asked in different surveys whether they are prepared to pay higher prices for environmentally or socially responsible products. The answer is always yes, they are. But in practical purchase situations they tend to forget their preparedness, as cheap prices attract them too much. The questions of the surveys should be changed to something like this: 'This product has been manufactured responsibly and is sold at normal price. Are you willing to buy a cheaper product which is manufactured irresponsibly?' See more arguments for this opinion in Table 4.1.

*'This product has been manufactured responsibly and is sold at normal price. Are you willing to buy a cheaper product which is manufactured irresponsibly?'*

**Table 4.1** Ethical and unethical low prices

| |
|---|
| **When the low prices are based on:** |
| • innovations; |
| • advanced technology; |
| • energy and/or material efficiency; |
| • mass production and; |
| • short distribution channel, |
| They are **ethically low prices.** |
| **When the bargaining in manufacturing and distribution goes 'under critical point',** **as concerns:** |
| • quality of raw materials; |
| • protection of environment; |
| • product safety; |
| • work safety and other working conditions; |
| • remuneration; |
| • social security and; |
| • labour rights as a whole, |
| The process ends up with **unethically low prices.** |
| Ethically low prices should be called **normal low prices.** |
| Unethically low prices should be called **too low, unacceptable prices.** |

# 4.8 Carbon and Water Footprint in Product Labelling

## 4.8.1 Carbon Footprint

As climate change is such an exposed topic, the interest in $CO_2$ emissions has progressed from company level to products and services level. A Carbon footprint has been calculated on various products – in some cases it has even been marked on product packages. The UK retail chains, for example Tesco, have been forerunners of this development, though the speed of progress has been much slower than was originally promised. Calculation is needed, as it should cover the whole life cycle of the product, and consumers are not yet well aware of which footprint is good and which bad. If the carbon footprint of a product used in cookery is 180 grams of $CO_2$ emissions per 100 grams of the product (the life cycle ends on the shelf of the food store), how should one deal with this information if there is not very much comparable information available? And how many grams of emissions does one create when cooking at home?

The easiest carbon footprint that consumers have already learned to use and compare is the one for $CO_2$ emissions of cars, though the EU regulations for calculating them produce results that are about 20 per cent lower than those based on road tests. And one car brand invented a new way of marketing by announcing the emissions of their new hybrid model per person (17 g per person!). They did not say that the car is registered for seven persons and that the emissions do not depend very much on the amount of passengers.

There are many tools available for calculating the carbon footprint. I have not tested them, but you can try them:

CCalC-tool http://www.ccalc.org.uk/software.php

SULCA – Sustainability Tool for Ecodesign, Footprints and LCA (Life Cycle Analysis), developed by the VTT Technical Research Centre of Finland https://www.simulationstore.com/sulca

There are standards for calculating a product-specific carbon footprint: ISO 14067, of which there are not yet many applications, and PAS 2050 in the UK and the Carbon Trust certification based on it. An international organization, PEF World Forum (www.pef-world-forum. org), has been established to develop calculation models and exchange experiences.

Here is the link to the ISO 14067 standard: http://www.iso.org/iso/home/news_index/news_archive/news.htm?refid=Ref1643

Product-specific carbon footprints will become more common in business-to-business trade as the products are offered to professional buyers, who have much more knowledge of the subject and who can include environmental criteria in their competitive tendering. The environmental product declarations by Ruukki are one example of this trend: http://www.ruukki.com/b2b/support/certificates-and-declarations, another one is the Finnish office furniture manufacturer Martela: http://martela.com/carbon-footprint. Martela's corporate responsibility specialist **Anne-Maria Peitsalo** explains why and how Martela has incorporated carbon footprint calculations into their product development.

## Anne-Maria Peitsalo: Carbon Footprint Calculations Are Part of Martela's Product Development Work

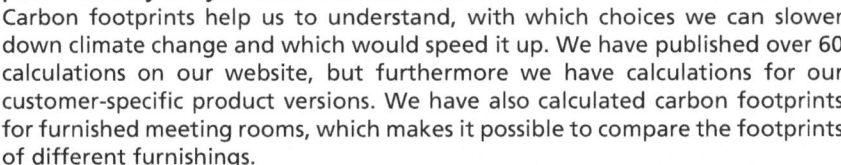

Martela is a listed Finnish company manufacturing office furniture. Anne-Maria Peitsalo is Martela's corporate responsibility specialist (http://martela.com/carbon-footprint).

**Martela has calculated the carbon footprint for over 60 products. Why did you start these calculations?**
Carbon footprints help us to understand, with which choices we can slower down climate change and which would speed it up. We have published over 60 calculations on our website, but furthermore we have calculations for our customer-specific product versions. We have also calculated carbon footprints for furnished meeting rooms, which makes it possible to compare the footprints of different furnishings.

We started in 2011 by hiring a student to calculate carbon footprints of Kari and Picco chairs as a thesis.

The thesis provided a theoretical background to our calculations and reference values for the results we got by somewhat easy calculations. The thesis also helped us in studying the environmental impacts of our supply chain of components. However, a thorough life cycle assessment takes time and is a laborious and expensive way of assessing a product's environmental impacts.

**Where can one find research data and similar calculations?**
On the Internet you can find British research reports, for example by Fira International Ltd and the British Contract Furnishing Association. The Centre for Remanufacturing and Reuse has done research on the climate impacts of furniture recycling. The climate calculator of the WWF Finland (http://climate calculator.net/en) is also suitable for calculating the environmental impacts of procuring furniture.

The emission values given by the WWF's calculator for product types are for example: electrically adjustable table 250, chair 30 and high cupboard 70 kg $CO_2$ e. Martela's own calculations for similar products are: Pinta EQ electrically adjustable table 76, JamesH chair and Combo cupboard 49 kg $CO_2$ e.

**How are the calculations made? Are there outsiders involved?**
The calculations are made as part of the product development work with the footprinter™ software. The software licence is chargeable and the software is updated annually with Martela's statistics of energy consumption, waste and so on. The licence holder, Natural Interest Oy, helps us in applying the calculation principles and in developing our calculations.

**How have your customers taken to the carbon footprint? Any other experiences?**
The calculations are on our website for the free use of customers. One of our big clients in Norway told us that the existence of the calculations was a crucial factor when they chose their supplier. When some customers have given us offer requests, we have attached calculations of the environmental impacts of the offered products to our offer. Many customers are, however, interested for example in the LEED certification, which gives a totally different content to the environmental assessment.

> **How do you plan to continue?**
> Calculation of carbon footprints develops all the time. The more specific the calculation practice is, the closer to the 'correct' value one can get. In practice, the calculations still have to use the material-specific generic coefficients. For the time being, we will continue calculating carbon footprints as part of our product development, because this give us a general view on the environmental impacts of our material and logistics options.

## 4.8.2  Water Footprint

The water footprint is a newcomer as to product information and probably even more difficult for consumers than the carbon footprint. In most of the developed countries, we are used to getting our water from the municipal water supply system, and shortage of water is a very rare incident. From the global perspective, there is shortage of water in many areas, and the situation gets worse.

Municipal water supply covers only part of the availability and use of water. Some companies calculate the product-specific use of water and amount of wastewater reliant on municipal water supply only, whereas those who promote a vegetarian diet and oppose the use of meat and dairy products calculate differently – in accordance with the calculations by the Waterfootprint organization, covering all forms of water – ending up with large figures. ISO 14046 standard tries to create a unified practice for the calculation: https://www.iso.org/obp/ui/#iso:std:iso:14046:ed-1:v1:en

Here some company examples:http://www.theheinekencompany.com/sustainability/focus-areas/protecting-water-resources; www.coca-colacompany.com/setting-a-new-goal-for-water-efficiency

In seminars I have seen illustrative examples of calculating a product-specific water footprint. It has been interesting to notice that as the networking of production means today that components of the products are manufactured in many countries, a big part of the water footprint of a product we have regarded as 'Finnish' is actually generated in Spain or even India.

Even though we have ISO standards for carbon and water footprints, their calculation and information used in marketing depend very much on the company's own expertise, as there is no certification for product labelling in this area. One day, the authorities in charge of consumer protection should offer a solution to this sometimes misleading marketing by requiring use of objective, highly reliable data. Meanwhile, some companies have proceeded voluntarily, such as Finnair, whose $CO_2$ calculation model has been assured by PwC.

### 4.8.3 Environmental Criteria in Public Procurement

The public sector's purchase of products and services can amount to 20 per cent of GDP. The public sector's role as a power player in the market is thus remarkable, especially when there is a demand for products that represent high efficiency in the use of energy and/or materials and for products with less harmful environmental impacts.

The EU Commission published a recommendation and guide on the use of environmental criteria in 2004. Still, the application of environmental criteria has gained ground very slowly. National governments have tried to speed up the development by obligating government offices and municipalities to take into account green-tech solutions in all public procurement.

About 75 per cent of public procurement takes place in municipalities. Of these purchases, more than half are purchases of services, the other half is consumer goods and maintenance of properties. As to environmental impacts, the most meaningful purchases are vehicles, electricity, heat, foodstuffs and food services.

## 4.9 Transport of Materials, Products and Employees EN30

Transport always creates significant environmental impacts: use of energy, emissions to air, maybe also emission to the water system, waste, noise and spills. The environmental impacts of transport are material indicators, especially in sectors in which the production requires large quantities of materials and in which large amounts of products are manufactured or bought for selling and then transported to all parts of the country and to other parts of the world. In some companies the employees travel a lot, and many of these trips are made by vehicles that have large emissions: by passenger cars and by air.

In economic responsibility, one indicator is to divide purchases between own country, other EU countries and countries outside the EU. The longer distance the purchased goods have to travel, the greater their environmental impacts are, depending of course on the mode of transport. Shipping has the lowest $CO_2$ emissions, but ships create, for example, plenty of sulphur emissions. Trucks are needed at least for part of the journey, use of air freight is quite rare. Air transport should not always be criticized – it is important to take into account the whole life cycle of the transported goods (see examples of cut flowers and cars later).

## 4.9.1  Purchase Delivery Transport

If environmental impacts of purchase transport are included in the buyer's environmental calculations, the seller and the buyer have to cooperate and decide on division on work, so that both of them do not calculate and publish the same emissions. This decision is usually based on the term of purchase/delivery (Incoterms). If the buyer acquires the goods 'Ex Works' (available at the seller's premises) and takes care of the transport, the emissions of the transport belong to the buyer. Accordingly, if the term of delivery is for instance DAP (Delivered at Place of destination), the buyer does not participate in organizing the transport and is not then responsible for the transport emissions. There are other terms where the seller and buyer share the emissions – the seller delivers the goods to the nearest port and the buyer takes care of the rest.

The international forwarding and transport companies can nowadays produce excellent statistics of the transported amounts and their emissions. Unfortunately, very few purchase deliveries have been taken into reporting, even though such deliveries from far away countries have often been heavily criticized, and in many cases with wrong arguments.

## 4.9.2  Delivery Transport

Collecting statistics of delivery transport becomes easier when organizing the transport is in own hands. The statistics should include the delivered amount of goods in tons – possibly also in cubic metres – and the kilometres driven. The use of fuel is also important but for some reason rarely reported. For example, training the drivers to adopt an economical driving style, aimed at reducing fuel consumption, is an important environmental action, complementing the optimization of transport routes and a high volumetric efficiency.

VTT Technical Research Centre of Finland Ltd has developed LIPASTO – a calculation system for traffic exhaust emissions and energy use in Finland: http://lipasto.vtt.fi/en/index.htm. I am sure there are similar systems available in other countries.

Many transport companies nowadays produce excellent travel-, amount- and emission statistics for their clients. When there are products of many customers in the same trucks, the best way of calculating the data is to sort out the transport company's division of sales between clients. If a company's share of the sales is 15 per cent, the emissions can also be assumed to be 15 per cent.

The latest trend is to offer 'carbon neutral' transport. The companies making carbon neutral offers do not claim that the emissions of their transport would have disappeared, but that they have compensated their emissions by paying a certain price per ton of their emissions to a carbon fund, which organizes projects in developing countries in order to decrease the emissions there. As climate change is a global problem, it is valuable to finance such projects, even from very far away. But in reporting, the company has to disclose their real emissions, and beside this they can say how much they have compensated and to what sort of project.

*The company has to disclose their real emissions, and besides this they can say how much they have compensated and to what sort of project.*

*Business travel* of employees is part of the transport entity, usually divided into air travel and use of passenger cars. If flight tickets are bought from a travel agent, it is possible to get a report of the air miles/kilometres flown by the company's employees, but on a smaller scale the companies can collect this information themselves. Use of passenger cars is easier to collect – if they are company cars owned by the company, annual data will always be collected; if they are leased cars, the leasing company will give the statistics. If the employees use their own cars, the data can be taken from the paid kilometre allowances.

Calculating the emissions is usually based on the amounts that the car manufacturers have declared for each model. If there is no car-specific data available (employees' own cars), it is possible to use the emission coefficients of a national research databank like the Finnish LIPASTO mentioned earlier. The environmental targets, of course, include replacing car and air travel with rail travel and replacing part of the flights with virtual meetings. The companies organizing such services can collect such data for their customers, who can disclose the data beside their air travel statistics. Here is a citation from Kesko's report 2015:

In 2015, the air miles of Kesko employees travelling for business totalled 8.0 million (8.1 million in 2014, 8.8 million in 2012). Encouraging the use of virtual meetings is one of the ways Kesko endeavours to decrease the amount of air travel. The amount of virtual meetings held via the Microsoft Lync application has increased by 19% since the previous year. In 2015, a total of 47,453 hours of Lync-meetings were held (39,924 hours in 2014). At the end of 2015, the Kesko Group had 26 Videra video conferencing facilities in use and the total duration of all video meetings between two or more facilities was 3,812 hours (4,341 hours in 2014).

As a retail group, Kesko has now also added the emissions of employee commuting and customer travel to stores. Such calculations are very challenging and it is not possible to reach a 100 per cent exact result, but they give an impression of the dimensions of these issues.

## 4.9.3  Transport Is Only Part of the Life Cycle

Cut flowers like Fair Trade roses, carnations and mixed bunches are flown every night from Nairobi airport in Kenya to both Amsterdam and London. Air freight is the only possibility for the Kenyan flower farms to sell their products to Europe. The lifespan of these flowers is around two weeks, so they need to be delivered to the stores within three to four days of being cut on the farm, and they require an unbroken refrigerated transport chain with a temperature of below 7°C. If air freight could not be used, the Kenyans could not dream of the European flower market.

In 2007, Dr **Adrian Williams** of the University of Cranfield in Bedford, UK compared, using the life cycle assessment method, the $CO_2$ emissions of Dutch and Kenyan cut flowers delivered to the World Flowers RDC wholesale company near London. In Kenya, the flower farms do not need energy in their cultivation – their greenhouses are used to protect the flowers from the sun. In Holland, a similar flower farm annually uses 800,000 cubic metres of natural gas and 1,200 MWh of electricity per cultivated hectar. The crop in Kenya is 70 per cent higher than in Holland.

The final result of the study was that the greenhouse gas emissions (of which $CO_2$ accounted for 90–96 per cent) created by the Dutch cut flowers were six times as high as those of the Kenyan flowers, in spite of the air freight. However, the margin of error of the calculation is +/– 30 per cent: http://www.fairflowers.de/fileadmin/flp.de/Redaktion/Dokumente/Studien/Comparative_Study_of_Cut_Roses_Feb_2007.pdf

In June 2010, the Greening of Industry Network held a conference in Seoul, South Korea. One of the speakers representing the South Korean car manufacturer Hyundai presented their carbon footprint calculation, which had already been extended to almost all car parts. The calculation looked very easy and plausible, even so plausible that I began to suspect whether it was reliable. The focus of the presentation was including climate change impacts in the factory investment calculations.

When Hyundai started to consider a new investment for enabling their business to grow, they had compared two options. The first one was to enlarge their manufacturing plant in South Korea and deliver the cars from there to the Rotterdam harbour in Europe on a cargo vessel designed for transporting cars. The second option was to start a new plant in the Czech Republic and deliver the cars by road to Rotterdam in car transport trucks. Though the emissions from shipping are usually regarded as very low compared to trucks, in this case the climate change impacts of the deliveries by road were much lower than the impacts of shipping from South Korea to Europe. Hyundai put their plant in the Czech Republic to use in 2009.

## 4.10 Screening of Suppliers Using Environmental Criteria EN32 and EN33

One of the new issues in GRI G4 recommendations is reporting on suppliers' environmental impacts. If the suppliers have been included in the company's value chain, it is presumable that their environmental impacts have been assessed as material issues and they have to be studied carefully. The task is not easy, and on this point many companies are tempted to make groundless statements: 'We presume that our suppliers comply with our environmental policy and minimize their environmental impacts, and we monitor our suppliers regularly, willing to learn how they work to reach our common goals'. The stakeholders ask rightfully, which concrete environmental requirements we have set for our suppliers, how we monitor their conformance in practice, and which facts we can present as results.

Unfortunately, GRI does not give good instructions on how this monitoring should be carried out. The first required indicator, EN32, is the percentage of new suppliers chosen during the year who have been screened, using environmental criteria defined by the customer company. The indicator EN33 should include more specific information about the significant actual and potential negative environmental impacts in the supply chain and actions taken: how the assessments are carried out, how many improvements have been agreed upon, and how many supplier relationships have been terminated as a result of assessment.

The essential problem is the diversity and inaccuracy of the assessment methods. GRI suggests that 'assessments may be informed by audits, contractual reviews, two-way engagement, and grievance and complaint mechanisms'. This seems like GRI would regard assessments made by the customer company as reliable information of the suppliers' environmental protection. Neutral third party audits are not required – though are not ruled out, either.

I am also a firm supporter of impartiality as concerns these challenging supplier assessments. Unfortunately, third party audits have to be tailored for each company, as the international sectoral cooperation and the standards for supplier audits are too scarce. Some examples, though. Fairtrade Labelling has used both social and environmental criteria for years in auditing their farmers. Business Social Compliance Initiative (BSCI), promoting social audits of suppliers for retail chains and the consumer goods industry, has developed a similar scheme for environmental audits, called Business Environmental Performance Initiative (BEPI – www.bepi-intl.org), which started at the end of 2014. BEPI concentrates on the manufacturing phase of products, not on the whole life cycle, taking the following issues into the assessments:

- environmental management system (compulsory)
- use of energy, transport, greenhouse gas emissions, other emissions to air
- water and wastewater
- waste management
- preventing pollution, chemicals
- preventing accidents
- preventing pollution of soil and ground water
- use of land and biodiversity.

The BEPI process has three steps: (1) self assessment, (2) remediation plan together with a BEPI consultant, (3) BEPI audit by a third party. The process lasts from two to six months, and the audited suppliers will get a quality rating: Minimum Practice, Good Practice or Leading Practice. BEPI follows the corresponding environmental principles of the Global Social Compliance Programme (GSCP), to which I will return in 6.2.

Customer companies' own monitoring of their suppliers may be reliable from the viewpoint of the companies' own quality control and risk management. In reporting, own monitoring is not convincing, third party audits should always be used, whenever it is economically and practically possible.

# 5

# Responsible Managing of Own Human Resources

Human resources are a major capital in any company, and the professional skills, welfare and job satisfaction of the employees are directly connected to the success of the company. In the traditional Finnish and European business culture, this has been understood for many years. In developing countries, many entrepreneurs still think that the business is most profitable when the employees are kept in bad working conditions and on extremely low salaries. I will return to this issue in Chapter 6.

In Finland and in most EU countries, employment is regulated by requiring labour legislation and nationally binding collective labour agreements. compliance with the regulations and agreements is controlled by public work safety inspectors and trade unions. Breaches will quickly get publicity as the media enjoys bringing them out into the open. In Finland, serious breaches are rare and public control is not affected by corruption or bribery. As concerns products made in Finland, the social responsibility of production can be proved just by complying with legislation. In some EU countries, and especially in developing countries outside of the EU, the legislation may by all means follow the ILO core conventions, but the control of labour terms and conditions is insufficient and disturbed by the corruptibility of the inspectors.

As stakeholders are interested in how workers' rights actualize all over the world, it is important to invest in their control whenever work in the risk countries is involved. I go deeper into this subject in Chapter 6.

© The Author(s) 2017

J. Kuisma, *Managing Corporate Responsibility in the Real World*,
DOI 10.1007/978-3-319-54078-8_5

Social responsibility in labour issues is directed by human resources policy, in which the company promises to follow certain principles in managing the staff and investing in its welfare and know-how. Typical performance indicators of social responsibility are:

- basic data on employees
- job satisfaction
- investing in health and safety at work
- accidents at work
- sick days
- investing in training (money and time)
- compensation and fringe benefits
- turnover of staff
- performance reviews.

In Finnish companies, basic data on employees is needed for many purposes, which means that the data is available and no new IT systems are needed. Collecting data on sick days and training days may sometimes be challenging, though.

Indicators of social responsibility affect each other as well as the profitability of the company. Improving job satisfaction usually leads to a decrease in sick days and staff turnover. Investing in precautionary occupational health care and safety at work decreases accidents at work and sick days. A decrease in sick days and staff turnover reduces costs; investing in training and job satisfaction improves productivity. Social indicators are thus worth careful and many-sided studying, as well as their financial impacts such as the costs of a sick day or of recruiting a new employee. It is possible to gain much more profit by good management and investing in employees. Research shows that investing in welfare at work can pay back five to six times the money invested.

# 5.1  Job Satisfaction

Job satisfaction is one of the most crucial issues of social responsibility and affects many other matters. GRI has never taken job satisfaction as a separate indicator, not in the G4 recommendation either, though it is nowadays commonly monitored in many companies. As I think job satisfaction needs to be addressed, regardless of GRI, I have earlier combined it with reporting on staff turnover and will do it again here.

*Job satisfaction is one of the most crucial issues of social responsibility and affects many other matters.*

Researchers as well as business executives have plenty of experience of how good job satisfaction inspires employees to high class performance, which makes sales grow, improves productivity, decreases sick days and staff turnover and improves profitability. On the contrary, if the working climate is bad and the employees are very unsatisfied with the company, department or manager, the employees' motivation and quality of work will suffer, there will be more short absences, and skilled employees will leave for better employers. All this will reduce profitability. Word about bad job satisfaction and working climate will spread easily outside of the company, which will make recruiting of new employees more difficult. Respectively, the spreading of positive information will increase the company's attractiveness as an employer.

Job satisfaction and working climate are worth monitoring, and the results should be compared with the development of other social indicators and profitability. The crucial problems will be revealed through monitoring and solutions to them can be sought. By repeating the monitoring annually, it is possible to see whether correct actions have been taken.

## 5.1.1   Job Satisfaction Indicators

Job satisfaction is monitored by annual surveys in which the employees can participate anonymously. The survey is usually carried out by a neutral research body and tailored according to the company's needs.

If the amount of employees is small, the survey assignment can be given perhaps to a business school or university student. It is also possible that somebody in the company carries out the survey, on the condition that the questions are carefully compiled and the respondents are guaranteed being able to express their opinions without being recognized. The scale of the scores is usually from one to five, five being the best score. Typical areas of the survey are satisfaction with:

* the company;
* own department/unit;
* cooperation and working climate;
* own manager;

- stress from work;
- getting recognition;
- compensation and fringe benefits;
- realization of equality;
- promotion possibilities;
- performance reviews.

In addition to the list above, the last few years have brought such new issues as commitment of employees and empowerment for achievements.

The results are usually divided by and talked over in each department/unit. However, the results cannot be divided into units that have five employees or less, as there is a danger that the respondents would then be recognized. In public reporting, results of the satisfaction with the company, own department, own work and equality are usually disclosed, the other issues are commented on mainly if there have been changes during the year. In big companies and units with over five employees, satisfaction with own manager can be included in the manager's incentives.

## 5.2    Basic Data About Employees (LA1)

Basic data about employees (amount, distribution of age and gender, duration of employment, basic education) do not directly describe the company's responsibility, but they give outsiders a picture of what kind of people the company employs. The GRI G4 recommendation suggests that companies report on the new employees hired during the year, because the information about their age and gender speaks of the company's ability to hire diversified and qualified staff and of the efforts to ensure equality.

GRI has for some reason removed from G4 the grouping of employment into permanent/fixed-term and whole-time/part-time. As the continuous use of fixed-term has often been regarded as contrary to labour contract law, the attractiveness of this subject has, in my opinion, not decreased in these economically difficult years. The public sector in particular should talk about their employment more openly and make sure that everything goes according to the laws and principles of responsible management. The latest statistics of the Finnish public sector show that 20 per cent of the government's employment and 22 per cent of the municipalities' employment are fixed-term contracts.

Part-time contracts have also raised critical discussion throughout the years. As we very well know, part-time work is typical in sectors where the need for workforce varies considerably between times of day and days of the week. The employer tries to match the service resources with the customer flow, in order to ensure the best possible productivity. Labour unions criticize employers for not giving their part-time employees enough working hours, which means that their salary is not enough for living. At the same time, there are plenty of students and other workers who favour short working weeks and find part-time work very important. A many-sided topic, for which it is difficult to find a solution that would satisfy all.

In spite of GRI, I would keep the percentages of both fixed-term and part-time employees in reporting – giving such 'additional' information is, by no means, forbidden. Low percentages do not reflect responsibility nor high percentages irresponsibility, but showing the percentages gives the stake-holders an opportunity to evaluate what kind of jobs the company offers and how they have developed in the last few years.

The GRI indicator LA1 suggests reporting on the number, age, gender and region of new employee hires during the year and the rate of employee turnover. I suggest that the percentages of fixed-term and part-time jobs are also reported. These figures can also be given for new employees, showing whether the amount has grown or diminished from the previous year(s).

## 5.3   Employee Turnover (Part of LA1)

Employee turnover and job satisfaction are to me fundamental indicators of social responsibility. *If the employees do not get along in the company, the work assignments and/or the superiors' way of managing are not motivating.* The wages and outlook for career development are bad, and there have been big changes in the organization, disliked by many. The most competent employees in particular leave the company if the demand in the labour market is heavy. And the other way around: if the employee turnover has been totally non-existent for years, there is a danger of getting into a rut at work, and the revival that new employees could cause does not materialize.

In some sectors – especially in those where young people often begin their work career and work, for example, while studying – a high rate of employee turnover can be very natural. Uneven distribution of employee turnover by age and gender can represent discrimination, and the turnover has direct impacts on wage and recruiting costs. Rumours about high rate of employee turnover and its reasons will definitely make recruiting of new employees more difficult.

Turnover rates are counted by comparing the amount of employees left during the year with the total amount of employees at the end of the year. The rates are counted separately by gender, by age groups (for example under 30 years, between 30 and 50 years, over 50 years) and by countries of operation. SMEs will get a pretty simple table out of this.

Again, it is possible to go beyond the GRI recommendation. Interesting additional information could be given by showing the percentages of employees leaving on their own initiative, on the employer's initiative (reasons based on the labour contract law) and for other reasons such as retirement.

## 5.4   Health and Safety (LA6)

Health and safety performance is a key measure of an organization's duty of care. Low injury and absentee rates are generally linked to positive trends in staff morale and productivity. This Indicator shows whether health and safety management practices are resulting in fewer occupational health and safety incidents. An evaluation of trends and patterns may also indicate potential workplace inequity.

### 5.4.1  Sick Days

Sicknesses of employees result in costs to the company. In Finland, the Ministry of Social Affairs and Health has estimated that the annual costs of sickness absences are about 1,600 euros per employee. Insurance companies and the Confederation of Finnish Industries have higher figures: 11 sick days on average, 350 euros per day, makes close to 4,000 euros per employee.

Sickness absences may increase due to accidents caused by poor work safety, working methods or conditions hazardous for health (such as exposure to chemicals), but also by problems between supervisors and employees, or between employees, and worsened job satisfaction caused by other reasons. Investments in improving the working atmosphere and job satisfaction, precautionary occupational health care and other welfare at work usually reduce sickness days and cut down the company's costs.

## 5.4.2 Accidents

Preventing accidents is an essential part of work safety. The starting point for prevention is recognizing dangerous situations and anticipating unpredictable situations.

Work safety law obligates the employer to investigate and assess the dangers at work systematically. If the employer has not enough expertise to assess the risk, external specialists should be used.

One of the Finnish insurance companies has calculated that in Finland around 130,000 injuries at work take place annually. One injury costs 6,000 euros on average, which means that the total costs are about 780 million euros. There are six 'productivity thieves' at the work sites: unnecessary injuries, needless and prolonged sickness absences, ineffective treatment of sicknesses and injuries, excessive or insufficient occupational health care services and deficiencies in welfare at work. And the sixth, the most expensive, are the premature retirements.

Professor Guy Ahonen of the Finnish Institute of Occupational Health has counted that as there are 190,000 persons on disability pension, the Finnish national economy loses 8 billion euros' worth of production potential annually. Adding in the costs of occupational diseases and nursing, the disability of persons of working age accounts for losses of 25 billion euros. The total annual wage sum and employers' social charges in Finland are around 100 billion euros, which according to Ahonen means that there is a huge productivity potential in welfare at work.

*In Finland, the disability of persons of working age accounts for annual losses of 25 billion euros.*

In Finland, occupational health care and nursing are usually well managed. It is profitable to invest in preventive occupational healthcare, Zero Accident campaigns and similar measures, as their costs will easily be covered by the decrease in sickness days. The employees regard good occupational health care and nursing services as fringe benefits, which have positive effects on job satisfaction.

Read more about the Finnish Zero Accident Forum:

http://www.ttl.fi/en/safety/occupational_accidents/zero_accident_forum/pages/default.aspx

### 5.4.3   GRI Indicators Emphasize Injuries at Work

GRI recommendations favour more reporting on injuries at work and on occupational diseases than on ordinary sicknesses. Indicators are:

- types of injury;
- injury rate ('the amount of injuries and fatalities in relation to the total amount of hours worked' in Finland usually in relation to million hours worked, which is quite a big figure for SMEs);
- occupational disease rate (the amount of occupational diseases in relation to the hours worked);
- lost workdays (due to injuries and occupational diseases), also in relation to the hours theoretically worked;
- absentee rate (all absenteeism in relation to theoretical workdays).

Collecting data on sickness days maybe difficult in the beginning. Companies tend to follow mainly those sicknesses that are reimbursed by the social security system on the grounds of the health insurance legislation, and the sickness days not entitled to daily allowances may not have been registered. In order to get the correct and exact picture of sicknesses, all sickness days, even those that last for only one day, have to be registered. The company has to build up a working system for this.

Even though sicknesses can very often be kept from occurring by preventive occupational health care, GRI does not suggest reporting on such health care and the funds used for it. Here again, I complement GRI Guidelines by suggesting that reporting covers both investments into occupational health care and development of sickness days, side-by-side. Performance indicators are then:

- total investment in occupational health care, nursing etc., calculated per employee
- preventive occupational health care's percentage of the total costs.

## 5.5   Training (LA9), Skills Management, Lifelong Learning (LA10)

Investing in employees' training has always belonged to good management, and it is appraised to improve a company's economic success. During the recession, opinions about the importance of training seemed to split into two extreme groups. The companies that decided to save on everything dropped all training totally out of their programme. The others – very often family-owned SMEs – trained their employees during the recession more than normally, 'because then we have time to develop the employees and the company, to make sure that we are highly competitive as soon as the economy starts growing and the business starts to flourish'.

GRI Guidelines instruct to report the *average hours of training per year, per employee, by gender and by employee category*. The bigger the company is, the more difficult it is to collect data on training hours, as there are many kinds of training, and no exact definition of it. It is easier to take into account participation in training events outside of the company than to decide which internal events and meetings can be regarded as training.

The company needs to decide which gatherings are internal training and which are other meetings, and develop a procedure with which the statistics can be collected. One problem in defining internal training is whether it should have a minimum duration – some companies use three hours' duration as the minimum.

It is also useful to collect data on how much money per employee is invested in training. This describes the scale of the financial investment but does not of course guarantee the quality or results of training.

Training programmes supporting lifelong learning have become more common in the rapidly-changing labour market of the twenty-first century. Employees have to be able to learn new matters continuously in order to secure their employment, and employers are expected to make big changes easier by offering, for example, retraining programmes or retirement planning for those soon facing retirement.

The GRI recommendation suggests that companies describe how they support their employees' lifelong learning both during employment as well as after it is finished, for example by:

- internal training
- supporting external training financially
- arranging possibilities for sabbatical periods
- retraining programmes
- reassignment training and transitional assistance programmes for employees whose employment has or will be terminated
- pre-retirement planning.

Big companies have saved lots of costs arising from disability pensions when they have been able to retrain employees who have a disability related to physical exertion (such as backache) to new occupations with no physical exertion.

## 5.6    Performance and Career Development Reviews (LA11)

The percentage of employees receiving regular performance and career development reviews by gender demonstrates the extent to which this system is applied throughout the organization and whether there is inequality of access to these opportunities. The reviews are usually connected with payment by results, which motivates employees and improves job satisfaction. In the review, the employees can present their own wishes and opinions on how the work should be developed and what their training needs are.

It is important that the reviews are based on criteria that everybody is familiar with, and that the reviews take place according to an agreed, annually recurring scheme, are documented and the documents then jointly approved. This helps to avoid situations where the manager thinks that the review has been carried out but the employee disagrees.

It is also absolutely important that the matters settled in the reviews materialize. In Finland, a survey was carried out in government institutions in 2014, asking the employees among other things how the performance reviews had been carried out. Only 13 per cent of the respondents found the reviews useful and half of them experienced that the reviews did not have any effects on the matters discussed. Hopefully companies will improve on this issue.

As said previously, the indicator here is the percentage of employees having received performance/career development reviews during the year.

## 5.7    Equal Remuneration for Women and Men (LA13)

GRI does not take a stand on reporting on actual wages – remuneration cannot be regarded as a corporate responsibility issue in countries where wages are regulated by collective agreements and employment contract acts. My recommendation is to report on such disputes over wages and other terms of employment that have been dealt with between the employers' federation and the labour union, in the district court or at an industrial tribunal. Reporting should then consist of the amount of and reasons for the disputes and the solutions, explaining in whose favour the case was closed. These disputes are often reported in the media when they have arisen, not necessary any more if they have been terminated in the employer's favour or as unsettled. Therefore, it is better to disclose the disputes openly rather than to keep silent about them.

The economic responsibility indicator EC5 recommends comparing standard entry level wages to local minimum wages. Many countries have introduced minimum wage legislation, which we do not have in Finland, as the collective agreements cover most of employment. In the human resource indicators the only recommendation concerning remuneration is LA13, the ratio of basic salary and remuneration of women to men by employee category, by significant locations of operation. I think this indicator has been included in the GRI recommendations since the beginning, that is since 2000, and for reasons that are easy to understand, but I have seen very few companies reporting on this.

A 'justifiable' explanation has usually been that there can be tens, even hundreds of job descriptions in the company, and reporting on wages by gender does not describe realization of equality. When talking about very standardized floor level jobs, the comparison between male and female workers' wages are more justifiable and gives pretty correct information on the subject. Some companies disclose the average wages of men and women at the company or corporate level, which is better than nothing.

Many countries have legislated Non-Discrimination Acts which give you more information about equality of remuneration and other issues at work. Here is the Finnish website, including information on legislation, research and different minorities: http://www.yhdenvertaisuus.fi/welcome_to_equality_fi/

## 5.8 Labour/Management Relations (LA4), Health and Safety Committees (LA5)

The GRI recommendation does not have much to say as to labour/management relations. The only subjects GRI has taken forth are 'minimum notice periods regarding operational changes' and 'the percentage of total workforce represented in formal joint management–worker health and safety committees'. In Finland, as well as in many other countries, the notice periods and other rules of the negotiations have been legislated and the subject has not been taken into collective agreements separately. The health and safety committees are also regulated by law.

Companies that have been reporting for a long time will have handled labour/management relations more extensively than GRI has recommended and can continue doing so. For example, they have included statistics about employee membership of labour unions (in countries where it is possible to get this information) and about the company's participation in the employers' federation, as well as a description of the workplace steward system and of national and international cooperation meetings.

GRI does not have a position on the disputes between employer and employee, concerning compliance with labour legislation, collective agreement or employment contract act. I return to these non-compliances in 7.4.

## 5.9   The Company's Attractiveness as a Workplace

I would like to comment on one more important subject that GRI does not speak of. Whenever a company is understaffed, it has to be an interesting, attractive and respected workplace in order to be competitive in recruiting new employees. Interest and respect consist of many issues, of which job satisfaction and investments in welfare at work are fundamental. Also, the image of the company's responsibility affects interest – young people want to have an employer that is respected by society, has a good reputation and can keep all important matters in good condition.

In many countries, surveys like 'Best Place to Work' are carried out, targeting students in vocational schools, polytechnics and universities, as well as young people who have already graduated and have worked for a couple of years. These surveys give useful information to develop management and employer images. The more companies subscribe to the survey, the lower the costs will be for each company.

## 5.10  Other HR Indicators of GRI

I have not commented on all HR indicators of GRI, as I think some of them will never be given much weight in the materiality assessment. Here is a list of those indicators I have left out:

- LA2: Benefits provided to full-time employees that are not provided to temporary or part-time employees
- LA3: Return to work and retention rates after parental leave
- LA7: Workers with high incidence or high risk of diseases related to their occupation
- LA8: Health and safety topics covered in formal agreements with trade unions

- LA12: Composition of governance bodies and breakdown of employees per employee category according to gender, age group, minority group membership and other indicators of diversity.

The next subject is not included in the actual indicators but is connected with job satisfaction, as well as with the attractiveness of the workplace.

Work-life balance is difficult at a certain stage of life and can cause problems both at work and at home. Some companies have solved these problems by developing flexible working hours and remote work possibilities at home and organizing work in a new way. One example of such development is the 'Crowded Years Initiative$^{TM}$' of Attorneys at law Borenius (Finland). They started an initiative for the simple reason that there was an increase in the number of lawyers, mostly women and generation Y'ers, leaving the firm. Many of them were juggling two jobs and living double lives – one as an employee and the other as a parent. The Crowded Years Initiative$^{TM}$ has shown promising results. There is a clear rise in female appointed partners in the firm since the onset of the initiative and a decline in female lawyers leaving the firm. Also statistics show that significantly more male lawyers are taking paternity leave. Borenius received glory in the IFLR Euromoney LMG's Europe Women in Business Law Awards 2014 by winning four categories: Finland – country award, best national firm mentoring programme, best national firm for work-life balance, and best national firm for women in business law:

http://www.borenius.com/2014/06/17/crowded-years-from-paper-to-practice/

http://www.borenius.com/2014/06/16/balancing-acts-by-the-dutch/

# 6

# Responsible Supply Chain

As it is nowadays typical to outsource production to cheap labour countries, or source from there components for production or ready-made products for sale in the developed world, the supply chain is a very central material aspect for many companies and has earned plenty of pages in this book.

I remember very well when I had to deal with responsibility issues in the supply chain for the first time. A journalist of a labour union journal called me in 1996 and asked whether we had found any child labour in Kesko's supply chain and how we prevent it. My answer in those days was that all suppliers have signed our purchasing contract, in which we forbid the use of child labour, and therefore we have not encountered those problems. Many companies have used this very feeble answer for years.

Quite soon we realized at Kesko that such documents signed by the suppliers do not give much credibility to our sourcing methods, and soon the discussion extended from child labour to overall labour conditions and labour rights. We started to plan a procedure of responsible sourcing based on third party auditing, and after two years we challenged all our competitors and other companies buying from risk countries to conform to our principles. The challenge brought forth 'The Responsible Importers Network' under the umbrella of the Central Chamber of

© The Author(s) 2017
J. Kuisma, *Managing Corporate Responsibility in the Real World*,
DOI 10.1007/978-3-319-54078-8_6

**121**

Commerce. Later, the network developed into the Finnish national chapter of Business Social Compliance Initiative (BSCI), of which I will say more later.

Responsibility for the supply chain has become one of the most important issues of corporate responsibility, in my ranking even beside climate change. Sourcing of products extends nowadays to all parts of the world, and it is no more limited to the actions of multinational companies or global brands. In all sectors and in all sizes of business, procurement can at least partly be directed to cheap labour countries, which adds reputation risks to the procedure. NGOs specializing in human rights and environmental protection, labour unions and other organizations monitoring company responsibility can easily use the worldwide online communication systems to shed light on violations of labour regulations and human rights, and the media will seize on them snappishly, as they offer interesting, negative news material.

## 6.1    In the European Union the Workers' Rights Are Respected – at Least in Theory

In Finland and other EU countries, it has been well understood that investing in employees' welfare and job satisfaction are crucial parts of corporate responsibility. Job satisfaction reduces sickness absenteeism and employee turnover, decreases wastage and improves quality, productivity and profitability.

Our frames of working are pretty clear: generally binding collective agreements and strict legislation define the terms, work safety inspectors and strong labour unions ensure that the terms are observed. The situation is more or less the same all over the European Union, though the member countries that have joined during the last ten years have not been able to raise their labour conditions and terms totally to the level of the old member countries.

Violations occur also in old member countries, especially if they have plenty of workers – partly illegal – who have come from outside of the EU. In principle, buyers do not have to control their suppliers' working conditions in the EU, as the control belongs to the authorities. BSCI keeps a list of risk countries where the control should primarily be focused. Of the EU countries, only Romania and Bulgaria are on the risk list.

## 6.2 In Developing Countries the Control of Labour Legislation is Insufficient

In poor countries the labour legislation as well as its control are insufficient, and the countries compete for foreign investments and jobs, even turning a blind eye to whether the laws and regulations are obeyed. Labour union movement is usually weak, in some countries even totally forbidden or part of the political party in power. In such circumstances, many companies – typically national SMEs, sometimes bigger companies – make the mistake of believing that insufficient control, low wages and primitive working conditions guarantee big profits for the owner. This may happen in the short term, but sooner or later the company will get into trouble, when the customers become stricter in requiring evidence for responsible operations. It would be worth testing whether the profits would after all be bigger if the company invested in the workers.

*It would be worth testing whether the profits would after all be bigger if the company invested in the workers.*

As production and sourcing of goods move over to countries where labour and other costs are low, the violations of labour rights become major reputation risks for the buying companies. In the age of modern online communication, the faults of a supply chain reaching all parts of the world can spread in a couple of minutes to both social and traditional media, if the observers of the faults wish to disclose them.

Thus the responsibility of the contracting partners has to be assessed, especially from the point of view of reputation risks, both before starting the cooperation and during the cooperation. When we are committed to acting responsibly, it means that our partners have to be responsible too, otherwise our reputation will suffer badly.

GRI G4 recommendations have taken indicators of environmental protection and working conditions in the supply chain into reporting. As concerns working conditions, they are:

- LA14: Percentage of new suppliers that were screened using labour practices criteria
- LA15: Significant actual and potential negative impacts for labour practices in the supply chain and actions taken

• LA16: Number of grievances about labour practices filed, addressed and resolved through formal grievance mechanisms.

I will handle the requirements for the supply chain more thoroughly later.

## 6.3   The Partners Have to Obey the National Laws and ILO Conventions – Nothing Special in That!

The requirements applied to the partners are documented on a more common basis in the company's Code of Conduct (principles of responsible business) and on a more detailed basis in the principles of responsible sourcing. The requirements have to be made clear to existing partners as well as to potential new partners. If the partners are companies in developing countries, the requirements will not be met quickly – a continuous development process is required.

This process needs a schedule. Some faults need immediate remediation, others need more time. It is important that the process continues and that the biggest risks are assessed first. Considering new partners, the requirements have to be fulfilled, if not before the partnership begins, at least soon after that. The supply of companies that have passed audits is nowadays extensive and gives the buyers plenty of possibilities to choose from.

Setting the requirements is easy in the sense that they all already exist. All companies that carry out responsible sourcing require the same minimum conditions: complying with the national labour laws and ILO core conventions, depending on which regulations are the more demanding alternatives from the employees' point of view. All companies have the same list of subjects to be monitored:

• freedom of association and right to collective bargaining
• equality, discrimination, treatment of employees
• working hours
• remuneration
• health and safety at work
• child labour
• forced labour and disciplinary measures.

The biggest problems are in complying with the regulations for working hours, remediation and health
and safety. Child labour and forced
labour cases are quite rare in the
export industry, but certainly child
labour comes up every now and then.

> *The biggest problems are in complying with the regulations for working hours, remediation and health and safety.*

Manufacturing companies do not always produce everything themselves, but they can have plenty of subcontractors. The more complicated the sourcing network is, the more difficult it makes the controlling
of it. For example, the Swiss Migros wants to know the next level
subcontractors of their potential suppliers, which means that the subcontractors need to carry out the self-assessment of the BSCI auditing
scheme. Migros then views these self-assessments together with the
supplier and those subcontractors that seem to be risky will be audited.
The process is pretty laborious and expensive, but because the biggest
part of Migros's assortment of products are their own brands, it is very
important for the reputation of Migros to manage the risks in their
production effectively.

I will now handle each subject on the monitoring list in more detail.

## 6.4    Minimum Requirements for Working Conditions and Terms

### 6.4.1    Freedom of Association and Right to Collective Bargaining

All employees should have the right to join the labour union of their
choice or set up one, and the right to bargain about their working
conditions and terms collectively through their representatives. The
partner company should respect this principle, inform the staff about
the freedom of association and explain that association will not have
negative consequences under any circumstances. The company should
not interfere in founding, operations nor governance of labour unions or
collective bargaining.

In the attached interview, Janne Ronkainen, Executive Director of the Trade
Solidarity Centre of Finland, comments on the labour unions' role in Africa.

### Janne Ronkainen: Unofficial Economy Is a Big Challenge in Africa

Janne Ronkainen is Executive Director of The Trade Union Solidarity Centre of Finland (SASK).

**The production in Asia has grown with immense speed in the last few decades. In what countries are labour unions influential and in what countries do they have the biggest problems?**

Asia has been the most challenging of all continents. The political system in China does not allow independent labour unions. In India, the strong caste system covers the whole of society, also the labour unions. They exist and are protected by law, but their working logic is based more on the traditional power structure than on genuine member democracy. As concerns the other big Asian countries, labour unions have a strong role in Indonesia and the Philippines. In Indonesia, labour unions have succeeded in raising the minimum wages of many sectors at the state level and in improving workers' social security. In China, the improvements in the standard of living and the workers' income have been the greatest. The social pressure has grown and led to unofficial strikes and other demonstrations, and the political powers have had to react by improving legislation, wages and working conditions.

**What is the situation in Africa?**

In the southern, eastern and partly also in western Africa, labour unions are notable societal actors, having also significant achievements in improving labour and living conditions. In South Africa and Namibia, labour unions have had a strong role in suspending apartheid and improving workers' standard of living, income and social security, in spite of many problems. Also in Zambia and Ghana, the labour unions have succeeded in improving the labour conditions and terms remarkably.

One of the big challenges in Africa is the considerable unofficial economy, the so-called hawker economy, which acts almost totally outside of all regulations. In some African countries, even 95 per cent of the workforce earns their income outside of the official economy. The unofficial economy, together with mass unemployment and non-existent hope for the future, finally led to the revolts in North Africa a couple of years ago. As concerns North Africa, the future does not yet look any better from the viewpoint of economy, employment, poverty or labour unions.

**Could Africa face similar development to that achieved in Asia?**

I used to be more optimistic about the development in Africa. The workforce will double, the age structure is very young and there is much space, remarkable natural resources and potential for agriculture. However, I have started suspecting whether we will in Africa see similar positive changes to those we have seen in Asia – extending to the poorer demographic groups as well. The problems in Africa are the almost total absence of occupational and other secondary education and the corrupted political elite. Many foreign companies that have invested in exploiting the natural resources in Africa bring most of the workers from other countries – China, Latin America, even Europe. The relatively good wages paid for such work do not channel into the local economy in the same way as they would if the wages were paid to local skilled workers. At the same time, the relations of such foreign workers with the local community will be weaker, and the companies will not invest that much in training, infrastructure and other reforms.

In countries like Myanmar, Singapore, Saudi Arabia and the United Arab Emirates, labour unions are totally forbidden, In countries like China, Laos, North Korea, Syria and Vietnam, labour unions are only allowed as subordinates of, and controlled by, the country's single-party system. And as surprising as it seems, the US has not ratified the ILO core convention on freedom of association and collective bargaining, and unionization there is company-specific. If the majority of the workers want to join a labour union, everybody will become a member and the company is thereafter 'unionized', but if the majority says no, then there will be no union in the company and nobody can join. In the US, only a little over 10 per cent of the workforce belong to labour unions, and collective agreements have been very rare for a long time.

If joining a labour union is difficult, the SA 8000 standard and some other auditing schemes accept the company-specific bargaining mechanism. The partner company must then let the workers choose freely their own representatives who will belong to the company's own bargaining and cooperation bodies. The company should guarantee that the workers' representatives will not have to face discrimination, harassment, bullying nor retaliations due to their activity, and that the representatives have the right to meet other workers at the workplace.

The late **Neil Kearney**, former President of the International Garment, Textile and Leather Workers' Federation and an active spokesman for the SA 8000 standard, once spoke at a conference about his experiences in China. The workers he met there had plenty of questions about the company-specific wage committee: What does the election mean? What should the workers' representative do? Can we choose more candidates than one? After some practice, the cooperation had started to go well.

In some Eastern European countries, the labour union movement has not succeeded in gaining a foothold as society has become westernized. In Finland, as well as in many other countries, companies are often expected to promote labour union membership to the workers, but this is very difficult, as belonging to unions is totally up to the workers to decide, as long as the employer does not prevent it. For buyers, the presence of a labour union that can affect the partner company's working conditions is usually a relief, because then the problems that the buyer and auditor should otherwise interfere with may already be solved at the workplace level.

See also ILO conventions 11, 87, 98, 135 and 154.

## 6.4.2  Equality, Discrimination, Treatment of Employees

In hiring, remuneration, access to training, promotions, ending of employment or retirement decisions, the partner company should not discriminate anybody due to gender, age, religion, race, caste, birthplace, social background, ethnic or national origin, nationality, labour union membership, political activity and opinions, sexual orientation, family responsibilities, marital status, nor for any other similar reason.

Discrimination is difficult to detect especially in own monitoring/auditing. Professional auditors are better at finding the problems in worker interviews. Pregnancy, which is not mentioned on the list above, is a typical cause for discrimination in female-dominated sectors.

See also ILO conventions 100, 111, 143, 158, 159, 169 and 183.

## 6.4.3  Working Hours

The partner company should comply with all national laws and sectoral agreements on working hours, days off and vacations. The permitted maximum amount of working hours is regulated by law but should never regularly exceed 48 hours per week, and the maximum for overtime work is 12 hours per week. Overtime work should be voluntary and a higher compensation should be paid for it. When the company falls under such a collective agreement that represents most of its workers, and overtime work is needed to get over a short-term demand peak, the company can skip the 'voluntary rule' and require overtime work based on the collective agreement. In this case also, the special arrangements must fit into the maximum hours regulated.

After six successive working days, the employee is entitled to at least one day off. There are exceptions to this rule only if both of the following conditions are realized:

• The national law allows to work more than six successive days without a day off
• A freely negotiated, valid collective agreement allows the working hours to level out and includes enough resting periods.

Violations of working time regulations come up too often, as they would require continuous control on the part of the labour inspectors, and the resources are insufficient for this. In the audits,which are carried out quite seldomly, the compliance with working time regulations is examined, among other things, with the help of rosters, payroll accounting and worker interviews, but the situation can change weekly, even daily. The workers do not always object to illegally long working weeks and overtime work, because they are poor and want all the income they can get. Often, the long working days and weeks are caused by increased demand, which the employer does not believe will continue year round and therefore does not dare to switch the factory into two-shift work. This would enable compliance with the working time legislation and give employment to new workers, but would at the same time lower the income of the existing workers.

**Doug DeRuisseau**, Senior Advisor of Social Accountability International (www.sa-intl.org) once related, on the Q&A section of the SAI website (the comment is no longer there), his experiences of what excessive overtime work can cause: 1) labour costs per unit increased, 2) injuries at work grew in number, 3) productivity declined, 4) quality got worse. The closer contacts the company has with the contract companies, the more these subjects should be discussed in striving for successful cooperation.

See also ILO conventions 1 and 14 and ILO recommendation 116.

## 6.4.4 Remuneration

I address remuneration here in detail, as it is nowadays a fundamental subject in the production and sourcing networks around the world.

The binding collective agreements that we Finns are so familiar with are rare in other parts of the world, as the share of the unionized workers is smaller or the labour unions are company-specific, as in the US. If there are no collective agreements, the remuneration of the workers is typically regulated by minimum wage legislation, which has often fallen behind the living costs development due to high inflation rates.

For example in the US, the basic minimum wage is 7.25 US dollars an hour. President Barack Obama suggested that it should be raised to 10.10 dollars, but Congress was against the initiative. There are differences between states. At the beginning of 2016, the two exceptions under the federal minimum wage were Georgia and Wyoming (5.15 USD). In 31 states, the minimum wage was higher than the federal minimum, the highest being Washington DC (10.50 USD) and California and Massachusetts (10.00 USD). California will raise the minimum wage to 15.00 USD in 2022, New York from 9.00 USD to 15.00 USD in 2018. Minimum wages in all states are listed here:

http://www.ncsl.org/research/labor-and-employment/state-minimum-wage-chart.aspx

In Bangladesh, the miserable working conditions and terms led to raising of the minimum wage in November 2013 from 29 euros to 51 euros per month. The wages in Bangladesh are still lower than elsewhere in Asia.

We have seen the first signs of clothing production in Africa. In October 2014, H&M was reported to have three contract manufacturers in Ethiopia, where the minimum wage was then 28 euros per month. H&M promised that their partners would pay more, at least 30 euros (!) per month (this news was on the website of the Central Organisations of the Finnish Trade Unions SAK in October 2014, but is no longer there). One of the partner companies is owned by an extremely rich Arab sheikh, who also has business in Sweden. The Swedish TV4 has produced a 22-minute documentary on the cooperation between the sheikh and H&M, showing that there are many other issues to be discussed in the business relations with Ethiopia, besides just the low wages. In May 2017, the documentary was still available on YouTube: https://www.youtube.com/watch?v=5-ImoKhymL4.

According to social standards and auditing schemes, the wage paid for normal working hours should at least conform to the legal minimum wage and the standards of the industry sector. All illegal, unauthorized or disciplinary subtractions are forbidden (In some countries, the national law can allow disciplinary subtractions under a collective agreement).

The company should ensure that the wages and other benefits are clearly and regularly specified to the workers and paid according to the law and in a way that suits the workers. Compensation for overtime work has to be paid according to the national law. In countries where overtime work is not regulated by law nor by collective agreement, the workers should get compensation as an extra payment or according to the common practice in the industry, depending on which choice is more advantageous for the workers.

In situations where the legal minimum wage or the typical wage in the industry does not cover living costs and does not leave any additional income for the workers, the partner company should pay the workers *adequate wages* to satisfy basic needs.

## 6.4.5  The Importance of a Living Wage

There is an old ILO convention on minimum wage legislation but no stand on the wage extent, which would be impossible to take into global negotiations. In the UN Universal Declaration of Human Rights, 'just and favourable remuneration' has been defined as one of the rights, but there is no clear definition of what that would mean in practice.

In the last two decades, for example when drawing up the Social Accountability SA 8000 standard, it has become popular – and for a good reason – to talk about *living wage* or *basic needs wage, BNW*. I have collected a summary of living wage definitions and calculations from the most common social auditing schemes. In Table 6.1, I have marked Asia Floor Wage Alliance's (AFWA) comparisons between legal minimum wage and living wage in six Asian countries. In 2005, trade union movements and other organizations working for labour rights founded AFWA, which aims at a living wage being paid in the Asian clothing and textile industry. AFWA bases their calculations on the assumption that an adult requires 3,000 calories a day to be able to carry out his/her work. We Europeans think that 2,100 calories would be the correct amount, which means that the correct living wage would be about 30 per cent lower than that counted by AFWA. In Table 6.1, I have added my own calculations of living wages which are still remarkably higher than legal minimum wages.

All companies operating in developing countries or buying from them must nowadays take a position on the sufficiency of the wages paid. I do not think a Finnish company would have anything against the workers earning living wages. The stakeholders often insist that the buying companies should make their supplying partners pay clearly more than minimum wages to the workers making products for such responsible clients. In practice, it is possible to control only the suppliers' compliance with minimum requirements on remuneration, not any individual wage arrangements. It is not realistic to pay higher wages to some workers participating in the production of some named products – it is uncertain that such raises would be directed evenhandedly to the correct workers and that they would actualize in full extent. It is also extremely difficult for one single company to pay clearly higher wages than the common practice in the industry and country. Development of wages is dependent on the updating of minimum wage laws, negotiations between employers and employees and competition between companies and between countries – not on the positions taken by foreign buyers.

In my opinion, the AFWA's living wage calculation model, based on needed calories and purchasing power parity, is so far the best model, on the condition that AFWA gives up the 3,000 calories which now makes the calculations implausible. As commonly binding collective agreements exist only in a few countries, and it seems difficult to get a living wage voluntarily into companies' wage policies without fruitless bickering and varying results,

**Table 6.1** Living wage calculations

| Country | Minimum wage | Living wage (AFWA) | Minimum wage as % of living wage | Living wage (JK) | Minimum wage as % of living wage |
|---|---|---|---|---|---|
| China | €174.60 | €376.07 | 46% | €263.25 | 66% |
| India | €51.70 | €195.30 | 26% | €136.71 | 38% |
| Bangladesh | €49.56 | €259.80 | 19% | €181.86 | 28% |
| Cambodia | €72.64 | €285.83 | 25% | €200.08 | 36% |
| Sri Lanka | €50.31 | €259.46 | 19% | €181.62 | 28% |
| Indonesia | €82.14 | €266.85 | 31% | €186.80 | 44% |

This table describes the difference between the minimum wage and living wage (per month).

The living wage has been calculated by using the purchase power parity. The minimum wages are from the year 2015. Asia Floor Wage Alliance (AFWA) has used 3,000 calories as the daily need for nutrition. I (JK) have used 2,100 calories, otherwise the calculation is the same.

it would be easier to proceed by developing minimum wage legislation. What if AFWA's model was modified so that in each country the government took FAO's calorie recommendation as basis, and define the family like AFWA does, use purchasing power parity in which food would make up half of the monthly costs, and commit to updating such a legal minimum wage annually with an inflation remediation? Could an international agreement on such national procedures be based on the national implementation of the UN Business and Human Rights document? Governments have their own responsibilities for putting human rights into effect, and adequate remuneration is an essential human right.

I have collected the living wage definitions of the major social auditing schemes.

### Living wage definitions of major social auditing schemes

**SA 8000 Standard**
The audited company and the auditor should together estimate the living wage case by case, by examining the family sizes, amounts of wage earners, living costs etc. The wage should cover basic needs and keep the wage earner and his/her dependents above the poverty line, and additionally there should be some extra money left over for contingencies. Living wage level should be reached in 18–24 months. The wage instructions of SA 8000 leave plenty of room for interpretation and subjects for controversy.

**Ethical Trade Initiative (ETI)**
According to the ETI Code of Conduct, companies should pay at least the minimum wage prescribed by law or the 'standard wage' of the sector, depending on which one is higher. The wage should always cover the basic needs and leave over some money for contingencies.

**Business Social Compliance Initiative (BSCI)**
The BSCI Code of Conduct takes the position that companies should 'respect the rights of the workers to receive fair remuneration that is sufficient to provide them with a decent living for themselves and for their families', and specifies that the wage must at least comply with the minimum wage legislation or the wage defined in the collective agreement of the sector, depending on which one is higher.

**Fair Wear Foundation (FWF), Fair Labour Association (FLA)**
Both instruct that the wage must be at least the minimum wage by law or the 'standard wage' of the sector, depending on which one is higher, and the wage should cover the basic needs of the worker and his/her family and leave some money for contingencies.

**Worldwide Responsible Accredited Production (WRAP), Electronic Industry Citizenship Coalition (EICC)**
Both instructions are satisfied with the minimum wage by law.

**Fair Trade**
Fair Trade certification is based on the minimum wage or the 'standard wage of the sector', depending which one is higher. The living wage instructions include nutritious food, decent accommodation and other necessities, and costs of families have been examined in pilots organized in four countries. No universal definition has been given, but if the farmer is found to pay 'non-living wages', he is made to negotiate with the workers about raising the wages step by step.

**Asia Floor Wage Alliance**
AFWA has its own calculating model:

- The worker's wage should be sufficient to sustain himself/herself and two other 'consumption units' (one unit = one grown-up or two children)
- A grown-up worker's daily need for food is 3,000 calories
- In Asia, half of the monthly income is spent on food.

The calculations use the World Bank's purchasing parities, which make comparisons between countries easier. The food basket and other comparisons are often disputed, especially the daily need of 3,000 calories – FAO's recommendations to Asian countries are based on 2,000 – 2,100 calories.

## 6.4.6 Health and Safety at Work

In developing countries, there are plenty of shortcomings in work safety. Single accidents are not necessarily brought to the buyer's knowledge, but notices of bigger accidents will spread quickly all over the world. For example, the sad news from Bangladesh – the fires in the clothing factories and collapses of factory buildings – have caused big headlines, and also the buyers have been required to prevent similar cases in the future. This is a challenging requirement, as the problem has not been in the social audits' area of responsibility but in the breaking of building regulations, which has most probably been due to building inspectors being bribed. How else could one build a nine-storey-high factory on soft ground with a permit for four storeys?

The partner company has to secure a safe and healthy working environment for its workers. The company has to efficiently prevent accidents and injuries arising from work by intervening in the work safety risks in advance and by following up the typical accidents and their reasons in the sector. In order to ensure health and safety at work, the company should define clear instructions and procedures concerning personal protection equipment, clean toilet premises, access to clean drinking water, decent storage space for food when needed and so on. If the company has arranged accommodation for the workers, it has to take care of the cleanliness and safety of the accommodation and see that it meets the workers' basic needs.

All workers must have the right to avoid a threatening serious danger without asking permission from the company. All procedures at work and conditions in the dormitories that violate basic human rights are forbidden. Young workers in particular should not fall into dangerous, insecure or unhealthy situations.

Management should name their representative who will be responsible for all employee health and safety issues. All employees should get regular and documented health and safety training, which should be given separately to new employees at the beginning of their employment. The company should have procedures for detecting, preventing and eliminating health and safety threats.

See also ILO conventions 155 and 184 and ILO recommendations 164 and 190.

### 6.4.7  Child Labour

According to an estimate by the ILO, 168 million children were working in 2012. Of them, 85 million were at dangerous work, half of them at agricultural work on family farms, the rest in mines and factories. Although the figures are big, there has been significant improvement since 2000, when 246 million children were working and 171 million at dangerous work. As to girls, the decrease is 40 per cent, as to boys, 25 per cent.

In the social audits, child labour has not often been detected – it is more typical in companies working in the home market and in agriculture rather than in export business. Especially in agriculture, it can be difficult to draw the line between child labour and working for the family. The basic rule is that the children have to be able to go to school, even though they help on the farm.

Use of child labour is prohibited according to what has been regulated in the ILO and UN conventions and national law. The most demanding rule is the one that should be followed. Usually a child is defined as being under 15 years of age, and those between 15 and 18 years are young workers. The ILO has given some poor countries (50 countries) the right to lower the age limit to 14 years. However, in some countries like in China, the age limit is 16 years.

All exploitation of children and working conditions that resemble slavery or are hazardous to the children's health, are prohibited. The rights of young workers should be protected. If children under the age limits are detected working, the company should have principles and practices according to which a plan can be drawn up in order to remediate the children's position and to document the actions taken. The company must give enough financial and other support to these children, so that they can go to school till the end of their compulsory education and until they are no longer children according to law.

The company can employ young workers, but if they are still within the range of compulsory education, they can work only outside of school hours. The school and work hours of a young worker – adding in the time needed for transportation – may not exceed ten hours per day, and the work hours may not exceed eight hours per day. Young workers are not allowed to work night shifts.

See also ILO conventions 10, 79, 138, 142 and 182 and recommendation 146. (On the ILO website www.ilo.org you can find a list of the countries that have exceptions to the basic age of 15 years, i.e. 14 or 16 years).

## 6.4.8 Forced Labour and Disciplinary Measures

All forms of forced labour, including monetary deposits or custody of identity cards at the beginning of employment, are prohibited, as well as using prisoners at work, which violates basic human rights. The partner company or any other party acting as an agent in recruiting workers may not take into custody part of the worker's salary or other benefits, possessions or documents in order to force the worker to continue working for the company.

Workers should have the right to leave the work site after the working time, and they should be free to end their employment, provided that they inform their employer about it within reasonable time.

**Doug DeRuisseau** (of Social Accountability International) once had to answer the question as to whether an armed guard standing by the gate of a dormitory represents forced labour. Doug's advice was that if the guard stands facing away from the building, he protects the workers' safety and does not let any trespassers in. But if he stands facing the dormitory, he probably wants to prevent the workers from leaving the area, which is against their rights.

The company or the agent recruiting workers should not participate in human trafficking or support it. The company should treat its workers with appreciation and respect. The company should not maintain nor accept physical discipline, psychological or physical force, or verbal insults.

In many EU countries, as well as in the US, there are illegal immigrants who work for a low wage and in poor conditions, because if they complain to the authorities, they will be deported from the country. Such an exploitation of paperless workers can be compared to forced labour.

See also ILO conventions 29 and 105.

## 6.4.9  Controlling Must Be Plausible

Environmental audits of suppliers are challenging but feasible. The requirements can be defined quite accurately, and the objects inspected are production processes, raw materials, components, waste management and so on – facts that very seldom change. Audits can be carried out by the buying company, though neutral third party audits are always more credible in customer communications and other interaction with stakeholders.

Controlling working conditions and terms is more difficult, as it is a question of the workers' position. Working conditions do not change from one day to another, neither do the working terms, but the workers change every now and then, and there can be big differences in their treatment.

A lot of information can be retrieved from the work-related documents, but the best information source is the workers themselves, which makes the worker interviews inevitable. It is also necessary to collect information from outside the company, for example from NGOs and authorities. To read the documents as well as to carry out personal interviews, one has to master the local language. Therefore, the inspections made by the buying company can only extend to exploring the production facilities and to interviewing the English-speaking management representatives. It is of course possible to use an interpreter, but then it is difficult to control whether the translations are truthful.

Neutral third party audits of working conditions have grown considerably in number, both for credibility and practical reasons. For this purpose, the social standard Social Accountability SA 8000 was developed, with the intention of placing it on the level of ISO 9000 and ISO 14000 as a certifiable standard. There are other similar auditing schemes that do not result in certification. The audits are conducted by professional auditors working for international certification bodies and speaking the local language. They have been trained, for example, to avoid the pitfalls in studying the documents and interviewing the workers.

## Nilambar Bhunya: The auditing industry has to get rid of some still existing defects

Nilambar Bhunya is an independent CSR consultant, auditor and trainer, based in Kolkata, India, associated for example with Wethica as their Lead Compliance Auditor.

**Has the interest of suppliers grown in social auditing in the last few years? Do they already proceed without the buyers' requirements, or does the process always start from the buyer's request?**
There are differences between regions. Some Bangladeshi factories and many south Indian factories realized real need for compliance. They started linking social audit findings, corrective actions with sustainable business. Most of the north Indian factories believe auditing is an overhead.

**What are the biggest problems in getting the audit carried out and then passing the audit?**
1. Getting real picture of labour management
2. Conducting successful off site interviews
3. Identifying fake documents and coached workers
4. Incompetent auditors
5. Corrupt auditors

**There are many social auditing schemes that have almost the same requirements as SA 8000 and a common Internet-based databank of supplier audits for the members who can save a lot of money through such cooperation, and the suppliers can avoid overlapping audits. Are there still too many schemes, and do you find some of them more successful than some others?**
1. Currently there are very few initiatives to avoid audit overlaps
2. Auditing and certification is a business, to sustain that you need audits. That could be the reason for not having such initiative.

**What about a buyer who is from a sector (for example furniture) that does not have any possibilities for cooperation in auditing? Which third party audit could he make use of, as all except SA 8000 seem to work on the "members only" principle?**
Unfortunately this is the scenario. IKEA have their own IWAY compliance structure which is very comprehensive and robust. They can extend that for their competitors too but it needs independent monitoring body. Presently there is no tailor-made BSCI or structure for furniture industry. Recently I audited 12 furniture units in the UAE – they were following Dubai/Abu Dhabi local laws as well as accepted industry standards. I did that for a brand against their brand Code of conduct.

**What will the audit market look like in the next 5-10 years from now?**
1. People have started to understand the loopholes of the auditing industry. Many have realized the business motives behind that.
2. More and more people will go for handholding continual improvement plan along with audits.
3. More stress will be given on training and self-auditing.

Before the actual audit, the working conditions can be monitored, which consists of reviewing the main points of the audit and drawing up, on the grounds of the detected deficiencies, a remediation programme, whose implementation will help to pass the audit and lower its costs.

For a single company working alone, it is pretty difficult to control the responsibility of the product and component manufacturers. Neutral third party monitoring and auditing companies can be used, but whenever all buyers are doing approximately the same thing, tens of audits are carried out at the manufacturers annually, which is quite a burden to the manufacturers and a big cost to the buyers. Therefore, cooperation with other similar buyers is useful in monitoring and auditing, as it is then possible to carry out the audit in the manufacturing company only once and upload the audit report into a common database, to be used by any of the buyer companies in the scheme.

Next, I present basic information about the neutral auditing schemes and give you my opinions on their pros and cons.

## 6.5   Social Auditing Schemes

All of the most common auditing schemes control compliance with the national labour laws and ILO core conventions, depending on which ones are more demanding from the workers' point of view in the country in question. An essential part of the schemes is the Internet-based database, which gives the members the possibility to share audit results. This helps them to avoid overlapping audits and saves a lot of costs and work.

In principle, the audit costs belong to the manufacturer, who orders the audit and can use it in business relations with all clients. Sometimes, a contracting partner or a retail chain wants all their suppliers to pass the audit as soon as possible and pays the auditing costs.

### 6.5.1  Social Accountability SA 8000 Standard (www.sa-intl. org)

SA 8000 has been composed like the ISO standards, but it has not been developed by ISO but by a multistakeholder association, Social Accountability International (SAI), and it has received plenty of funding from the US federal government. SA 8000 is the only social auditing scheme that issues public certifications regarding inspections of working conditions and terms. The certifications cannot, however, be found on the SAI website but they are on the website of Social Accountability Accreditation Services, which is a sister organization of SAI, training and accrediting SA 8000 auditors: http://www.saasaccreditation.org/?q= node/23

On 15 April 2016, there were 3,727 SA 8000 certified companies in 69 countries and 65 sectors, and these companies employed somewhat over two million workers. Asia had 53 per cent of the certifications, Europe 42 per cent. Italy had 1,081 certifications, India 953 and China 654.

The results are really modest, taking into account that SA 8000 was introduced in 1997. SA 8000 certification is regarded as very expensive – most of the costs arise from the large number of interviews required – and difficult due to the management system requirements. An entrepreneur who has started their business by buying first one sewing machine, then another, then tens of them, has not been able to develop themselves to a good management system planner, even after having grown to be an export company. Only a couple of Finnish companies have required use of SA 8000 standard from their suppliers – the certificates are accepted, though.

## 6.5.2 Ethical Trading Initiative (ETI), SEDEX Database (www.ethicaltrade.org, www.sedexglobal.com)

Ar around the time as SA 8000 was introduced, the British (retail trade, industry, trade unions, NGOs) developed their own auditing scheme, whose content is pretty much the same as that of SA 8000. The database SEDEX (Supplier Ethical Data Exchange) and the auditing scheme SMETA (Sedex Members Ethical Trade Audit) have been developed for the common use of buyers and manufacturers. In addition to the auditors, all members can upload audit reports to the database. There are 38,000 member companies in 30 sectors in over 150 countries. The member companies employ over 10 million workers.

The SMETA scheme does not require third party audits. This means (at least to me) that one has to be careful in using the audit results, and it is important to find out how the audit has been carried out. SEDEX does not accredite any auditors, so the members are free to choose their auditor. Audit results are not public, and SEDEX does not disclose how many manufacturers have passed the audits.

### 6.5.3   Business Social Compliance Initiative (BSCI) (www.bsci-intl.org)

BSCI cooperation was started at the beginning of the 2000s on the basis of the auditing scheme developed by German department store and clothes store chains. In 2003, the scheme was relocated to Brussels under the management of the Foreign Trade Association. When Kesko joined BSCI in 2004, there were around 30 members from a few European countries. In June 2016, BSCI had over 1,800 members: import companies, retail chains, brands among others. There is an own auditing scheme for primary production as well.

BSCI audits are from the workers' point of view practically the same as the SA 8000 certification. BSCI does not require the management system, but it can be developed at 'the best practice phase', which will then lead to SA 8000 certification. BSCI has a cooperation agreement with SAI, and only SA 8000 trained auditors accredited by SAAS can carry out BSCI audits.

In May 2016, BSCI and SEDEX signed a memorandum of understanding to co-develop projects and programmes that enhance the sustainability efforts of their memberships: 'The partnership will see the two organisations working more closely together, leveraging their joint strengths to drive scale within the responsible sourcing industry and creating numerous benefits for the memberships of both. This will establish a firm base and mutual understanding which can be further built upon to continue the collaboration in future' (press release, 26 May 2016).

BSCI helps companies to be audited by providing them – through their BSCI membership – with the BSCI Handbook, which includes among other things instructions for self-assessment. The buyers get their own handbooks. Getting audited and listed in the BSCI database requires cooperation with a BSCI member. There are over 32,000 audited suppliers in the database, but it can be used only by members. As outsiders cannot get information on BSCI audited companies, the audits cannot be utilized in consumer information and marketing.

BSCI organizes annually many training and information events for suppliers all around the world, especially in Asia. In its annual report, BSCI publishes audit statistics, from which one can see that the major deficiencies of the audited companies are in working hours, remuneration and work safety issues.

NGOs – for example the Clean Clothes Campaign – willingly criticize BSCI for being a business-drawn initiative, which has not taken NGOs nor

trade unions into their decision-making. This critique reflects mainly dis-
agreements about exercise of power. BSCI governance bodies have no effects
on the quality of audits or through this on protecting workers' rights. The
auditing companies compete against each other on reliability and quality.
Bad companies are knocked out soon, because unreliable data has no value in
this market. There have been some
cases where the auditors have suc-
cumbed to accepting bribes, but it
has quickly led to the sacking of
these auditors.

*In some cases the auditors have suc-
cumbed to accepting bribes, but it has
quickly led to sacking of these auditors.*

## 6.5.4 Fair Wear Foundation (FWF) (www.fairwear.org)

The Fair Wear Foundation is based in the Netherlands. It has 80 member
companies in seven European countries: clothes retailers and brands. Some
trade unions and NGOs like the Clean Clothes Campaign also participate in
their activities. FWF's Supplier Code of Conduct has the same content as the
other schemes, but the carrying out of audits and audit reporting are
different.

FWF approves of self-made audits. They can be carried out by audit teams
consisting of different backers, or the audits can be carried out by professional auditors – same certification bodies as are used in third party auditing.
FWF then audits the completed audits without notification, in order to
check that FWF's audit rules are followed. Also Clean Clothes accepts
these audit options and even praises the competence of self-made audits
and team audits. This is a very special trajectory: at the end of the 1990s,
Clean Clothes and similar NGOs criticized self-made audits and insisted that
monitoring of the supply chain should be given to neutral, professional
auditors.

On FWF's website, one can find each member's Brand Performance
Check Report, whose content has been built differently from the other
schemes, and the results cannot be compared with companies that work
with SA 8000, BSCI or ETI/SEDEX. It is difficult to get the big picture of
FWF's results in supplier audits.

## 6.5.5 Fair Trade Labelling (www.fairtrade.net)

There are over 1.2 million Fair Trade farmers and workers in 70 countries.
Their umbrella organization, Fairtrade Labelling Organizations International

(FLO), has drawn up auditing criteria for 20 primary product groups and for different producer organizations. There are criteria for working conditions and terms, as well as for environmental issues and the same social criteria as in BSCI and other similar audits. Farmers have a strong representation in FLO's administration.

Fair Trade certification is carried out by the independent FLOCert, which was established by FLO and has continent offices in South Africa, India and Costa Rica, these having regional offices in many countries. The certification entitles producers to use the Fair Trade label, which is well-known all over the world. Fair Trade certification is the only one in the world that has been able to take the results of social and environmental audits into product labelling. The scheme is valid only in primary production, not in industrial manufacturing.

FLO specifies for each product a minimum price (guarantee price), which is public and which is supposed to be higher than the world market price of the product. Small producers have sold about two thirds of their production as Fair Trade products, big farms about one third. Sometimes the Fair Trader price is too low, and the producers have sold their product without the Fair Trade certificate at a higher price.

As part of the price, FLO has also specified the Fair Trade Premium, a separate sum that the buyer pays above the guarantee price or market price, and the Fair Trade producers' co-op or the bigger Fair Trade farm use the sum for social or economic development of the community. The premium is usually between 5 and 30 per cent of the guarantee price, and it is presented for every product on FLO's website. For example, in Kenya on the Fair Trade cut flower farms the premium has been used to cover costs of the schools built for the workers' children and to acquire computers for the leisure premises.

In 2015, the sales value of Fair Trade products in Finland grew by 6.9 per cent to 173.5 million euros. The sales per capita – 32 euros per year – is the fourth highest in the world. The Fair Trade label is recognized by 92 per cent of Finns and 79 per cent know what it means. There are over 1,700 Fair Trade products available, of which more than half also have the Organic certificate.

## 6.5.6  Other Schemes for Monitoring Labour Rights

There are many other monitoring schemes in use to control suppliers in developing countries:

**WRAP** (Worldwide Responsible Accredited Production, www.wrapcompliance.org), mainly working with US clothing brands, follows the same requirements as the other schemes, provides the suppliers with material for self-assessment, uses third party auditors and publishes the audited factories on its website. There are three different certificates: Silver, Gold and Platinum. Silver class allows more deviations from the requirements than the others, not however from the 'Red Flag' requirements such as prohibition of child labour and forced labour. There are over 2,200 WRAP-audited companies which employ almost 2 million workers.

*Fair Labor Association* (www.fairlabor.org) consists of 40 big clothing and sports brands like Nike, Adidas, New Balance, Puma, Kathmandu, Hugo Boss, H&M and partly also Apple and Nestlé. The monitoring principles are the same as everywhere, but FLA highlights its development programme (Sustainable Compliance methodology) in its information. Audits are carried out usually by monitoring/auditing companies accredited by FLA, but sometimes FLA's own employees participate in the audits. FLA is criticized for letting the big member companies affect the audit results – one example of this was Apple's supplier Foxconn, which had big problems in China. FLA publishes summaries and examples of the audit results but not a list of audited suppliers.

*International Council of Toy Industries ICTI* (www.icti-care.org) has its own development and auditing programme, ICTI Care, and the corresponding organization for the electronics industry, *Electronic Industry Citizenship Coalition EICC* (http://www.eiccoalition.org/), has its own, too. The principles and procedures are the usual ones.

ICTI has actively improved work safety, but its members have problems with working hours. ICTI audits classify working hours in four groups, in which the weekly maximum hours are 60, 66, 72 and over 72 hours – quite far from China's new legislation and ILO's maximum hours. There are 1,100 ICTI-certified manufacturers in 12 countries, employing 600,000 workers and supplying 900 toy brands. Suppliers can be searched for on a public database by name.

EICC has developed an own risk assessment tool, self-assessment procedure and audit scheme, which requires use of third party auditors. Results are not disclosed.

The big brands of the food retail and consumer goods industry (35 members, such as WalMart, Tesco, Carrefour, Migros, Ahold, Marks & Spencer, Unilever, Chiquita, Dole, Starbucks, IKEA, Walt Disney and HP) have established a scheme called *Global Social Compliance Program GSCP* (www.gscpnet.com). GSCP has thorough instructions for monitoring the supply chain, including risk assessment, self-assessment forms, auditing instructions and so on, everything based on the same universal principles implemented by similar schemes.

Those schemes that demand third party audits have accredited international certification bodies and similar companies for this work. GSCP also approves, though under strict conditions, auditors who work for an NGO, a trade union or an industrial organization. There is a danger that such backgrounds can make the audit results distorted. Hopefully, that will never happen.

GSCP started publishing its tools at the end of 2008 and has proceeded in stages. So far, they have not established a common database for audits, and they have not reported any facts on progress – a big ship moves very slowly.

## 6.6    Summary of Responsible Sourcing

As you will have noticed when reading my descriptions of the various schemes monitoring working conditions and terms, there are so many such schemes – too many. When SA 8000 standard was introduced, its purpose was to rationalize evaluation of suppliers so that all monitoring could be done in the same way in all sectors, all over the world. The certifications and other audits would be available for all buyers, and the manufacturers could get rid of all those separate audits organized by each of their tens or hundreds of clients.

Unfortunately, this has not been the case. SA 8000 standard turned out to be too expensive and demanding for the SMEs in developing countries, and the big brands that are in a crucial position just did not make use of SA 8000. One reason for this may be that the names and addresses of the SA 8000 certified suppliers are publicly available on the SAAS website, and only a few brands and retail chains are excited about such transparency. Thus the suppliers have to – depending on the sector – continue participating in the numerous audits, each of which may be carried out differently, even though the issues that should be monitored are in practice the same for every supplier.

What about the countries in which proper labour laws exist and suppliers comply with them, terms of employment are regulated by binding collective agreements and the standard of living is quite high? In these countries, approximately all companies could get the SA 8000 certification and all farmers could get the Fair Trade certification. Maybe that was the reason why ISO did not want to extend their standard collection to certification of minimum requirements, a completely different concept than certifying best practice. I do not know whether they have been even asked.

Now, we are again facing the fact that the working conditions and terms of manufacturing companies in risk countries are monitored by about ten pretty professional international certification bodies, and some smaller ones in addition. European buyers have wanted to develop a more practical scheme (BSCI) out of SA 8000, but it has not been good enough for the British nor their American colleagues. The US consumer brands have two monitoring schemes of their own, the British SEDEX/SMETA now has plans to cooperate with BSCI. Hopefully this will succeed and take one step towards rationalization.

In Europe, part of the clothing business (a small part though) has wanted its own monitoring scheme (FWF), and the big retail and industry brands in Europe and the US have not wanted to join the SMEs but they have established their own GSCP, which is supposed to become the best scheme in the world. Also sectoral schemes have been set up (ICTI Care, EICC), and they are useful cooperation as such, though the principles and methods of monitoring should not depend on the industry sector.

Due to all these individual schemes, pointless overlapping costs arise, but I guess we just cannot help it. And when development of a responsible supply chain started criticizing buyers of self-made audits and requiring neutral information instead, now even NGOs (Clean Clothes among others) often prefer their own audits to those carried out by certification bodies. No doubt this playing field is quite disorderly, but fortunately the majority of the schemes are based on third party audits, which I definitely support.

However, I do make a stand on the publishing of the audit results. If a consumer considers buying a product and wants to know where it has been produced and whether the responsibility for the production has been verified, it is very difficult to get such information. This kind of answer is now offered: 'yes, the manufacturer of this product has passed the social audit, so that everything is in order, but for competition reasons we cannot say who this manufacturer is'. This is a real shame, and shows that as concerns consumer information, no progress has been made at all. Though the buyers have invested in neutral third party monitoring, consumers are not informed of the audit results, and have to continue trusting the buyers' word. SA 8000 has the only public list of certified suppliers, but this does not help much, because there is no SA 8000 label on the products. The same with other social audit schemes – no information on products. Fair Trade products are the only ones that have the label, but Fair Trade works only with primary products, not industrial products.

Recently, some pioneers have started to publish names of their suppliers on their websites, but they do not disclose audit results nor information about which products come from these suppliers, and the manufacturer's name is very seldom marked on the product. For example H&M has such a supplier list: (http://sustainability.hm.com/en/sustainability/downloads-resources/resources/supplier-list.html), as well as Nike: http://manufacturing map.nikeinc.com. In Finland, Kesko Group has only supplier names from each country on its list: http://www.kesko.fi/en/media/news-and-releases/news/2015/purchasing-chain-of-clothes-and-shoes-made-transparent/, whereas Stockmann department stores have a more detailed list with detailed addresses: http://www.stock manngroup.com/en/supplier-and-factory-list.

*Though the buyers have invested in neutral third party monitoring, consumers are not informed of the audit results.*

## 6.7    How to Proceed in Developing Responsible Sourcing?

In Table 6.2, I have described a thorough development process for responsible sourcing. SMEs can manage with a more straightforward plan. As this process is more or less about managing reputation risks, it is worth *assessing the risks in sourcing.* A common rule is that there are no social or environmental risks when buying from EU countries, and the monitoring should then be directed to purchases from outside of the EU. BSCI has placed on their list of risk countries only two from the EU – Romania and Bulgaria – but there can also be risks inside the EU, for example in the following cases:

• the company does not have a functioning system for work safety nor environmental management;
• the company uses hazardous subjects or processes;
• the company uses untrained cheap labour and seasonal workers;
• the company has human rights issues;
• the company uses plenty of cash.

As soon as the risks have been assessed, the next step is to define *sourcing principles,* which should express the core issues of responsible sourcing and which should be presented to existing and future suppliers. If necessary, more detailed requirements can be published separately regarding each field of corporate responsibility.

**Table 6.2** Suggested action plan for responsible purchasing management

| Suggested Action | Remarks |
| --- | --- |
| 1) Revise Supplier Requirements in your Code of Conduct. | Simple description of the principles applied to business partnerships, the reasons why, and the expected results for both parties. |
| 2) Decide on basic requirements on economic, environmental and social responsibility = Supplier Requirements. Tie the requirements with UN, ILO, OECD and GC conventions and guidelines. Put the requirements on the website and start sending them to existing and potential suppliers. | *Economic*: compliance with financial legislation, good reputation, pays taxes, bills, salaries etc. *Environmental*: stand on laws, standards, management systems, certifications. Some basic indicators at the beginning, more strict requirements later on. *Social*: ILO conventions/national legislation, special attention to work safety, systems/certifications. |
| 3) Produce a simple questionnaire for collecting basic information of suppliers on your database. | In addition to financial figures, information of management systems, certifications and reporting. |
| 4) Develop a check-list for assessing the suppliers: - divide all requirements into 5–10 subquestions - give points (e.g. scale 1–5) to each subquestion - decide the bounds for your rating (Approved, Approved with Remarks, Limited Approval, Banned). | Two check-lists may be needed for environmental issues: the basic list and a more demanding list. |
| 5) Decide which part of the check-list can be given to the suppliers in advance (pre-assessment) and which will be used at on-site assessments. | The final check-list can possibly be given to the suppliers as such, without a need for two different lists. |
| 6) Divide your suppliers into categories, based on importance / product grouping. | This should explain, which categories are prioritized in the assessment plan. |
| 7) Define risk suppliers. | Give the buyers a list of risk descriptions, all of which would lead to assessment. |
| 8) Develop a supplier database in your IT system. | |
| 9) Collect an assessment handbook of all measures to be taken. | This could be in the Intranet. |
| 10) Decide in which cases external third party auditors or NGOs are used. | In cases where stakeholders could have very critical opinions on your own assessments, external audits are recommended. |

*(continued)*

**Table 6.2**  (continued)

| Suggested Action | Remarks |
| --- | --- |
| 11) Train your own auditors (and before that, inform the whole buying organization of the decided system).<br>- ISO 14001, SA 8000, OHSAS? | Choose the ones with enough experience and best motivation, favour use of audit teams. |
| 12) Start the work through pilots. After the pilots, begin with the most important suppliers in the risk category. | A limited amount of assessments in each important product sector. |
| 13) Start collecting the data into the supplier database. | Each assessment will end with an assessment report that should be stored in the database and be accessible to all buyers.<br>The rating of suppliers could also be seen separately, not having to look at all individual reports. |
| 14) Start reporting on your assessment results in your annual CSR report. | The total amount of suppliers, the definition of risk supplier, the amount of suppliers in the risk category, the amount pre-assessed/assessed, the results of the assessments, plans for next year. |

Next, the suppliers should be grouped according to their importance and assessed risks. Monitoring has to be targeted to key suppliers and biggest risks, as the resources seldom are sufficient for handling a very big group of suppliers.

After this, it is time to decide on *how the monitoring should be carried out*. It is possible to examine on one's own the economic responsibility issues, as well as compliance with environmental requirements, because the raw materials used and production technology are usually permanent. Tailor-made environmental audits can also be ordered from a neutral party. Examining the workers' position on one's own is very difficult, and the stakeholders do not trust the usual story that 'we visit the factories regularly, make ourselves acquainted with the working conditions and interview workers, and because we have cooperated with this supplier for years, we know the circumstances and procedures of the company in question very well, and everything is in order'.

Merja Räsänen, partner of Nikolai Sourcing Ltd, describes in her interview how monitoring is carried out in practice.

## Merja Räsänen: Monitoring Has a Genuine Impacton Working Conditions

Merja Räsänen is partner and director of consumer goods trade at Nikolai Sourcing Ltd. Nikolai Sourcing has offices in Beijing, Shanghai, Hong Kong, New Delhi, Dhaka, Stockholm and Helsinki.

**Nikolai Sourcing has long experience of monitoring working conditions. In what parts of the world have you been working, in what kind of companies, and what is the background and training of your monitoring staff?**

We have offered monitoring services since 2008, when we set up a monitoring team at our Shanghai office. Most of our work takes place in China and Taiwan. As our customers come from many different sectors, we have carried out monitoring in very different production plants. The main focus has all the time been on textile, bag and shoe factories, but we have also monitored furniture factories and the chemical industry.

One of the core prerequisites for success is an experienced, qualified monitor. The training backgrounds of our monitors are very different, and it is not possible to become a monitor straight from school. Very often the career has started in other inspections like quality or environmental auditing. Nikolai Sourcing has hired only experienced monitors who have worked for international companies in assessing social responsibility. This has brought us versatile know-how and knowledge. Our employee turnover has been low, which has made long-term working possible.

**How is monitoring carried out in practice, what issues are reviewed in it?**

The monitoring process moves on like auditing: first the startup meeting at the factory, then the interviews with workers and management and inspections of the documents, the factory and the dormitory, if any.

Monitoring ends in reports, of which the most important is CAP (Corrective Action Plan), introducing to the factory in plain language what shortcomings and deficiencies they have, how they should be corrected and in what schedule. CAP is an important document and supervision tool for both the factory and the buyer. On follow-up visits, the monitors check how the corrective actions named in the CAP have been carried out. The report also includes pictures in which it is easy to see both shortcomings and successes.

**What are your experiences of monitoring? What shortcomings do they mainly reveal? How well have the monitored companies passed the actual audits?**

Over the years, we have the seen the main shortcomings in the Chinese factories: too much overtime work and insufficient compensation for it, problems in remuneration and work safety. Monitoring can reveal the shortcomings to the factories and advise what should be done to get things right. We can clearly see that monitoring helps the factory to prepare themselves for international audits. The monitor's advice and support helps in carrying out corrective actions and creating the right attitude towards responsibility, which has a genuine impact on the improvement of working conditions and responsibility of operations.

**How much does a typical monitoring cost?**
The costs depend on the basis of the monitoring. Some companies have their own Code of Conduct against which the monitoring and the report are carried out, or Nikolai Sourcing's own monitoring practice can be used. In 2016, the monitoring cost was 590 euros per day plus travelling costs. Such a low cost should not be an obstacle to ordering the service that gives the buyer information about the factories and helps in controlling the development of their working conditions.

The best solution is to become member of an appropriate cooperation group like BSCI or similar groups – the possibility of using a common supplier database is one of the biggest advantages of such cooperation.

If a supplier offers an audit report of a scheme other than the one you have joined, you can accept it if the audit has been carried out by a third party and there are no crucial deficiencies in the scheme (like the non-acceptable working hours of the toy industry). Such an offer is however quite rare, because all schemes intend to limit their information to paying members only, and audit reports are normally not freely available.

When it is not possible to find a suitable cooperation group, the monitoring also has to be carried out on one's own as concerns working conditions and terms. In such cases, it is also possible to use the services of neutral monitoring companies – though their monitoring is not as comprehensive and thorough as the actual audits, they serve the purpose of avoiding reputation risks very well.

After risk suppliers have been monitored/audited, the *performance indicators* of responsible supply chain are the amount of monitoring and/or audit assignments in relation to the amount of risk suppliers, and the audit results grouped into 'Approved', 'Approved after agreed remediation' and 'Rejected'.

### 6.7.1   GRI's Instructions for Screening Suppliers Are Non-specific

GRI recommendations suggest that companies report *the percentage of new suppliers that have been screened using labour practice criteria (LA14)* and *the significant actual and potential negative impacts for labour practices in the supply chain and actions taken (LA15)*. According to GRI, the percentage of screened new suppliers is counted from those 'with which the company negotiated or made a contract during the year and which were then screened using labour practice criteria'. Some instructions are given for screenings, which according to GRI can be carried out 'by supplier audits, contract inspections or other means of supplier cooperation or through official grievance mechanisms'. GRI does not take a stand on whether the audits and inspections should be neutral or self-made, which is a remarkable weakness in the instructions. GRI does not, either, recognize the practical situation that in sectors that have several seasons in a year, it is not possible to start acquiring neutral audit results before starting the business – as a condition for starting – if no such audit has been carried out before in the supplier company. Therefore, the buyer has to take the risk of starting the business first and then waiting for a couple of months before the operations of the supplier can be proved responsible. Of course, it is possible to look for the needed information months, even a year in advance, but in practice this is unrealistic.

I regard GRI's instructions on monitoring the working conditions as too vague and non-specific. Time will show how many companies are happy with reporting on such an important issue with such non-specific content or even want to hide behind the vagueness and avoid looking for reliable data and reporting on it.

*I regard GRI's instructions on monitoring the working conditions as too vague and non-specific.*

## 6.8   Human Rights Related to Sourcing

Human rights are discussed much more among the companies which operate in poor countries or buy from them than those companies based in rich countries. Human rights aspects are based mainly on the UN Universal Declaration of Human Rights and its adaptation to business, as well as on the Declaration on Fundamental Principles and Rights at Work defined by the ILO. Drawing the line between labour rights and other human rights can sometimes be difficult – if the subject has to do with the company's operational or reputation risks, it is worth following and studying more than just the ILO conventions.

There is of course plenty of information about the human rights issue on the Internet. I give you just three links here.

The first one is the website of the United Nations Office of the High Commissioner on Human Rights: http://www.ohchr.org/Documents/Publications/GuidingPrinciplesBusinessHR_EN.pdf

The second one is The Human Rights and Business Country Guide, which is a partnership initiative hosted by the Danish Institute for Human Rights in collaboration with partners around the world: http://www.bghr.org/

The third one is Business and Human Rights Resource Centre, which has for example tens of videos for those who want to study the subject from many angles and listen to expert presentations: http://business-humanrights.org/en/videos.

GRI has taken human rights as a separate reporting item with the intention that, in addition to sourcing, they apply also to the own operations and employees of multinational companies. I have earlier covered nearly all reporting items that GRI has included in the human rights area, so here I give only the list of the GRI indicators:

- HR1: Total number and percentage of significant investment agreements and contracts that include human rights clauses or that underwent human rights screening;
- HR2: Total hours of employee training on human rights policies or procedures concerning aspects of human rights that are relevant to operations, including the percentage of employees trained;
- HR3: Total number of incidents of discrimination and corrective actions taken;
- HR4: Operations and suppliers in which the right to exercise freedom of association and collective bargaining may be violated or at significant risk, and measures taken to support these rights;
- HR5: Operations and suppliers having significant risk for incidents of child labour, and measures taken to contribute to the effective abolition of child labour;
- HR6: Operations and suppliers having significant risk for incidents of forced or compulsory labour, and measures to contribute to the elimination of all forms of forced or compulsory labour;
- HR7: Percentage of security personnel trained in the organization's human rights policies or procedures that are relevant to operations;
- HR8: Total number of violations involving rights of indigenous peoples and actions taken.

This subject has been under public discussion mainly on issues concerning ownership and use of land – it applies to few big companies and the complaint and legal proceedings can be lengthy. It may be problematic to get neutral information about the treatment of indigenous peoples in the supply chain, as these issues are not part of the standardized audit processes:

- HR9: Total number and percentage of operations that have been subject to human rights reviews or impact assessments;
- HR10: Percentage of new suppliers that were screened using human rights criteria (such as labour rights LA14);
- HR11: Significant actual and potential negative human rights impacts in the supply chain and actions taken (such as labour rights LA15);
- HR12: Number of grievances about human rights impacts filed, addressed, and resolved through formal grievance mechanisms.

In reporting, it is useful to keep the human rights and labour rights in the same 'package' but analyse them nevertheless in two parts. The first one should include issues that apply to the own company, like training of human and labour rights and risk assessments, the second one deals with issues that apply to existing and new suppliers.

# 7

# Social Impacts

The word 'social' has often been connected to labour issues, but I use it in the same sense as GRI does, that is, describing the company's impacts on local, regional, national, perhaps even international society.

## 7.1 Relations with Local Community SO1, SO2

A company always has impacts on the *local community* where it operates. It can use the region's natural resources in its production, it can be a significant employer and taxpayer, it can cooperate with local enterprises and so on. By acting responsibly the company earns a good reputation, which makes the reforms and expansions of its operations easier.

Accordingly, polluting the environment or getting involved in corruption builds an irresponsible image, which makes cooperation with stakeholders difficult. Often, when a company has acquired land areas for its disposal, the disputes with the local inhabitants over land use have raised much publicity in the media. Also, the impacts of mining companies on the neighbourhood have been under vivid discussion. As usual, the negative impacts have been much more visibly exposed than the positive ones.

According to GRI, companies should report (SO1) on operations which interact closely with the local community, and carry out impact assessments

© The Author(s) 2017
J. Kuisma, *Managing Corporate Responsibility in the Real World,*
DOI 10.1007/978-3-319-54078-8_7

on and development programmes for this cooperation. Reporting should include social and environmental impacts, equality impacts, development programmes coming from local community needs, stakeholder interaction plans, broadbased groups consulting the local communities, processes taking into account fragile groups, grievance mechanisms and so on.

The list looks laborious and bureaucratic. Very big companies can probably carry out such cooperation programmes with local communities, and it is wise for them to do so. One good example is the Finnish/Swedish pulp and paper company StoraEnso, which has many operations in developing countries and has put a lot of effort into community relations which are very important for them, as they need to acquire land for their forest plantations.

They have all necessary documents collected into a download centre: http://www.storaenso.com/about/download-center?topic=2cb0d995-9de2-4a27-af55-2bbaa7e91a29

In their sustainability report, there is plenty of information about community engagement, from page 21 onwards: http://assets.storaenso.com/se/com/DownloadCenterDocuments/Sustainability_Report_2015.pdf

And there is a separate policy document concerning wood and fibre sourcing and land management: http://assets.storaenso.com/se/com/DownloadCenterDocuments/Policies_Wood_and_Fibre_Sourcing_and_Land_Management_2016_english.pdf

Smaller companies do not have the need for such detailed reporting on local community relations, but it is OK to present more modest actions if the subject is regarded as material.

The indicator SO2 describes how a company identifies and manages its own negative impacts on the local community. This may also include the intensity or severity, likely duration, reversibility and scale of the impact.

## 7.2   Corruption and Bribery SO3–5

The companies in Finland, as I believe in all EU countries, have decided on zero tolerance to corruption and bribery, in their principles as well as on a practical level. Companies that operate particularly outside of Europe have experienced problems in implementing zero tolerance – in some countries it is very difficult to succeed in business without bribing – and unfortunately some incidents also inside the EU have been in the headlines, though not too often.

I guess everybody has seen the Corruption Perceptions Index of Transparency International, published annually (http://www.transparency. org/cpi2015#results-table). The Index is a useful starting point when evaluating the circumstances in which the partner companies in each country operate. The Index covers mainly the public sector, though. I made some comments on the issue in 1.4.10.

In Transparency's 2015 Index, Denmark was the least corrupted country. Next best were Finland, Sweden, New Zealand, Netherlands, Norway, Switzerland, Singapore, Canada and Germany. The US was number 16, France 23, Spain 36, Hungary 50, Greece 58, Italy 61 and Turkey 66. India and Brazil were number 76, China 83, Vietnam 112, Russia 119, Bangladesh 139, Venezuela 158. The least corrupted African countries were Rwanda (44), Namibia (45) Ghana (56), South Africa and Senegal (61). The worst countries on the list were Sudan, North Korea and Somalia. The 2016 Index was not yet published in November 2016.

Transparency's country reports (National Integrity System Assessments) include plenty of detailed information about the crucial corruption and bribery problems detected in each country. When I participated in an EU training project on responsible public procurement, I studied the country assessments of a couple of EU member countries in Eastern Europe and noticed that public procurement is almost always on top of the problem list. Those who wanted to promote their business did not necessarily pay bribes, but instead they arranged deals with the buyers' relatives and friends. It has been estimated that in these countries corruption has raised the prices of public procurement by 20–25 per cent. Quite a cost for the taxpayers.

*It has been estimated that corruption has raised the prices of public procurement by 20–25 per cent. Quite a cost for the taxpayers.*

The GRI recommendations have three indicators to describe corruption and bribery:

- SO3: Total number and percentage of operations assessed for risks related to corruption and the significant risks identified;
- SO4: Communication and training on anti-corruption policies and procedures;
- SO5: Confirmed incidents of corruption and actions taken (were employees dismissed or disciplined, were contracts with business partners terminated or not renewed, were there public legal cases against the company or employees).

I have so far never seen reporting on corruption incidents, only on risk assessment and training. It is very difficult to disclose the incidents, as their treatment in the media is very tough, as of course it should be. Sometimes, publishing of these incidents is important for future business, for instance some certification bodies in Asia have very quickly announced that they have dismissed auditors who have been caught taking bribes. I have persuaded a couple of companies to report on what type of bribery and corruption requirements they have faced, but worry about their own safety and their families' safety has prevented such first steps of transparency on this subject. From this point of view, GRI's indicator SO5 does not seem very realistic.

Sometimes, it seems difficult to draw the line between corruption and bribery. One subject for discussion is the so-called facilitation or kickback payments, which are a much bigger problem to companies than bribes, as they are associated with the progress of permission and other documents and actions in practice. The difference between a bribe and a facilitation payment is clear. A bribe is a payment, for example, to a public officer for the purpose that they would do something that they are not permitted to do. A facilitation payment is a payment to the public officer for the purpose that they would do what they are supposed to do faster.

Facilitation payments are prohibited by law in many countries, but for example in the Foreign Corruption Practices Act of the US, they are accepted under certain preconditions. The zero tolerance principle does not accept facilitation payments nor presents which are larger than 'normal public relations' allow.

Whenever a company has many activities between buyers, sellers and public authorities, it is useful to draw up for internal use quite detailed instructions on what is allowed and what is forbidden. When drawing up the instructions, one should get acquainted with the sections concerning bribery in the national criminal law. In the Finnish criminal law, a bribe differs from a present in the way that a 'bribe is a benefit without legal rights that aims at getting the person that is bribed to favor the donor in his/her work task or position of trust' or 'the donor aims to influence a public officer in his/her position'. GRECO, the anti-corruption body of the European Council, has demanded that Finland should define the difference between bribe and present more clearly in criminal law.

Finally, a story that describes cultural differences. The Commission on Business in Society of the ICC held its meeting in an African country – I decided not to mention the name of the country here. On the day preceding the meeting, the national ICC chamber organized a seminar on corporate responsibility and some of us gave presentations there. The morning hours of the seminar were dedicated to the corruption and bribery theme. The discussion was bustling, the participants representing companies took up the subject seriously and were passionate about wanting to get rid of corruption. At the lunch table, I sat next to the interpreter (French/English) of the seminar, a lady in her early sixties, who told me that she was a Doctor of Law by education. She was very surprised that there had been so much discussion about bribery in the seminar – she had never thought that bribery was a problem in her country: 'When I drive my car, a police officer often stops me and wants to see my driving licence. I give him my license, which has a cover, and there is a banknote inside. The officer gives my licence back – the banknote is no longer there – he touches the peak of his cap, says 'Have a nice trip', and the traffic flows well. What's the problem?'

'Confronting corruption', an article by **Ravi Venkatesan** (McKinsey Quarterly, January 2015) makes interesting reading. Mr Venkatesan has been CEO of Microsoft India and member of the board of directors of Volvo and is nowadays chairman of the international Social Venture Partners network:

http://www.mckinsey.com/insights/corporate_social_responsibility/ Confronting_corruption?cid=other-eml-alt-mkq-mck-oth-1501

## 7.3   Political Contributions SO6

Financial support from companies to political parties and candidates has been a common and critical subject in the media, on the supposition that the company aim behind their financial support is to affect the opinions and decisions of politicians. In some extreme cases, the support has been regarded as bribery. Those companies following the GRI recommendation have had to report their political contributions since the beginning of the GRI history, that is since 2000, but all companies have not done this and they have been forced to disclose their donations only when the media has started to investigate the subject.

Campaign fund-raising is today regulated in Finland as well as in many other countries. According to Finnish regulations, one donor can donate to a candidate, the support team of the candidate and other organization working solely for the support of the candidate not more than 3,000 euros in the municipal elections, 6,000 euros in the parliament elections and 10,000 euros in the European Parliament elections.

The recipient must disclose the donor's name if the donation is at least 800 euros in the municipal and parliament elections and 1,500 euros in the European Parliament and presidential elections. All donations received have to be reported to the State Finances Inspection Office to be published on their website.

Transparency of political contributions seems to be important in democratic countries. I do not recall having seen a more thorough listing of political donations, nor a more open presentation of own political goals than what I found on Microsoft's website (https://www.microsoft.com/about/csr/transparencyhub/political-engagement/). Also, in the US there are restrictions on political donations – companies cannot support the candidates of federal elections financially, whereas in state and local elections they can. Microsoft reports on their donations every two years.

### 7.3.1  A Company as a Political Donator

In Finland, the costs of political contributions are not deductible in the company's taxation, as such costs are not affiliated with the company's business. You should make yourself acquainted with the tax regulations of your own country.

Political parties, candidates and their support teams also look for funding by offering various items for sale. Such cost deductions in taxation can be judged in many ways. The basic rule is that the company can deduct only the costs that are affiliated with their business.

The costs should then not be higher than the current price paid for similar products or services. Advertising in political newspapers and seminar costs can be deductible if the company's presence in the newspaper can be compared to commercial advertising and if the seminar is affiliated with the company's business and the participation fee is not higher than the current price.

Even though costs of minor amounts are deductible in taxation, they are not deductible if they have been given for political purposes.

## 7.4  Breaches of Legislation

Indicators of social performance include breaches of competition legislation (SO7) and other non-conformances with laws and regulations, as well as fines or other sanctions (SO8). GRI addresses other laws with the following indicators:

• PR2: Total number of incidents of non-compliance with regulations and voluntary codes concerning the health and safety impacts of products and services during their life cycle

- PR4: Total number of incidents of non-compliance with regulations and voluntary codes concerning product and service information and labelling
- PR7: Total number of incidents of non-compliance with regulations and voluntary codes concerning marketing communications
- PR8: Total number of substantiated complaints regarding breaches of customer privacy and losses of customer data.

GRI also deals separately with breaches of environmental legislation (EN29) and of laws on products and services (PR9).

As I mentioned when describing the relations between employees and employer (LA4), this GRI recommendation does not include reporting on employment disputes related to labour law, collective agreement or labour contract. In my opinion, this subject is an essential part of human resource management and worth reporting, which needs nothing more than to disclose what kind of disputes between labour unions and employer associations have been taken to negotiations, to either district court or industrial tribunal, and which party has won the case.

I think all breaches of legislation should be disclosed in one package, except the breaches of environmental legislation (EN29). It depends on the company and the sector, whether breaches are regarded as material issues – my feeling is that they should always be disclosed, as well as of course the positive result that no breaches have occurred during the year.

In addition to breaches of laws and regulations, GRI includes introduction of grievance mechanisms and amounts of complaints received.

# 8

# Product Responsibility

The interest in corporate responsibility is transferring to product information whenever collecting product-specific data is possible.

*Health and safety impacts of products and services on customers* (PR1–2) is regulated by strict legislation and directed by many recommendations – like the OECD Guidelines – and by companies' own voluntary principles. Especially for foodstuffs and electronic devices the safety requirements are very strict and breaches have been presented visibly in public. Product responsibility includes impacts on health and safety, packaging labels and other product information, as well as regulations on marketing and privacy protection of customer data. Breaches of product responsibility can lead to product withdrawals, fines or damages, and they bring costs and harm the company's reputation. Complying with regulations reduces breaches and protects the competitiveness of the company and job satisfaction of the employees.

*Product information* (PR3–4) – part of product responsibility – is regulated in many countries by national legislation, and the EU has its own standards for declaring the consistency, origin and other details of products.

*Marketing communication* is regulated by consumer protection legislation and complementary instructions by the consumer ombudsman and by sector-wise recommendations and international guidance such as the OECD Guidelines and the ICC Code of Marketing and Communication Practice. The GRI recommendations include information on sale of banned

© The Author(s) 2017

J. Kuisma, *Managing Corporate Responsibility in the Real World*,
DOI 10.1007/978-3-319-54078-8_8

or disputed products (PR6) and non-compliance with regulations and voluntary codes concerning marketing communications (PR7).

*Protecting customers' privacy* is also included in many countries' legislation. Privacy protection is related to confidentiality, safe storing of customer data and using of the data only for purposes that have been agreed on. In the last few years, the subject has been in the public eye, as customer loyalty programmes have become more common. GRI recommends the reporting of the number of complaints received (PR8).

*Customer satisfaction* is an important indicator for all companies and can be regarded as one of the material issues of corporate responsibility. Customer opinions are monitored by collecting customer feedback and by carrying out customer satisfaction surveys, whose results should be reported on (PR5). According to my experience, companies present ways of monitoring opinions: participation in the sector's mutual surveys, execution of own tailor-made surveys and the 'mystery shopping' procedure. Numerical results are, however, disclosed only when own results are better than those of competitors or at least comparable. GRI recommends clearly that the results of the surveys and the essential conclusions should be reported. Hiding bad results does not comply with the transparency requirements of CR reporting.

# 9

# Materiality Assessment in a Matrix

When all performance indicators of the GRI recommendations have been reviewed, given weightings and placed in the table presented in 2.8.2, the indicators should be shifted to a matrix (see Fig. 9.1) in order to perceive the materiality.

The materiality assessment is an essential part of the GRI recommendations. There is a huge number of suggested indicators, and it is not possible nor sensible to report on all of them, but every company has to recognize the issues that are the most important, most material for themselves and their stakeholders, and concentrate on those issues. The purpose is to visualize, with the help of the materiality matrix, which issues are material and which also are related to the company's activities but are not important enough to be continuously monitored and reported on. Some companies leave the immaterial issues out of the matrix. In my opinion, it is important to present them as well, so that the reader can with one glance see how the company has structured the big picture. The problem is that the amount of immaterial indicators can be considerable and there will be a crowd in the lower left corner of the matrix. Therefore, every company has to find a compromise and decide what is sensible. Later, in collecting the GRI Index, it is possible to concentrate on material indicators only.

If weightings have been given on a 0–10 scale, the most material indicators are usually the ones that have received a weighting of 6 or more, from the

© The Author(s) 2017                                                    **165**
J. Kuisma, *Managing Corporate Responsibility in the Real World*,
DOI 10.1007/978-3-319-54078-8_9

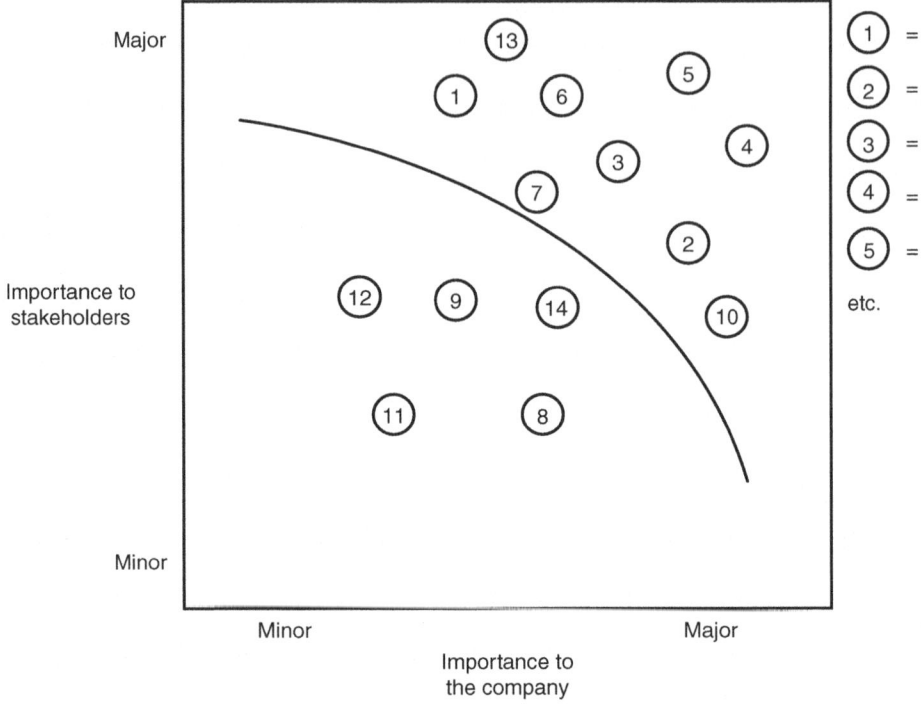

**Fig. 9.1** Presenting the results of the materiality assessment

company itself or from the stakeholders. A weighting of 5 can sometimes be considered as material and kept in monitoring and reporting – weightings lower than 5 are in principle not reported on. However, it may be sensible to monitor and report on some of them, perhaps when they are related to some of the material indicators and complement them. For example, the basic information of employees is worth reporting, even though it would not be regarded as material. Those indicators that have received zero weighting have no importance whatsoever or no connection to the company's activities, and they have therefore been left out of the matrix, For example, an auditing company or a law firm may not have very much to do with biodiversity or environmental responsibility in the supply chain, if we are not inclined to be pedantic.

In a big corporation consisting of many subsidiary companies and many lines of business, it is probable that some indicators are valid only in some parts of the corporation. For example, corruption and bribery issues are material only in some countries of operations, and the risk of child labour is material only in sourcing certain products from certain countries. All such differences cannot be presented in one corporate level matrix – if, for example, the risk of child labour is included in the matrix, it is advisable to explain in a footnote, in which operations the risk is material.

Instead of GRI indicators, some companies present entities like 'Welfare at work' or 'Material and energy efficiency'. Such a description is clear and sufficient for an ordinary reader of the report, but it does not comply with GRI's efforts to make companies assess the materiality of the GRI indicators. For example, the entity 'Welfare at work' consists of many separate indicators, which can have different weightings, but if they are all taken under one main title, they are regarded as equal. To be precise, one should at least say which indicators the entity consists of: LA1 Employee turnover, LA6 Sick days and accidents at work, LA9 In-service training, LA10 Lifelong learning and LA11 Performance and career development reviews.

# 10

# Management Principles Guiding Corporate Responsibility

The *stakeholder assessment* has consisted of recognizing the stakeholders and their expectations and requirements of the company, considering with which actions the company will respond to them and discussing which indicators will be used for monitoring the performance of the actions. The *materiality assessment* has covered all areas of corporate responsibility – in the scope that GRI has defined – and the material issues and indicators have then been chosen. After all this, it is time to give promises about developing corporate responsibility and draw up an action plan for the next few years, based on the materiality assessment and promises.

In order to bring forth concrete results, the promises have to be concrete as well. Beautiful words and wishes do not benefit the company or its stakeholders. If one promises anything, one has to measure the results and prove how the promises have been kept.

## 10.1 Public Management Principles Are Important

In order to make the employees aware of what should be done to ensure responsibility and to enable the stakeholders to keep track on which promises the company has made and how these promises are kept, public management principles guiding responsibility are needed. Such principles exist in many companies, but they have not been published and outsiders then know nothing

© The Author(s) 2017                                                        **169**
J. Kuisma, *Managing Corporate Responsibility in the Real World*,
DOI 10.1007/978-3-319-54078-8_10

about their existence or contents. I noticed this once again when I searched many company websites and tried to find links to principles. Transparency of operations is an essential feature of corporate responsibility and introducing the management principles is an important part of such transparency. Defining the principles belongs to the tasks of the CR steering group.

Developing the set of principles usually starts by defining 'Principles of Responsible Business Conduct', the so-called 'Code of Conduct'. The Code consists of the company's policies and instructions for the situations that arise in its operations and stakeholder relations, requiring responsible actions. If the company has international commitments, they are also entered in the common principles.

The common principles are specified with more detailed principles, policies and guidelines whenever needed, such as:

- governance principles (listed companies)
- risk management principles
- human resources policy
- health and safety policy
- environmental policy
- principles of responsible sourcing
- product policy /product statements
- communication policy
- principles of sponsoring

*Principles* present on a common level the company's standpoint on certain subjects, *policy* is a more detailed description about how the company will act in respect of the subjects. All principles and policies are worth publishing on the company website in a way that they are easily found.

Common principles should be approved by the board of directors. Some of the complementing principles (like governance and risk management principles) are approved by the board, the others by the management board. All employees should be familiarized with the common principles. The training of specific principles – like principles of responsible sourcing – should be targeted to those employees who work with the subject in question.

All management principles guiding corporate responsibility are clear promises on which actions will be taken and what kind of results are sought. Therefore, it is necessary to avoid giving beautiful but empty promises, whose results can never be measured. For example, it is difficult to prove the promise 'we serve our customers honestly and kindly and act ethically', as well as 'all our suppliers and contractors have to comply with our environmental policy'. On the contrary, the following type of promises are measurable: 'We invest in welfare at work, job satisfaction and work safety' and 'We reduce our emissions by optimizing our transport and by cutting the fuel consumption of our vehicles'. It is, of course, not possible to find indicators for every single sentence, but the basic rule is: 'Do not give any promises whose realization you cannot prove'.

*It is necessary to avoid giving such beautiful but empty promises whose results can never be measured.*

## 10.1.1  Code of Conduct

The big multinational companies in particular nowadays have a so-called Code of Conduct as their guideline. The Code of Conduct explains to the employees and other stakeholder groups – customers, suppliers and other partners – how those working in the company should and will act in different situations.

The structure of a typical Code of Conduct is:

- complying with the laws
- responsible economy
- promoting competition
- conflicts of interest
- customer relations
- relations with partners
- good working community
- environmental responsibility
- implementation of the principles

When formulating the text, it is important to remember that even though the principles are common and not very detailed, they are promises whose realization must be monitored and reported to stakeholders.

The Code of Conduct usually gives the stakeholders a possibility of notifying about any grievances and breaches arising. There are different procedures for this purpose. The primary choice is always contact with one's superior, but it is often necessary to give the notification so that the identity of the notifier can be kept as confidential as possible. For such purpose, notification procedures have been developed and placed on the company intranet, or notifications can be sent to a neutral external party.

Here are two examples:

http://www.vaisala.com/en/sustainability/responsiblevaisala/codeofcon duct/Pages/default.aspx

http://martela.com/files/media/Responsibility/martela_corporate_code_ of_conduct_2016.pdf

### 10.1.2 International Commitments of Corporate Responsibility

Whenever a company is multinational (according to OECD's definition, a company that operates in two countries is already multinational), it should consider voluntary commitments to common and sector-specific international agreements and initiatives:

- UN Universal Declaration on Human Rights and Convention on the Rights of the Children;
- UN Principles on Business and Human Rights;
- UN Principles for Responsible Investments;
- ILO Convention on Fundamental Principles and Rights at Work;
- OECD Guidelines for Multinational Companies;
- Codes and recommendations of the International Chamber of Commerce ICC.

Of these, the ILO Convention can be regarded also as legally binding, because its requirements have been included in the labour laws of most countries. OECD Guidelines – though they are only instructions – resemble sections of law and give possibilities for complaints. The others are more or less voluntary commitments. I have presented these commitments earlier in 1.5."

## 10.2  Environmental Policy

Most companies have taken care of the environment well without detailed policies. For an outsider, it has been difficult to determine whether the actions and results presented are true, if the company has not clearly and publicly presented the promises and objectives.

Promises concerning the protection of the environment are given in the environmental policy. This describes which are the most significant environmental impacts of the company, with which actions the company is going to reduce them and how performance should be monitored and reported on. Measuring the results is essential, and again it is not sensible to make empty promises whose realization cannot be monitored or proved. If a company wants to get their environmental management system certified against ISO 14001 or EMAS (the EU's Eco Management and Audit Scheme), a written environmental policy is necessary.

The environmental impacts vary from one company to another. Therefore, every company has to define their environmental policy according to their own starting point, impacts and actions.

I have chosen some model policies here, not as the best practices, but as homework for you. Go to these web pages, read through the texts and analyse the policies from the point of view of which promises you think are measurable and which are just empty words.

http://www.lassila-tikanoja.fi/en/company/corporate-responsibility/code-of-conduct/Pages/environmental-policy.aspx

http://cdn.ek.aero/english/images/environment_policy_tcm233-658143.pdf

http://www.finnairgroup.com/linked/en/yhteiskunta/Finnair_Environmental_Policy.pdf

https://www.jal.com/en/csr/environment/vision/

http://www.burberryplc.com/documents/corporate_responsibility/global-environmental-policy.pdf

http://company.marimekko.com/sustainability/environment

http://www.kesko.fi/en/company/policies-and-principles/environmental-policy/

## 10.2.1 HR Policy

As with environmental issues, most companies do take care of their employees well without detailed written policies. But for an outsider, it has been difficult to determine whether the actions and results presented are true, if the company has not clearly and publicly presented the promises and objectives.

The basic principles and objectives of human resources management are introduced in the human resources policy. Many countries will face a labour shortage as soon as the populous generation born in the 1940s and 1950s retires – though sometimes it seems as if such a situation just always remains far into the future. The surveys studying the attractiveness of workplaces show clearly that young job applicants value responsible companies and want details on their promises and results. The human resources policy – like the environmental policy – should mainly introduce the kind of promises whose realization can be measured.

There are significant differences in the structure and tasks of the staff in different companies. Therefore, each company has to emphasize their own needs and focus areas in their human resources policy. Big companies may need to define a separate health and safety policy and a related action plan.

Here is the same exercise as with the environmental policies:

http://www.orion.fi/en/Orion-group/Sustainability/policies/human-resources-policy/

https://corporate.vattenfall.com/sustainability/policies-and-management/human-resources-policy/

https://www.neste.com/fi/en/node/18049

http://www.kesko.fi/en/company/policies-and-principles/hr-policy/

http://www.veolia.com/en/veolia-group/careers

## 10.2.2 Principles of Responsible Sourcing

Principles of responsible sourcing consist of common requirements such as complying with legislation and prohibition of bribing, commercial requirements like quality, technical and environmental requirements, requirements on product safety, and product responsibility and deliveries. If the biggest part of sourcing is directed to EU countries, the reputation risks of sourcing are minor and responsibility does not need to be highlighted in the sourcing principles. Whenever products are made, or some stages of production are carried out, in developing countries, the suppliers are regarded as risk suppliers, in which case social requirements are added to the principles. The basic standard is that the suppliers should comply with national labour laws and the ILO core conventions, depending on which rules are the most exacting from the workers' point of view. Such sourcing principles directed mainly at foreign risk suppliers are often called Supplier Code of Conduct.

It is difficult for a single company to monitor a supplier's compliance with the social and environmental requirements in a supply chain that extends to far away countries around the world. Therefore, international sector-specific cooperation is almost indispensable for developing this monitoring, especially as it is important to work with neutral third party auditors and to create a common database in order to avoid auditing the same factories many times. Unfortunately, this kind of cooperation is not possible in every sector. At the moment, the most important organizations developing supplier monitoring and auditing are:

- Business Social Compliance Initiative (BSCI), headquartered in Brussels at the Foreign Trade Association, which in November 2016 had almost 2,000 members – mainly European retail groups, consumer goods industry, brands – and over 20,000 suppliers in the databank;
- Ethical Trading Initiative ETI in the UK (very few British companies take part in European cooperation initiatives such as BSCI), with less than 100 members and the audit databank SEDEX, which has the major retail chains and their suppliers as members, somewhat over 36,000 companies;
- ICTI Care Process (ICP), run by the International Council of Toy Industries (ICTI), with about 100 leading companies from the toy sector.

If a company belongs, for instance, to BSCI, their sourcing principles should comply with the BSCI Code of Conduct.

I have addressed monitoring and auditing in detail in Chapter 6.

Some examples of sourcing principles:

http://martela.com/files/media/Responsibility/martela_social_require ments_on_suppliers_2011.pdf

http://www.fortum.com/SiteCollectionDocuments/Corporation/Code% 20of%20Conduct%202012/suppliers_CoC_eng.pdf

https://www.neste.com/en/corporate-info/sustainability/sustainable-sup ply-chain/supplier-requirements

http://www.novonordisk.com/sustainability/actions/Responsible-Business/Responsible-sourcing.html

http://eu.patagonia.com/pdf/en_US/Patagonia_COC_English_02_13.pdf

http://www.woolworths.co.za/store/fragments/corporate/corporate-index. jsp?content=../article/article&contentId=cmp205999

This includes both social and environmental responsibility.

## 10.2.3 Principles of Risk Management

Written, public principles of risk management are normally part of the management system of large listed companies, but any kind and size of company can of course make use of them. Though the management principles guiding responsibility should normally be publicly available, it is possible to leave risk management principles out of the public package if the company is not looking for interest from investors. Strange enough, GRI does not require presentation of these principles in reporting – though disclosures of management approach are required on many occasions, which is almost the same thing.

In listed companies, risk management can be regarded as part of the implementation of corporate governance principles. Risks are usually divided into strategic, operational and finance risks. Risks other than economic impacts should be taken into account. A reputation risk arises if the company's actions are in conflict with the expectations of the stakeholders, such as customers or shareholders. The most typical reputation risks are associated with the operations of the suppliers and subcontractors: bribery, corruption and other economic malpractices, violations of environmental regulations and labour rights.

I have addressed risk assessment earlier in 2.5.

## 10.2.4  Product Policy, Product Statements

In some sectors, the companies will face questions asked by customers – consumers as well as b-to-b buyers – regarding the production conditions or origin of the products. The companies are expected to give clear stands on these questions: 'what is your stand on fur production, living space of broilers, transports of beef cattle, hormones and antibiotics in raising cattle and fish, genetic modification, endangered fish species, forest certification, protection of rainforest, recycled raw materials and so on. These questions are based on the customers' own 'ethical principles', which exist in abundance and which impact purchasing behavior. Consumers are nowadays very individual and the segmentation of marketing is therefore not that easy. The target group 'mothers at the age of 30–40 years, with university degree, living in the capital area' has been disturbed by 'consumer tribes' that have spread all around Europe: friends of organic food, vegetarians, vegans, opponents of furs, protectors of animals, carbon footprint followers, opponents of motoring, human rights activists, health-conscious and so on. Companies can also have similar principles, often based on the principles of the owners: we sell neither tobacco nor alcohol, we do not sell adult entertainment material, and so on.

If the company finds such statements important from a customer relations point of view, they are definitely worth defining and publishing. Some examples of such statements are:

• Products made of tropical wood should be FSC- or PEFC-certified

- Our restaurant conforms to the guidelines of the WWF Consumer's Seafood Guide. All tuna that we sell is proved to be sustainably fished by MSC certification
- Our meat originates from cattle that eats fodder which has not been genetically modified
- The jeans we sell have not been sandblasted
- We do not sell fur products
- We use only RSPO-certified palm oil.

## 10.2.5 Communications Policy

Very few companies have published a written, public communications policy on their website, nor is it among the management principles listed in the GRI recommendations. However, communications are a very fundamental part of corporate responsibility in the sense that a responsible company should act as openly and transparently as possible. From this point of view, the communications policy should be much more visible.

As concerns openness of communications, listed companies are more advanced than other companies, due to the high standards set for their communications, but their standpoints are mainly related to governance principles and financial information. Other companies do not have such burdens and they can therefore define quite simple communications policies.

The basic contents of the communications policy are:

- Basis of communications, for example values and strategy
- The company's position on the tasks and goals of their communications
- Common principles, such as reliability, openness and quickness
- Focuses of communications
- Positions on commenting on confidential and incomplete issues and on competitors' business
- Responsibilities of communications

## 10.2.6 Sponsoring Principles

Big as well as small companies are frequently asked to cooperate with many kinds of non-profit organizations, athletic clubs, individual sportspersons, artists and others. The larger the company, the more useful the publicly available sponsoring principles are for this cooperation, so that the parties involved already know in advance what can be expected from the company.

Sponsoring principles explain:

- what is meant by *donations* (decision by the general meeting, does not include mutual cooperation) and by *sponsoring* (mutual cooperation, which supports the company's business and makes the company and/or its products better-known)
- what is the procedure of donations and to which purposes donations are made
- which organs/persons of the company process sponsoring proposals
- what kind of sponsoring suits the company's values, strategy and responsibility principles and what goals does the company set for sponsoring

It is nowadays difficult to get companies to participate in charity projects, as mutuality is regarded as a prerequisite for stakeholder cooperation. Donating money to a project that has nothing in common with the company's operations is not common – often the companies also feel that such projects should be funded by tax revenues. Donations for example to a children's hospital or disaster aid are of course important, as long as they do not play the main role in corporate responsibility. Sponsoring – funding a project that is clearly related to the company's operations – is more easily arguable.

> *Donations for example to a children's hospital or disaster aid are of course important, as long as they do not play the main role in corporate responsibility.*

## 10.3  Standards Assisting Management Principles

Corporate responsibility should rest on accountable facts. Though the company itself may be responsible and reliable, own reassurances are not sufficient in every situation. Therefore, certificates given by neutral certification bodies on compliance with international standards, as well as the neutral product labels proving responsibility, have gained more importance in managing corporate responsibility.

ISO standards are the best-known international standards. Those standards serving corporate responsibility include the following:

– *ISO 14001* environmental management standard is used in over 170 countries, and there were over 300,000 certifications in July 2016. It was revised in 2015, as well as the quality standard ISO 9001, and it will have a three-year transition period. The key changes relate to increased prominence of environmental management within the organization's strategic planning processes; greater focus on leadership; addition of proactive initiatives to protect the environment from harm and degradation, such as sustainable resource use and climate change mitigation; improving environmental performance added; lifecycle thinking when considering environmental aspects; addition of a communications strategy.

In addition, the revised standard follows a common structure with the same terms and definitions as a number of other management system standards such as ISO 9001. This makes them easier, cheaper and quicker for those companies who use more than one, not to mention helping out the auditors.

By implementing ISO 14001, environmental management becomes systematic and goal-directed, even though the mere use of the standard does not guarantee good results.

The EU has developed a similar certifiable management system EMAS (Eco Management and Audit Scheme), which is commonly used for example in Germany.

SMEs very seldom have a certified environmental management system. Some companies claim that they comply with ISO 14001, but their system has not been certified. However, the only possibility for proving the compliance is the neutral certification.

– *OHSAS 18001/18002* Occupational health and safety management standard, which will be replaced by ISO 45001 standard which is currently being developed by a committee of experts.

– *ISO 19600* Compliance Management Standard was published at the end of 2014. ISO 19600 provides guidance for establishing, developing, implementing, evaluating, maintaining and improving an effective and responsive compliance management system within an organization.

– *ISO 22000* sets out the requirements for a food safety management system and can be used for certification purposes. It maps out what an organization needs to do to demonstrate its ability to control food safety hazards in order to ensure that food is safe. It can be used by any organization, regardless of its size or position in the food chain. The ISO 22000 family contains a number of standards, each focusing on different aspects of food safety management. ISO 22000 is under revision, the final updated version is expected early 2017.

– *ISO 27000* family of standards helps organizations keep information assets secure. Using this family of standards will help the organization manage the security of assets such as financial information, intellectual property, employee details or information entrusted to you by third parties.

ISO/IEC 27001 is the best-known standard in the family, providing requirements for an information security management system (ISMS).

– *ISO 31000 Risk management – Principles and guidelines* provides principles, framework and a process for managing risk. It can be used by any organization, regardless of its size, activity or sector. Using ISO 31000 can help organizations increase the likelihood of achieving objectives, improve the identification of opportunities and threats and effectively allocate and use resources for risk treatment.

However, ISO 31000 cannot be used for certification purposes, but does provide guidance for internal or external audit programmes. Organizations using it can compare their risk management practices with an internationally recognized benchmark, providing sound principles for effective management and corporate governance.

– *ISO 26000* is a social responsibility standard which provides guidance rather than requirements, so it cannot be certified to, unlike some other well-known ISO standards. Instead, it helps clarify what social responsibility is, helps businesses and organizations translate principles into effective actions and shares best practices relating to social responsibility, globally. It is aimed at all types of organizations regardless of their activity, size or location.

The standard was launched in 2010 following five years of negotiations between many different stakeholders across the world. Representatives from government, NGOs, industry, consumer groups and labour organizations around the world were involved in its development, which means it represents an international consensus.

ISO 26000 is a guide for those who have started to make themselves acquainted with corporate responsibility, and for those more experienced who want to improve their procedures. The standard consists of terminology and principles of corporate responsibility, involving the stakeholders and seven core subjects:

1. Governance of the company
2. Human rights
3. Labour practices
4. Environment
5. Fair ways of acting

6. Consumer affairs
7. Participation in the activities of the local community and developing them.

The problem with ISO 26000 is – as already said – that it has been named as an ISO standard, which usually means possibilities for certification as proof that the company complies with the standard. However, ISO 26000 is a guidance standard which cannot be certified to and whose compliance cannot be proved in any other way, because the standard does not include exact requirements or indicators for measuring.

In spite of this, there have been efforts to certify compliance with ISO 26000 (in Denmark, Spain, Austria and Italy, for example), even though ISO has forbidden this. These efforts may be due to the fact that the certification bodies earn money out of certifying compliance with standards, and the possibility of getting certified to ISO 26000 has clearly interested a large number of companies. Some certification bodies now offer 'training on introduction of ISO 26000'.

*There have been efforts to certify compliance with ISO 26000, even though ISO has forbidden this.*

The Dutch standardization organization NEN has developed procedure instructions NEN-ISO 26000 (NPR 9026) to complement ISO 26000. The instructions describe the process with which a company prepares and draws up an assurance – a self-declaration – that they comply with ISO 26000 principles and instructions. In my opinion, such self-declarations do not match with the normal assumption of how standards are used.

GRI, although it is a reporting scheme, offers companies a much more precise and measurable management system for corporate responsibility, so that ISO 26000 does not bring any added value to companies that implement GRI thoroughly. GRI has published a guidance document on the joint use of GRI and ISO 26000, which is worth studying if one aims to use both in own development work. If a company is not yet ready for reporting, it is possible to get the hang of corporate responsibility by exploring ISO 26000. In the EU directive on non-financial reporting, coming into force at the beginning of 2017, ISO 26000 has been mentioned as one possible reporting frame, which could cause quite a mess, as ISO 26000 does not have any performance indicators.

(Most of the ISO standard presentations above are based on ILO's own texts on their website www.ilo.org)

*Social Accountability SA 8000* standard was developed at the end of 1990s as a continuation of ISO 9001 and ISO 14001 standards. It is the first certifiable social standard, which enables auditing of working conditions and terms, especially in countries whose own labour laws and control are insufficient. SA 8000 is based on the requirements of national labour legislation and the ILO core labour standards. SA 8000 has been highly appreciated among the NGOs, as it is a so-called 'multi-stakeholder initiative' – stakeholders have been able to participate in the drafting and decision-making of the standard. However, the results of SA 8000 are quite modest, as the manufacturing companies in developing countries have found it too expensive and difficult to comply with, due to the strict requirements on management systems. The most SA 8000 certifications – surprisingly enough – have been achieved in Italy. I addressed SA 8000 and similar social auditing schemes (BSCI, ETI/SEDEX, FWF etc.) in Chapter 6.

ISO now plans to publish ISO 20400 standard on sustainable procurement in 2017. This will be a guidance standard, which means that it is not possible to obtain certification. As the certifiable social standard SA 8000 has existed for almost 20 years and all social auditing schemes are based on third party auditing, though not certifying of supplier factories, ISO attends this market extremely late, giving no specific value to the buyer/supplier relation. Those of you who have risk suppliers, should of course get acquainted with ISO 20400, but concentrate on third party audits of suppliers against one of the advanced social auditing schemes.

## 10.3.1 Product Certifications

There is strong demand for neutral information about company responsibility, and also about product responsibility.

The selection of product labels is becoming abundant. There are many kinds of organic labels, Fair Trade, EU Flower, Nordic Swan, forest certification behind wood products and paper, sustainable fishing (MSC), environmental certificates for buildings, carbon footprint, water footprint and who knows what. All these neutral labels are important and useful, as long as their contents have been decided in a wide mutual agreement and there are not too many identical labels whose contents are, however, a bit different. Consumers have to know and understand the contents of the labels before they can trust them.

I addressed the labelling of responsible products in 4.7.

# 11

# Drawing up the CR Action Plan

As soon as the material issues and the indicators for them have been chosen and the necessary promises for each area have been presented in the publicly available management principles, the management model of corporate responsibility is almost ready – only actions and reporting are still needed.

The action plan (target plan) can at first focus on approximately the ten most important issues, on which the stakeholder groups expect to get visible results as soon as possible. There are also issues of which the stakeholders' expectations are not as strong as the company's own needs to increase their performance and improve profitability. In SMEs, for example, improving energy efficiency or waste management does not significantly impact the state of the environment, but it reduces the company's relative environmental impacts and costs.

The actual plan should be scheduled for the next three years, so that the realization of the targets is monitored and reported on annually. At the first stage, the CR action plan can be separate from other planning, but step by step it should become part of the company's normal annual planning. This means that the structure of the CR action plan should be similar to other annual planning.

As companies often have different ways of presenting their planning, here is a simple model for the contents of the CR action plan:

(1) **Subject**
A title for the entity that is being developed; for example, 'Energy efficiency'.

© The Author(s) 2017
J. Kuisma, *Managing Corporate Responsibility in the Real World*,
DOI 10.1007/978-3-319-54078-8_11

(2) *Actions*

A compact description of which actions have been planned; for example, 'Energy reviews, introduction of geothermal heating at two premises'.

(3) *Performance indicators*

GRI indicators used for monitoring the results, in the above mentioned examples this would be total consumption of energy kWh and specific consumption $kWh/m^2$.

(4) *Targets*

Numerical targets for the results. It is difficult to analyze whether the targets have been reached if they have not been described numerically or otherwise accurately defined. For example, 'Cutting specific energy consumption' is not a sufficiently accurate target; it should be defined as 'Cutting specific energy consumption from the current 250 kWh per square meter to 200 kWh per square meter'.

For many companies, setting of numerical targets seems to be difficult, even when it is a question of financial targets. If areas of corporate responsibility are not yet that familiar, the target setting may be difficult in the beginning, and the targets are often quite modest instead of very demanding. As the action plan is monitored every year, it is easy to set new targets if the previous ones have been found to be incorrect. In a couple of years, the target setting will become familiar and more accurate.

(5) *Schedule*

In which schedule the targets should be reached, divided into several years when needed. In the example above, 'building of geothermal heating in 2018, cutting specific energy consumption by the end of 2019'.

(6) **Responsibilities**

Each action/target should have an owner – the department/team/person who is named as responsible for the actions and targets (see Table 11.1). Companies very seldom seem to name the responsible actors in the publicly available action plan. Publishing the actors adds to the weight of the target and it is worth showing at least in internal communications. As concerns external communications, leaving out the responsible actors may show discretion in case no results are achieved. I have seen some companies even publish the names of the persons who should be responsible for certain actions. This seemed quite cruel, as the results seldom depend on one person only, and the persons may change during the year.

**Table 11.1** Action plan

| Subject | Actions | Indicators | Targets | Schedule | In charge |
|---|---|---|---|---|---|
| Energy efficiency | Energy reviews, geothermal heating at two premises | kWh kWh/m$^2$ | Reduction of total energy use from 12,000 to 10,000 kWh and from 250 kWh to 200 kWh/m$^2$ | Building of geothermal heating by the end of 2018, reduction of specific energy use by the end of 2019. | Environmental manager & property manager |
| etc. (approx. ten important subjects) | | | | | |

Again, I wanted to search company websites in order to find simple, manageable action plans. To my surprise, very few companies have disclosed any action plans at all. There are some very short ones and then some enormously long ones – the longest I found was 36 pages.

The action plan – there can be other names: 'responsibility programme', 'responsibility promises', 'target plan' – is a summary of the company's fundamental plans and numerical targets as to corporate responsibility, and it should be easily found on the website. I have suggested displaying it on the second level of the Corporate Responsibility menu, so that it can be immediately seen when opening the CR pages. However, many companies have the action plan only in their CR report, and even there it may be difficult find.

As I have said, one of the biggest shortcomings of the plans is that they do not show clearly how the results are measured, which then means that also the targets are mainly verbal, seldom numerical. And none of the companies have named the responsible actors, or I am sure they have done this internally, but they do not show them in public – not even the department that is responsible.

Some of the links I have here represent good examples, some still leave room for improvement. Google gave me plenty of Japanese companies which seem to make their plans in a systematic way, but they often seem to include everything possible in the plan, whereas my suggestion is to start with the ten most important issues.

http://www.lassila-tikanoja.fi/en/company/corporate-responsibility/
http://www.ngk.co.jp/english/csr/web/environment03.html
http://www.itochu.co.jp/en/csr/activities/actionplan/
https://www.marubeni.com/csr/group/action_plan/
http://www.nikon.com/about/csr/environment/promote/action_plan/
index.htm
http://www.toshiba.com/csr/env_5th_environmental_action.jsp

# 12

# Reporting on Performance

As soon as the material issues and indicators are known, promises have been given, measuring of results and execution of the action plan have started, the company is finally prepared to start public disclosure of promises, actions and results. Reporting is instructed by accounting legislation, accounting committees (in some countries there are such committees giving more specific instructions on how the law should be interpreted) and the international GRI Guidelines.

I do not address accounting legislation here, as there are many books for just that purpose, and there will be national amendments, due to the EU Directive on non-financial reporting. I concentrate on the GRI Guidelines as the basis for reporting, but as I have already gone through all GRI indicators when addressing materiality assessment, I do not repeat them.

## 12.1 Outline of the GRI Guidelines

The *GRI Recommendation (Reporting Principles and Standard Disclosures)* consists of the following sections:

- purpose of the recommendation, instructions for use and principles of reporting;
- instructions for describing common management practices and principles;

© The Author(s) 2017

**187**

J. Kuisma, *Managing Corporate Responsibility in the Real World,*
DOI 10.1007/978-3-319-54078-8_12

- instructions for presenting management principles (management approach to each area of responsibility) and performance indicators;
- positions on how the UN Global Compact, OECD Guidelines and the UN Principles on Business and Human Rights are linked with GRI reporting.

Moreover, the recommendation includes a large *Implementation Manual*, in which all details of reporting are addressed really thoroughly.

The GRI recommendations is quite a package for reading and exploring; it may at first seem an impossible task. But when one remembers that every company can adapt GRI to their own needs and concentrate on their own material issues, the package will already become much lighter. SMEs should not be afraid of the extent of the recommendations – they can learn how to find the areas that best suit their responsibility efforts.

It is not possible to give a detailed breakdown of GRI in this book. Anybody can download both documents mentioned on the GRI website www.globalreporting.org. The recommendations have 94 pages and the manual 266 pages – there are 58 potential issues for reporting in the section 'Management and other issues' and 89 on the indicator list – there really is no shortage of material! Those who are responsible for financial reporting in listed companies are used to working with an extensive amount of detailed data, but as concerns amount of information, GRI has developed very close to the IFRS standard if not beyond it.

The earlier versions of GRI described compliance with GRI (In accordance with GRI) on three different levels: A, B and C. The new G4 recommendation does not include these levels, but the 'In accordance' feature can now be described on two levels: either Core (the basic level) or Comprehensive (covers about everything). Both levels have been accurately instructed, indicator by indicator – which issues should be reported in order to comply with the level requirements and which issues have been included in the potential assurance of the report. This procedure is much better than the earlier one which gave the companies the possibility of assessing their level themselves. Time will show how many companies can come up to the Comprehensive level, most companies will get somewhere between Core and Comprehensive. To study the requirements of both levels, go to www.globalreporting.org.

GRI has published ten sector-specific, complementary reporting instructions. They used to be called Sector Supplements. Now that they have been updated with G4, they are called Sector Disclosures.

The CR steering group, and especially the person in charge of the group and reporting in practice, should read through all GRI material – as reading progresses, they will notice which issues are material for the own company and which can be left out. The chairman of the group as well as the members and those who participate in collecting the data for the report should master the contents of GRI pretty well, but it is however probable that they will all concentrate on their own area of expertise and not the whole text.

The major working language of GRI is English, but the texts have been translated into 16 languages. In addition to English, there are translations into six other European languages: French, German, Greek, Polish, Spanish and Turkish. One can also find detailed GRI handbooks available by searching the web.

Developing corporate responsibility is long-term work which has not got very much in common with the quarter year economy. GRI recommends that the results are disclosed in at least three-year time spans, but many issues need an even longer trajectory. For example, developing the labour conditions and terms in the supply chain to the average EU level may take as long as a generation, though some individual companies may change faster.

## 12.1.1 Standard Disclosures of the GRI Recommendations

The general standard disclosures are divided into seven areas:

1. Strategy and analysis of the material issues, risks and opportunities
2. Organizational profile (14 different items)
3. Identified material aspects and boundaries
4. Stakeholder engagement
5. Report profile, comparison with GRI recommendation (Core or Comprehensive), assurance
6. Governance (22 items)
7. Ethics and integrity.

The need to describe the management approach has grown in the G4 recommendations, and almost all the 22 items of governance describe in detail what the board of directors does, for example: 'Report the process for delegating authority for economic, environmental and social topics from the highest governance body to senior executives and other employees', or 'Report the measures taken to develop and enhance the highest governance body's collective knowledge of economic, environmental and social topics'.

All topics brought up are good and important, but GRI's approach on the Comprehensive level is clearly more familiar to listed companies than to SMEs.

In some governance items, GRI goes even further than what has been customary in financial reporting and what the stock exchange rules require. GRI has clearly wanted to show that corporate responsibility should be taken visibly onto the agenda of the board and top management. At the same time, by having brought up so many details about governance, GRI has wanted to be developed closer to the financial reporting based on the IFRS standard. GRI has participated in the work of the International Integrated Reporting Council (IIRC), which aims at combining financial reporting and non-financial reporting into integrated reporting. I return to integrated reporting later.

So, how can a listed company or a big non-listed company manage all this information? The bigger the company is, the more it reports on the strategy, basic facts and governance also in the annual report and board of director's report. If non-financial CR reporting is carried out separately from financial reporting, one has to avoid overlaps and see in which part of the CR report it is possible to point to the financial report, and vice versa. If the financial and CR reports are published under the same covers as one report (which does not yet mean it would be an integrated report), the overlap problem does not necessarily exist, but as the amount of pages that can be used is limited, it is difficult to comply with the GRI Comprehensive level. Many indicators have to be disclosed with a couple of sentences – by combining some subjects it may be possible to keep the length of the text reasonable. I can bet that very few listed companies are able to report GRI's standard disclosures perfectly enough to reach the Comprehensive level, but anyway, it is good to comply with GRI as much as possible.

For small companies, compliance with GRI's management and governance recommendations is more difficult. The financial reporting of these companies is usually quite scarce, and it would be odd for them to publish more information about corporate responsibility than they publish about their economic success and future prospects. The board of directors of an SME, especially of a family enterprise, usually consists of a couple of persons only, and the GRI recommendation on governance is very much overscale for such companies. Therefore, SMEs and other even bigger companies will settle for Core-level reporting. Thus, of the governance issues only G4-34 *Governance structure (Board of Directors and its committees)* will be taken into reporting – though handling other issues is not forbidden.

Also, the following can be left out of reporting: G4-2 *Assessment of key impacts, risks and opportunities*, G4-57 *Seeking advice on ethical and lawful behaviour* and G4-58 *Mechanisms fo reporting concerns about unethical or unlawful behaviour*. In other respects, the Core and Comprehensive requirements are the same.

## 12.1.2  Fundamental Issues of Management

Reporting on the basic data and governance of the company is routine work – more fundamental issues in describing the management approach to corporate responsibility are:

- strategy of corporate responsibility (see 2.3.3)
- stakeholder assessment (see 2.4)
- presentation of common management principles and specific principles for sectors (DMA = Disclosure on Management Approach) (see 10.1, the specific DMAs are disclosed at the beginning of each sector of issues)
- assessment of material CR issues and their performance indicators
- definition of the company's value chain in reporting (which are the boundaries of our CR work).

## 12.1.3  The Pain of Starting the Reporting

Over the years, starting the reporting has been the issue, especially for smaller companies, which has retarded developing corporate responsibility: 'We have worked actively in the area of corporate responsibility, but we are not yet ready to report on it'; 'We have too many important development projects and we have to prioritize – a CR project does not have room on our agenda right now, maybe after a couple of years'. And often, top management thinks that reporting is an expensive operation. These are typical and understandable attitudes, but as CR is not a fashion but has come to stay, permanently, why not start to work with it right away!

An old Chinese saying is: 'The best moment for planting a tree is 20 years ago. The second best is today'. This saying fits well together with starting the CR reporting. The GRI recommendations are now 16 years old, before that environmental reports were already published. There has been enough time to consider the matter, now it's time to speed it up! If the necessary stakeholder and risk assessments and SWOT analysis have been carried out, with or without the help of this book, GRI indicators have been listed in order of importance, own value chain has been defined and action plan has been drawn up, the material for reporting is almost ready. Surely, the data can be collected easily and reliably.

As I have stated before, the data for reporting on economic responsibility can be taken from the bookkeeping, the statistics needed for human resources are for the most part available, as well as at least part of the environmental and product safety data. With good luck, there are statistics for almost all issues that have been found important in the materiality assessment. And even if some data is still missing, *it is always worth starting the reporting from the first possible calendar year.* Often companies have waited and waited to get everything as complete as possible. Now it is better to think the other way around: corporate responsibility is based on transparency of operations, whereupon it is useful to introduce issues that are in progress and show where we are now and how our operations develop step by step each year.

### 12.1.4  Reporting Software Saves Work

When the data cannot be collected directly from the company's information system and the pieces of data are here and there around the organization, collection of data can require an immense internal email traffic, which creates big challenges for the person in charge of reporting. If the amount of information is growing year by year, reporting software planned to support the GRI scheme could be a useful purchase – and such software can also be bought as a service (paid for monthly or annually). Such software collects all required data from the company's other systems – like HR systems – and the owner of each set of statistics can enter their own data into the reporting software, which then makes all necessary additions and other analyses.

All GRI reporting software has been checked and 'certified' by GRI, and they are listed on the GRI website: https://www.globalreporting.org/report ing/reporting-support/certified-software-and-tools/Pages/default.aspx).  GRI does not recommend any software, nor is GRI responsible for their quality, GRI just checks that all software on their list complies with the GRI recommendations. In July 2016, there were 14 certified software companies on the list.

### 12.1.5  Profitability Aspects Are Worth Taking Along

I have always claimed that corporate responsibility actions and reporting save so much money that the costs can be covered and profitability can be improved. How big the savings are depends of course on the starting point. Sometimes, for example, energy inspections of badly constructed premises can bring forth really significant savings potentials against very small investments. Sadly enough, the profitability aspects are often forgotten or neglected, even if most of the environmental and human resources indicators are clearly profitability indicators as well: material, energy, water and waste management costs, costs arising from sick days, accidents and employee turnover, costs of withdrawal of products and so on.

In the future, whether the reporting develops towards integrated reporting or – as the EU directive on non-financial reporting already suggests – towards being part of the board of directors' report, CFOs of big companies will have to take responsibility for CR reporting as well. Therefore, it would already be useful if the CFO and the person now in charge of CR reporting could start training how to monitor CR performance and financial per-formance side-by-side. I will relate one example, where the CR indica-tors and financial indicators are very closely related.

> *it would be useful if the CFO and the person now in charge of CR reporting could start training how to monitor CR performance and financial performance side-by-side.*

Use of energy and emissions caused by the production of energy are fundamental environmental indicators, and energy purchases cost a lot of money. In integrated reporting, energy issues – if energy is a material issue – could be addressed like this (data from the three last years):

- amount of purchased energy (MWh)
- costs of purchased energy (€)
- investments in improving energy efficiency (€)
- estimated savings potentials of the investments (€) and payback times (years, months)
- environmental profile of the purchased energy (renewable, non-renewable, nuclear power)
- greenhouse gas emissions caused by the production of the purchased energy (tn $CO_2$)
- potential emission trading or compensations of emissions in projects in developing countries (€).

All the data I have suggested exists, but the companies do not usually want to disclose for example the energy costs, even though the use of energy is disclosed precisely, because outsiders could then count how much per kWh the company has paid for the energy. By the way, I find it very strange that companies do not need to present energy costs or other significant environ-mental costs in the notes to financial statements, not even when the costs are millions or tens of millions of euros. On the other hand, the (listed) companies have to give very precise information on the board members' allowances. I would think that the shareholders would be very interested in following how much money has been spent on energy and what has been done to save these costs, even if they do not follow the consumption in kilowatts that closely. Adding the economic requirements into energy use would certainly motivate actions to save energy.

In Chapter 2, I addressed just about all GRI indicators by commenting on their contents and also somewhat on their use in reporting. As I have earlier mentioned, it is not possible to go into details of GRI reporting in this book – GRI has published plenty of instructions for that purpose. I settle only for a couple of complementing views, which do not seem to come up in the 'official' instructions.

## 12.1.6  Indicator Protocols

Especially in big companies, plenty of people participate in collecting the data for reporting, and many of these people can change jobs during the year. Introduction of reporting software helps the work in practice, but if no software is available (and even if it is), it is useful to draw up content instructions for the material indicators used in reporting. These 'Indicator Protocols' can be drawn up by the CR coordinator – one A4 sheet for each indicator – and the protocols should be stored in the information system at a location that is easy to find. Most of the information needed for the instructions can be taken from the GRI disclosure guidance. Unambiguously documented instructions help all parties to understand the aspects in question and the need for collecting the data always in the same instructed manner.

The content of the instructions would be standardized and consist of the following parts:

- GRI number and name of the indicator
- Common relevance/reasoning of the indicator
- Relevance/reasoning of the indicator for our company
- Weights given to the indicator by our company/our stakeholders
- Compilation of the indicator: for example waste divided by type and disposal method: recovered waste, landfill waste, hazardous waste
- Information system or other statistics, from which the data for reporting can be retrieved
- The owner of the indicator (for example environmental manager).

## 12.1.7 Style of Reporting

Those of you who have read many CR reports must have noticed that many companies think they have been pretty successful in developing corporate responsibility. Just about all of their plans have come true, there are no problems, and many of the companies – even in the same sector – are leading companies of the sector as to sustainability, or at least aiming at winning that position.

I do not find reporting plausible if everything goes well. It is not necessary to seek and present problems involuntarily, but when it is a question of such a big entity, there surely are shortcomings and failures. All in all, reporting must rest on facts – not in the way that you review your actions with plenty of beautiful sentences and give a couple of facts between the reviews, but the other way around: you should present primarily the facts and then explain what is behind them if needed. It does not make sense to present claims that make the reader ask 'Can you prove your claim?' – the proof must be already visible. The facts speak for themselves. You can comment on the changes from the previous year and give reasons for them, but avoid praising yourself and your achievements. It is the reader's duty to determine what they think about your progress. One good piece of advice on the style of reporting is, 'Use as few adjectives as possible'.

*I do not find reporting plausible if everything goes well.*

As I am an extremist in emphasizing the facts, I have started to like the reporting model that starts by describing the actions in the fundamental areas, like in the annual report, adding some statistics to demonstrate the descriptions. The actual introduction of results would be placed after the annual report and would include all material performance indicators presented very compactly. Such a presentation is similar to the structure that big companies are already used to – the annual report plus the notes to the financial statements – and would bring CR reporting closer to financial reporting, as it should.

Some companies publish separate CR reports, others have included CR issues in the annual report, either clearly as a separate section or merged with the annual report if responsibility is regarded as the basis of business (for example a waste management company promoting circular economy). I have not yet seen any company include the CR indicators in the notes to the financial statements, though I think they will belong there, sooner or later. Another question is as to how this could succeed in practice, as both the financial statements and 'CR statements' consist of loads of data. But if this information was made available on the website, such a data package would be controllable, and it would be easier to search for the details of own interest without being strained by all the other material.

At the moment, combining the CR report and annual report may bring forth a strange situation. If the CR text is very accurate, fact-based and even assured, the text in the annual report can be a much more lively description of the company's strategy, achievements and future goals, without the auditors having read and approved that text. Very few readers notice this difference, but maybe it would be better to develop the accuracy of the annual reports to meet similar requirements to GRI reporting, than vice versa.

I always disliked digital reports, thinking that their readability was bad and they were difficult to use. Nowadays, digital reports have improved and it is easier to find all the information I am interested in. A downloadable PDF version should still be given as a choice, though its use will probably decrease year by year.

Some companies have added videos to their digital reports. In some cases – on the condition that the amount and lengths are reasonable – they give good possibilities for illustrating subjects that are otherwise difficult to describe. One good example is the Finnish pizza chain Kotipizza Group – nowadays a listed company – whose CEO **Tommi Tervanen** writes in his blog (named the best business blog in Finland in 2015) at least once a month and often uses videos. One of my favourite videos there is a Greenpeace video on fishing tuna in the Maldives. With this six-minute video, Tommi Tervanen wants to show the difference between the old non-sustainable net fishing and the MSC-certified pole-and-line fishing. Kotipizza Group buys MSC-certified tuna from the Maldives: https://www.youtube.com/watch?v=HP6rYThJWUg

*In some cases videos give good possibilities for illustrating subjects that are otherwise difficult to describe.*

## 12.1.8 So, Who Would Read the CR Reports?

For as long as CR reports have been published, there have been claims that nobody will read them, at least not in their entirety. The new versions of the GRI recommendations have always increased the information collected in the report. When I wrote my first GRI report for the year

2000, I managed to give quite comprehensive data in just 42 pages. Today, the reports typically have 100 pages or more. I have even seen reports with over 200 pages.

*Journalists*, and other parties who study company behaviour like *analysts*, use the reports as their source of information like reference books. The *CR experts of competitors* read the reports thoroughly and compare their own plans and performance to those disclosed in these reports. The *students* who attend CR courses in universities and polytechnics are interested in the reports, not only for their studies, but also from the point of view of their future work careers, as they want to work for a responsible, reputable company. The *suppliers of goods and services* glance through the reports in order to see whether they can find visions and plans that will affect business relations in the future. Only a small number of *shareholders* have so far been interested in the subject, but taking more CR information into the annual report may increase their interest. And of course the *employees* of the reporting company study the content of the report, especially the parts concerning their own areas of responsibility.

The attractiveness of the report depends very much on how the report has been compiled. If the readers are required to read the whole report, it cannot be too long. As the report is often used as a source of information, for searching for individual facts, the report should be user friendly so that it is easy to find the needed data quickly. Some target groups – like consumers – could benefit from an abbreviated wrap-up report, consisting of the subjects that interest consumers most.

There are different approaches to developing reporting. Some reporters are passive and restrict their work to the needs of the own CR and communications teams. Here, the report has to be produced quickly, efficiently and with as little money and fuss as possible, to be published on the website and the printed versions stored on the archive shelf, without much further use. This is just like one would buy a new car but try to avoid driving it.

At the other extreme, the development process of reporting is taken as a unique opportunity to collect, combine and compare new information, analyse development trends and the importance of information to the company and its stakeholders. The stakeholders expect the company to present a transparent plan for carrying out changes and improvements. Open disclosure of development in the report tells the stakeholders that the issues are taken seriously. The importance of goals will be emphasized also inside the company and will lead to more efficient work. The information produced by reporting will also be used as a tool by top management: in strategy work, risk management, goal setting, assessment of resources needs and alignment of resources.

## 12.1.9   Assurance of the Report

The history of auditing accountancy and financial statements of limited companies is in its current form more than one hundred years old. The need for auditing is seldom questioned, especially when it is based on legislation.

As CR reporting becomes more common, and the use of CR reports extends to investor and customer relations, it would seem self-evident that also such reports describing the company performance with many different first-rate indicators would be audited – in GRI language 'externally assured'. However, this is not the case.

My estimation, based on various sources (GRI, PwC etc.) is that around 30 per cent of GRI reports have been externally assured. GRI recommends assurance but does not require it. The EU directive on non-financial reporting that came into force in 2017, will not require assurance of data, either – such requirements could still be taken into national legislation, but I doubt it. We will hopefully see the contents of all national laws in 2017.

The assurance can be directed to the whole report, to some parts of the report or to a certain calculation. For example, the airline Finnair has had the information and the calculation method of their Emission Calculator assured externally. The assurance does not take a stand on the results but on the extent, validity and reliability of the data published, as well as on its compliance with GRI.

It is possible to comment on the results in the public assurance statement, but the results are more often addressed in the internal assurance report given to the company's management.

Assurance is not cheap, but it is possible to cover the costs with the benefits received from it. Assurance improves the quality, reliability and feasibility of the CR data, streamlines the management systems and practices behind the data and data transfer and gives direction to risk management actions. All in all, assurance adds much to the credibility of reporting compared to leaving the reader dependent on the data given by the reporting team and on the statement of the top management, no matter how professional and reliable the company's own people are regarded.

The GRI website offers a check-list of issues that the company considering buying assurance services should take into account. I do not go deeper into the assurance principles and practices here – my opinion is that assurance of the CR report is indispensable if you want to make the external use of the report successful (think, for example, of giving the assured report to a development bank when you apply for funding, or to a big b-to-b customer company that wants proof of your company's responsibility!)

## 12.1.10 GRI Content Index

GRI reporting has always included the GRI Content Index, with which the reporter presents how the own reporting complies with GRI recommendations. Previously, there were three levels to describe this 'in compliance with GRI': for beginners level C, for somewhat advanced reporters level B and for thorough GRI reporters level A. The companies could either choose their level themselves, ask GRI to give the rating or take it as part of the assurance and get a +/- mark after the rating. This meant that a thorough, externally assured GRI report was awarded A+.

In the latest G4 recommendation there are two levels: 'Core' and 'Comprehensive', and GRI has now compiled a check-list for the level assessment which enables the reporter to see what 'in compliance' on both levels means, as to general standard disclosures (strategy, organization, governance and so on) and specific standard disclosures. The instructions for the content index are found in G4-32: *Report Profile*. Of the indicators, those that have been assessed as material are taken into the index. In exceptions, some material indicators can be left out, but then there have to be justifiable reasons for such exclusions. Assurance of reporting is presented in the index indicator by indicator, as assurance can cover only part of the report.

The content index is made in the form of a table and shows where the reported topics are located, with page numbers and links. It makes the finding of information easier, gives outsiders an outlook on how the company complies with GRI, and shows whether there are still shortcomings in the report. For own employees, the content index is a tool with which it is possible to internally assess the quality and extent of the report in respect of the GRI instructions.

The content index has always been detailed and has required a lot of space in the report. I doubt whether there are many readers who would go through the index thoroughly. Therefore, regardless of how the report is published, it is practical and acceptable to publish the content index on the company website, where it is easy to find with a www-link given in the printed report or digital report.

I give you only these two examples, as the index is so standardized that it always looks approximately the same:

http://www.lassila-tikanoja.fi/en/company/annual-report-2015/responsi bility/reporting-on-corporate-responsibility/Documents/GRI_Index_2015. pdf

http://www.stockmanngroup.com/documents/10157/19127/Stockmann +CSR+2015.pdf/9747e232-32fe-4ba7-9177-23d93dc3a791 (GRI Index is at the end of the report)

## 12.1.11  How to Use the Report

The best moment of the reporting process should not be the release day – the report should be continuously used from that day till the release of the next report, like driving that new car every day. Here are some principles of successful use:

> *The best moment of the reporting process should not be the release day – the report should be continuously used from that day till the release of the next report.*

- The report should be distributed and discussed in stakeholder and shareholder meetings. The fundamental results should be included in the information material given out to investors and analysts, in order to expand their understanding outside of the traditional financial indicators.
- The report should be included in the welcome material for new employees and distributed to potential employees, for example at recruiting events organized for students and other candidates. Many of these attendees are interested not only in the economic benefits but also in the corporate culture, values, equality, investments in welfare at work and in job satisfaction.
- The report should be linked with the company's communications plan.
- The report should be distributed to major suppliers of goods and services and to b-to-b customers if there are any. A good report answers most of the questions arising in such connections.
- The top management of the company should take up the report thoroughly and use the results presented in the development and planning processes of the company. As a method, materiality assessment suits not just reporting but also many other processes that need both internal and external opinions to identify business opportunities and risks.

• The report can create a competitive spirit between the different units of the company, especially when the responsibility indicators are applied in the incentive system and the employees are thus encouraged to aspire to better results.

## 12.2 The Future of CR Reporting

### 12.2.1 EU Directive on Non-Financial Reporting

The GRI Guidelines were published in August 2000, and so far four versions have been published. In some countries, CR reporting is already obligatory by law and many stock exchanges around the world have decided to require GRI reporting. In the EU, reporting has been voluntary, though the demands for compulsory reporting have been loud for over a decade. Finally, in April 2014 the directive on non-financial reporting was approved:

http://eur-lex.europa.eu/legal-content/EN/TXT/?uri=CELEX%3A32014L0095

At this stage, the directive covers the following: 'Large undertakings which are public-interest entities exceeding on their balance sheet dates the criterion of the average number of 500 employees during the financial year'. We have seen some countries give other criteria beside the amount of employees (turnover 40m euros, balance sheet 20m euros) and definitions for 'public-interest entities' (such as listed companies, banks and insurance companies). The national laws based on the directive were supposed to be approved before 6 December 2016, and before that same date, the EU Commission was supposed to give more instructions on how the directive should be implemented. There was a clear conflict between these two schedules – this way it was not possible to take the Commission's instructions into account in drafting the national legislation.

On 21 December 2016, the national law had yet not been approved in Finland – the law proposal of the Council of State had been given in October, and no national changes are proposed to the EU directive. The EU Commission does not collect development in different countries on their website. The instructions from the EU Commission are expected to be passed in the spring of 2017 (!).

It has been estimated that the directive will apply to around 6,000 companies in the EU, but as the extent still seems to be a bit unclear, I advise everybody to check, what has been said in the national law and in the EU Commission's instructions.

The problem of the directive seems to be that it does not define any precise indicators with which the non-financial performance should be disclosed. This will leave the reporting vague and varied and the results cannot be compared between companies as each of them can choose the indicators that suit their own business best. And the directive also approves as acceptable reporting schemes such as Global Compact and ISO 26000, which have nothing to do with reporting. Personally, I do not understand what benefit we could get out of such reporting legislation that does not say exactly what should be reported.

*What benefit could we get out of such reporting legislation that does not say exactly what should be reported?*

As said, the EU Commission has been obliged to draw up more precise instructions for the reporting. I suppose the purpose is to write down some general and some sector-specific performance indicators. The instructions will, however, be recommendations, not binding rules. This means that if binding rules are needed, the indicators should be taken into national legislation. In the schedule now valid, the EU instructions do not help in compiling the national laws, and I predict that the national laws all over Europe will follow the undefined policy of the directive and will not include any performance indicators.

w?>Different countries may end up with different solutions if the public officers in charge of this issue in the member countries do not find a common solution to be adapted in the legislation all over the EU. It seems that we are still quite far from the accuracy required in the accounting legislation, though the original idea was to raise the status of non-financial reporting very close to that of financial reporting.

In spite of all this, if the EU Commission and especially the European Parliament consider at the end of this decade that the directive has been successful, I predict that the European Parliament will make the next move and suggest that CR reporting should be extended to smaller companies. This could mean SMEs, which are now defined in the EU as companies that meet two of the three following conditions: employees between 50 and 250, turnover between 10 and 50 million euros, balance sheet between 2 and 10 million euros.

As said, follow the information your national ministry in charge of these issues has (hopefully) given out in late autumn of 2016. One thing is already certain: if a company begins or continues GRI reporting, the directive will not change anything.

## 12.2.2  Next Steps for GRI

GRI has updated its recommendations every three or four years. In 2017, there is no new version in sight.

The Transition to Standards Project was initiated in November 2015 by the Global Sustainability Standards Board (GSSB). The original GRI G4 Guidelines are evolving into a set of modular, interrelated GRI Sustainability Reporting Standards (GRI Standards). The changes mostly involve improving the structure and format of the content from G4. This is intended to make the GRI Standards easier to keep up-to-date, and even more suitable for referencing in policy initiatives around the world.

The GRI Standards will include all the main concepts and disclosures from G4, enhanced with a more flexible structure, clearer requirements and simpler language. The transition aims to make the GRI Standards more accessible for reporting organizations and policy-makers, and so to encourage more consistent, higher quality sustainability reporting, focused on material issues.

The GRI Standards were published in mid-October 2016. It was not possible to include them in this book, but at first glance this is not a problem. Though the standard structure is different from the GRI Guidelines, the indicators used in reporting are more or less the same, they have just got 'new numbers' for identification. As the standards should come into effect in reports published after 30 June 2018, there is plenty of time to study them, though GRI also encourages starting to use the standards earlier. GRI has made a tool to help transitioning from G4 to GRI standards, showing the G4 content and standard content beside each other.

The project 'GRI's Sustainability and Reporting 2025' was designed to promote an international discussion about the purpose of sustainability reporting and disclosures, looking ahead to 2025. Over a 12-month period, thought leaders in various fields were interviewed on subjects ranging from data technology to society and business development scenarios, with the aim of identifying the main issues that will – or should be – at the centre of company agendas and their public reports. Throughout 2015, GRI generated articles, videos and analysis papers based on these interviews, and disseminated them to its global network of more than 20,000 organizations and individuals. The final digital publication, 'The Next Era of Corporate Disclosure: Digital, Responsible, Interactive', presents a roadmap for the future of reporting and can be found through this link: https://www.globalreporting.org/resourcelibrary/The-Next-Era-of-Corporate-Disclosure.pdf

On the GRI website there are plenty of interview videos that shed light on what different parties are thinking about the future of reporting.

I cannot avoid telling you this setback I suffered in looking for interviewees for this book. I asked GRI headquarters to answer four short questions related to the next steps of GRI. After having waited for almost one month, they finally answered and regretted that they were not able to provide input on this occasion: 'Due to a lack of resources in-house and nature of the book, we usually refrain from contributing to "for profit" materials whenever possible'. Having worked with GRI reports for over 15 years, I was of course very disappointed to learn that I did not get the interview, because this is a 'for profit' book.

I think GRI's existence is totally dependent on the business world, and all GRI reports are part of companies' 'for profit' efforts, as the reports tend to ensure and improve the companies' reputation, accountability, profits and share value. I assume that GRI does not like my open critique, but openness and transparency are fundaments of corporate responsibility and GRI reporting. If GRI was logical, they would neither give interviews to the media nor speak at conferences, as media companies and conference organizers are as much 'for profit' companies as the publishing houses.

## 12.2.3  Integrated Reporting

In 2010, I participated in an international conference, where the CEO of GRI at that time, **Mr Ernst Ligteringen**, predicted that by 2015 GRI would have succeeded in becoming mainstream in most big companies, and that by around 2020 the new mainstream would be integrated reporting. At the time of that conference, Accounting for Sustainability (UK), International Federation of Accountants and GRI established an organization to develop integrated reporting, called the International Integrated Reporting Council (IIRC). The work started as a pilot project in 2011, and in April 2013 IIRC published the first draft framework for comments and after the comments the Integrated Reporting <IR> Framework in December 2013.

The original idea of integrated reporting was, in my opinion, to combine financial reporting and CR reporting so that it would be possible to describe how corporate responsibility, especially social responsibility and environmental responsibility, are related to financial results and vice versa. In many sectors – for example pharmaceutical, food and forest industries, environmental services, energy production – corporate responsibility is an essential, inseparable part of the business, and it is natural that everything should be reported in the same 'package'. My assumption was that the <IR> Framework would be a reporting scheme which instructs how to disclose the indicators of the financial statement and the GRI indicators 'side-by-side' and how to describe how they are related. The starting point was challenging, because the financial statement is legislated and the CR reporting has been voluntary. Anyway, the target was to make these two reports gradually merge into one single report, presenting the company's performance from all necessary angles.

However, IIRC started to develop a process which would bring forth an integrated report on how the strategy, governance, operations, results and future views create value for the company in the short, medium and long term. The scheme is based on the impacts of operations on six different capitals: economic, manufactured, immaterial, human and social capital as well as natural resources, and the description of the mutual dependencies of these capitals. The framework defines the principles guiding the content of reporting and the content elements of reporting. The framework highlights the importance of the principles and does not give detailed instructions on the indicators but refers to existing reporting schemes like GRI.

According to IIRC, integrated reporting should not only explain how the company's operations affect the capitals but also describe the company's operational environment, resources and influence.

I find the offered <IR> framework complex and theoretical for the time being, and the targets of <IR> reporting are today mainly investors, financiers and other economic stakeholders. GRI reporting has aimed at interaction with all significant stakeholders and at presenting correctly how the company has earned its profits responsibly. It is difficult to picture that, for example, employees or NGOs could benefit from the effects of the company's opera-tions on the different capitals, not to speak of consumers. It is also difficult to picture that a financial management committed to the IFRS standard could strongly depend on the <IR> framework. I am sure the framework includes plenty of important issues, but so far it seems to me that <IR> cannot combine financial reporting and CR reporting, but has developed a third reporting scheme which is somewhere in between, bringing more added value to the financial analysis than to responsibility.

I do not suggest that you reject IIRC's initiatives right away. I encourage you to follow this development in the same way as GRI's development, because developing one single integrated reporting scheme is important for the future. IIRC's website address is http://integratedreporting.org/.

### Corli le Roux: Johannesburg Stock Exchange has motivated companies to become more sustainable

Corli le Roux is Head of Sustainability in the Capital Markets Division of Johannesburg Stock Exchange.

**Describe briefly the development of ESG reporting rules, both voluntary and compulsory, accomplished by JSE as well as the South African authorities.**

In South Africa, the *King Code on Corporate Governance* ("King") has improved best practices in governance and transparency; with integrated sustainability reporting covered since 2002 and integrated reporting since 2009. The JSE Listing Requirements require companies to report against the Code annually on an apply or explain basis. The *Companies Act* requires companies to establish a Social and Ethics subcommittee of the Board, which needs to report annually on the extent to which the company's activities are aligned with the principles of the UN Global Compact.

**How have the reporting rules changed the companies' performance?**

Combining mandatory and voluntary approaches provided significant impetus for the integration of key ESG issues into overall business strategies, across sector and size. While social issues have always been of significance in South Africa, given the country's unique history, governance is a very strong area for South African companies, with investors being willing to pay a premium for good governance practices. Environmental issues needed more focus particularly from sectors with minimal direct impacts, however, we have seen meaningful improvements in this regard.

**What were your main motives for starting the SRI Index? What has the SRI Index achieved and why did you start cooperating with FTSE?**

The JSE introduced the pioneering *Socially Responsible Investment (SRI) Index* in 2004 to assess corporate sustainability reporting. The initiative has evolved significantly with the FTSE/JSE Responsible Investment (RI) index series now rating the ESG reporting of many JSE-listed companies. South African companies compare strongly against other emerging markets as well as many developed markets.

The SRI Index aimed to recognize and incentivize corporate sustainability and transparency, and to mainstream responsible investment. It reinforced sustainability as a business and investment consideration and influenced the way that companies were managing and reporting on ESG issues, also leading to constructive debates – the mining industry following the Marikana tragedy in 2012 as an example.

The collaboration with FTSE Russell is a key development in the JSE's work. The FTSE ESG Ratings not only offer JSE companies the opportunity to be assessed against global best practices, but also enable more flexibility and expanded access to investment grade ESG data.

**You have supported integrated reporting since its launch. How well have the companies succeeded in applying <IR> reporting and what has been the influence of the IIRC scheme?**

Integrated reporting has been taken up widely given the apply or explain requirement for listed companies. It is not a requirement to follow the International <IR> Framework, although this is seen as the guiding framework by many larger and multinational companies. Integrated reporting enables companies to highlight material issues across the six capitals and to create better linkages between financial and sustainability policies, practices and performance. It will in due course enable better assessment by investors of the company's ability to create longer term value. The *Integrated Reporting Committee (IRC) of South Africa,* of which the JSE is a founding member, continues to provide guidance on particular elements of implementation, such as reporting on outcomes or linking strategy to performance. A Starter's Guide was issued by the IRC after the launch of the international <IR> Framework.

# 13

# Communicating Corporate Responsibility

SMEs are sometimes very laconic in presenting what they are doing. Unlisted companies do not have a compelling need to disclose their financial results or future plans. Even the ownership of the company can be left unclear to outsiders. As soon as developing CR comes along, the transparency requirements grow much stronger, as concerns economy and other areas of responsibility.

One of the basic principles of corporate responsibility is to present the company's operations and results openly, so that the actions are as transparent as possible and the stakeholders are able to assess the company's responsibility. Transparency means providing abundant information rather than scarce information. The CR report is usually part of abundant information, but web pages are needed as well, as there is often demand for some specific issue which can be difficult to find in the report.

*Transparency means abundant information rather than scarce information.*

## 13.1 Corporate Responsibility on the Company's Website

Corporate responsibility cannot always be found in the website's main menu, which means that one has to search for its startup page, especially if the front page is loaded with product information. Usually one has to click the title 'The company'. This title may not be in the main menu, either – sometimes

© The Author(s) 2017
J. Kuisma, *Managing Corporate Responsibility in the Real World*,
DOI 10.1007/978-3-319-54078-8_13

it has to be searched for among the small titles or site map located at the bottom of the front page. After this, the corporate responsibility title is usually found, if it exists. As a spokesman for corporate responsibility, I of course hope that finding this page is made easy.

The first steps to bringing corporate responsibility into communications is placing the title 'Responsibility' or 'Corporate Responsibility' (or 'Sustainability') on the main menu of the company's website, and under this title the basic issues of corporate responsibility: economy, human resources, environment, product safety and so on. It very often happens that when you start clicking the subtitles, you will find a half screen of verbal (and beautiful!) description on what the company is doing in that area of responsibility, without any facts and figures about the results. And from there onwards, the story does not continue. In my opinion, such a brief presentation does not comply with transparency requirements, nor does it satisfy the website visitor's hunger for information. If corporate responsibility work is taken seriously, there is definitely much more to tell.

An example from the other extremity is that too much information is offered and with such a structure that it is impossible to examine such information. Very often, it happens that after you have proceeded from one link to another, you get lost and have to find your way back to the beginning. For example, one of the European investment banks has on their website so many different principles and policies, position papers, reports, rules, instructions and whatever. Merely presenting the complaint mechanism requires ten sub-links. Having studied their pages, I finally found myself eight steps from the start, and I never managed to understand the logic of those web pages.

In giving out information, midway is the best: not too little, not too much, but just right. I find the three levels deep menu sufficient. Here environmental issues are shown as an example of the third level:


Corporate responsibility
    Managing corporate responsibility
    Economy
    Human resources
    Environment
        Environmental policy
        Environmental management system
        Materials

Energy
Water
Emissions
Waste management
Product development
Product responsibility
Community relations
Reporting
Action plan

In every section of the third level it is possible to offer a reasonable number of links to more accurate accounting reports, surveys, analysis and other additional information, on the condition that one can easily get back from them and does not have to continue further and further.

Subsections of *Managing corporate responsibility* are, among others, values of the company, vision of corporate responsibility, stakeholders, organization and management principles guiding corporate responsibility. As these principles are responsibility promises of the company, and the stakeholders will want to track their realization, they have to be easily found. I recommend that the principles are put into a separate menu at the edge of the responsibility front page, which would make the principles easily reachable.

Videos are not yet used too much in CR communications. I think they provide plenty of possibilities for invigorating and demonstrating CR information. Here are some examples from Finland:

http://www.kesko.fi/en/company/responsibility/ (Kesko is a major Finnish retail group. There are five videos on the front page)

http://www.martela.fi/vastuullinen-valinta ('Responsibility at Martela' video. Martela makes office furniture)

http://www.vaisala.com/en/sustainability/Pages/default.aspx (CEO **Kjell Forsén's** video presentation on the subject 'What Sustainability means in Vaisala'. Vaisala is a global leader in environmental and industrial measurement)

For those of you who have about an hour to spare, I recommend the presentation of **Ms Jill Dumain,** environmental strategy director of Patagonia, entitled 'Patagonia – why business is good for the planet' https://www.youtube.com/watch?v=wTdkHPeemME. Patagonia is a famous company in the sustainability circles and there are plenty of their videos on YouTube.

## 13.2  Communicating to Stakeholders

The responsibility web pages give the basic information about the company's responsibility work, the CR report discloses the actions and annual results more accurately. I have already addressed the use of the report and its different readers. Each stakeholder group has different needs for information, and only very few want to know everything. Depending on the size and resources of the company, responsibility communications should be tailored according to the interests of each stakeholder group.

*Employees* are naturally one of the most fundamental stakeholder groups, and they have to be aware of what is happening in the company. Employees should be provided with basic information about the procedures, management principles, essential results and future goals of corporate responsibility. Web pages and the CR report act as the basic material, but in internal communications, department meetings and other gatherings the important subjects can be addressed practically, looking at the subjects from each work assignment's point of view. Printed material can be made out of the management principles –the Code of Conduct in particular should be made known to all employees, including those who have just started in the company. Students are an interesting and interested target group, as they appreciate responsible, reputable companies when searching for jobs.

*Owners, investors and the analysts backing them* are mainly interested in how corporate responsibility affects financial results, reputation and risks, hence they need to get information on those subjects. This usually takes place in private meetings, and in listed companies the CR information should be included in a company presentation by the investor relations manager. Demand for such a presentation grows as investors commit to the UN Principles for Responsible Investment and act accordingly (see subchapter 1.5.5).

*Non-governmental organizations* usually have specialized in one of the CR subjects such as conservation of the environment, human rights or animal rights, and they want to get open information about their actions and results in these subjects. The CR report is a good tool for this purpose, but it is also useful to meet stakeholder representatives separately in order to discuss the subjects and add knowledge and understanding on both sides. NGO representatives usually have plenty of deep know-how in their own specialist field, and companies can benefit from constructive, regular interaction with them.

The *Media* is interested in corporate responsibility subjects and handles them mainly correctly and professionally, but unfortunately there are very few journalists who have specialized knowledge of these subjects. Journalists have complained that the CR reports are nowadays too extensive and they have never time to read them completely, but they use reports as reference books. A good report can offer them answers to almost any questions that come to mind. At a national level, it does not make much sense any more to organize a press conference where the new CR report is published, as reports have become so common that they have no news value and journalists do not care to come to such events.

*A good report can offer answers to almost any questions that come to mind.*

Newcomers from interesting sectors can be exceptions, and the regional and local newspapers have more interest in and space for reporting on the companies in their own area. For example, investments in the region, purchases from the region, jobs created, taxes paid and other subjects close to the regional/local people do interest readers more than, for example, material or waste statistics.

*Consumer customers* are interested in corporate responsibility at a mental image level, not requiring that much detailed information. Therefore, CR reports do not work that well in consumer communications. Consumers should get information about corporate responsibility in a very compact form and about subjects that affect their lives. Usually, for consumers the most responsible company is the one whose products or services they mainly use. They do not know very much of the competitors, and when participating in surveys, they would not feel comfortable if they had to answer that they find another company more responsible but favour this familiar one anyway. Product level information is more interesting to consumers than company level information – it is easier to understand the minor energy consumption of a single product than the energy efficiency of a company or the share of recycled materials in production.

## 13.3  Introduce Persons in Charge

Corporate responsibility consists of numerous details, of which very few are commercial secrets. Therefore, open presentation of information to those interested should be organized as well as possible. There is plenty of information on the web pages and in the report, but the possibility of contacting the persons in charge should be offered as well. Surprisingly, this is not self-evident in the world of today – probably due to problems of information security or fear that qualified employees could be recruited elsewhere. Persons in charge are seldom introduced, not only as concerns corporate responsibility, but almost as a common rule.

Anyone searching for contact details would rather find it directly on the website than over the telephone or through any other 'shot in the dark' which takes too much time. In some companies the only possibility of getting in touch with them is to fill in a form and then wait for the contact. If somebody is on the company's website searching for information, the need is usually acute and waiting would be frustrating. Therefore, the list of contact persons should be available on the website. Here are a couple of companies whose CR contact persons are easy to find:

http://www.fortum.com/en/sustainability/contact-us/pages/default.aspx

https://www.neste.com/en/corporate-info/who-we-are/contacts/sustainability-safety-and-environment-contacts-0

http://www.vaisala.com/en/sustainability/contacts/Pages/default.aspx

## 13.4  Corporate Responsibility in Marketing

GRI reports have existed for over 15 years, but responsibility is very seldom used as a theme of marketing and advertising. We have seen some corporate image advertising and more often marketing and advertising of environmental actions and achievements, but not much. I do not remember any marketing campaigns that I would like to show by way of recommendation. The ads have the same weaknesses as many CR reports: the world is beautiful, the sun is shining, birds are singing, fish jump, children laugh, food is healthy, water is clean, all waste has been collected and recycled and the emissions are close to zero. Nice but unrealistic – where are the facts that prove the claims?

In Finland, as well as in many other EU countries, consumer protection law is very strict and includes a very demanding clause that prohibits misleading marketing. It has been difficult to get the environmental claims indisputable. The safest solution has been to lean on neutral environmental labels and certificates in product marketing. As concerns social responsibility, the only neutral product label that exists is the Fair Trade label – other certifications and audits have not been adopted by marketing, for many reasons. And there are no practical indicators to prove that a company as a whole is responsible. The neutral index listings are the most applicable, but they apply only to listed companies and do not interest all customer groups. The indices and other listings do not have common content, and they can also be contradictory among themselves: the same company can be listed among the most responsible companies in the world as well as among the most irresponsible companies.

In some countries, the consumer authorities have published instructions for environmental marketing, which can normally be found on their website. I have not yet seen any similar instructions for corporate responsibility.

# 14

# Stakeholder Cooperation Revisited

One of the basic starting points of corporate responsibility is to take notice of the stakeholders' need to know if the company yields its profits in a responsible way. As I have described in subchapter 2.4, different stakeholder groups have different views on responsibility, each according to their own interests, and the companies' priorities also vary.

For those who want to develop stakeholder cooperation by 'half-scientific' methods, it is possible to apply the interaction process in accordance with the AA1000 standards. The AA1000SES standard (SES = Stakeholder Engagement Standard) defines principles for planning, implementing, assessing and communicating the quality and results of stakeholder interaction. The process is continuous and systematic, the fundamental parts being: involvement of stakeholders, informing, interaction, documentation of results, agreement on actions and communicating of results.

I have to confess that I have never managed to study the AA1000SES standard so thoroughly that I could claim to have used it at work. I see stakeholder cooperation as an interaction between people and find standardization of such interaction and drawing of elegant multistage process descriptions artificial. The same fits in theorizing corporate responsibility – the actions have started in the companies' practical life and the theories have tried to describe those practices in the academic language.

© The Author(s) 2017                                                                 **217**
J. Kuisma, *Managing Corporate Responsibility in the Real World,*
DOI 10.1007/978-3-319-54078-8_14

I remember the days when the Soviet Union and their planned economy still existed, and they sent people on study trips to Finland to explore new modern factories. A typical comment (if not an urban legend?) was that everything seems to work fine in practice, but does it work in theory? Many companies can claim that stakeholder cooperation works well in practice, but they have never thought whether it would comply with the AA1000SES standard.

*Many companies can claim that stakeholder cooperation works well in practice, but they have never thought whether it would comply with the AA1000SES standard.*

A simplified stakeholder cooperation process could look like this:

1) Identify the relevant stakeholder groups and place them in order of importance
2) Establish contacts with the stakeholder representatives, discuss the ways and goals of cooperation
3) Identify the expectations and requirements the stakeholders have of us and accordingly our expectations of the stakeholders
4) Agree on the actions with a common goal that both parties benefit from
5) Measure the results of the cooperation annually or by projects
6) Address the results together, make new plans, set new goals

The biggest problem I have always seen in measuring of results is not how the projects have been implemented, but communication in general (see sub-chapter 2.4.6). When the cooperation can be evaluated by development of sales, corporate image surveys, participant amounts of events and so on, measuring is possible. But what about maintaining regular conversation with the representatives of an environmental NGO, introducing the company's construction plans to the local community or participating in a campaign opposing harassment at schools by financially supporting the schools that have had effective programmes for this purpose?

Some companies report on this kind of regular cooperation in only verbal form, for example:

– *'We continuously follow what kind of topical issues and viewpoints our stakeholders take up and then evaluate them case-by-case';*
– *'The cooperation in environmental subjects has grown remarkably in our sector. We participate actively in cooperation via working groups, events and*

*seminars. Finding and sharing information and best practices benefits us all and especially our mutual environment';*
– *'We cooperate actively with authorities and NGOs. We network and intend to influence, in order to contribute to sustainable development'.*

I cannot claim that these descriptions are totally groundless. I have been in the habit of requiring numerical indicators for all promises and descriptions of corporate responsibility, so that the results can be concretely disclosed and their development followed. But I guess in reality statistics are not always available when describing stakeholder cooperation, and reporting has to settle for qualitative information.

If a company makes the mistake of describing cooperation in a too positive way, the partners will definitely protest (if they do not want to exaggerate, too). Anyway, I am not so certain about what constitute active, successful cooperation – how many questions should the stakeholders raise – 2 or 20?

# 14.1   Typical Weaknesses of Stakeholder Cooperation

**Wayne Dunn**, President and Founder, CSR Training Institute, former Professor of Practice in CSR at McGill University in Canada, once addressed the weaknesses and problems of stakeholder cooperation in one of the LinkedIn discussion groups. I made notes of his post and include these below.

## 14.1.1   Stakeholder Definitions Are Too Narrow

Too often important groups are left out of the definition, because companies do not identify them as their own stakeholders. As production and trade networks extend nowadays to all parts of the world, the authorities, associations and other organizations working with developing countries are usually forgotten. Such stakeholders could be, for example, the development aid programme of the foreign ministry; organizations working for children and families, like UNICEF, Plan, World Vision, Save the Children and International Youth Foundation; human rights organizations such as Amnesty and Oxfam; and Transparency International and its country organizations, fighting against corruption and bribery.

## 14.1.2  No Balance Has Been Found Between 'Defence' (Complying with the Norms) and 'Offence' (Strategic Opportunities)

It is not easy to be on the defensive for some issues and at the same time identify and develop strategic opportunities and added value through stakeholder cooperation.

## 14.1.3  The Company Takes the Defensive Position Too Early

Stakeholder meetings, especially meetings with the neighbourhood community, start too often in a negative atmosphere, particularly if the cooperation is at an early stage. Stakeholder representatives will unburden their discontent and complain about shortages and faults. The company representatives, especially those of the top management, will then start correcting the claims and steering their audience 'onto the right track'.

The complaints do not necessarily always result from what the companies are doing but from other tensions, though there are certainly often reasons for genuine complaints also. The company representatives should first concentrate on listening and waiting for the discussion to proceed from emotional positions to constructive proposals that benefit all.

## 14.1.4  Own Efforts Are Concealed

Companies engage with stakeholders in order to benefit from this. This target should not be concealed. Too often, companies emphasize that they are responsible and are cooperating only for the stakeholders' benefit. But if the company is regarded as a mere benefactor and the stakeholder as a mere target of charity, could the company cut off such cooperation painlessly if it had financial difficulties? It is better to confess the own pursuit of benefits and aim at cooperation that brings mutual benefits. And donating money is charity, not stakeholder cooperation as such.

> *Companies engage with stakeholders in order to benefit from this. This target should not be concealed.*

## 14.1.5 Communications Fail

Communications in stakeholder cooperation often fail. There is either too much or too little of it, it is too marketing-oriented or too plain, and it does not reach the correct target groups.

I also provide a link to the 2degrees' (a UK consulting company) most popular CSR webinar of 2014, entitled 'The future of reporting: How to build effective stakeholder dialogue to boost your CSR strategy': https://www.2degreesnetwork.com/groups/2degrees-community/resources/future-reporting-how-build-effective-stakeholder-dialogue-boost-your-csr-strategy_2/

# 15

# New Year Resolutions

Here I cite a French CSR consultant Marion Enzer, whose WiznessBlog (also came to my knowledge through LinkedIn) addressed developing corporate responsibility and reporting like New Year's resolutions in January 2015. We all can of course make this type of resolution at any time of the year:

http://publisher.enablon.com/blog/my-new-years-resolutions-as-a-sustainability-report/

## 15.1 Spend Quality Time with Friends

Actually, it is not a question of real friends but of stakeholders who should be engaged on a regular basis. Exchanges can be diverse (workshops, focus groups, phone or in-person interviews, online communications, meetings or events) but what's important is to share **quality time**, listen to their feedback, take notes of their requirements and take these into account.

## 15.2 Learn New and Exciting Skills

What could be more exciting than learning a new skill and becoming good at it? This year, this 'little something' is called **materiality**, which will help to stay focused on what's important for both my stakeholders and my business. Other exciting stuff to learn along the way: how to draw materiality matrices!

© The Author(s) 2017                                                                          **223**
J. Kuisma, *Managing Corporate Responsibility in the Real World*,
DOI 10.1007/978-3-319-54078-8_15

## 15.3  Lose Weight

With the concept of materiality put into practice, it is possible to focus only on the key material issues that are really important, and **avoid the non-essential topics.** This could save pages and pages of irrelevant content and help stay fit under...let's say...100 pages?

## 15.4  Be more Honest

The goal of the report is to present the key sustainability achievements of the company in the passed year...but also highlight the current and coming challenges to achieve the future goals. The report should **focus on what's good...and less good** in our operations, without doublespeak or unrealistic discourse.

## 15.5  Get Rid of Old Bad Habits

Starting the process too late? Not taking into account the stakeholders' feedback? Forgetting to add both quantitative and qualitative data? No! This year all of these bad habits will be left behind and the most basic **sustainability reporting best practices will prevail**.

## 15.6  Improve Grades

A grade is not an end in itself, but getting **recognition** from peers and experts in the field is still the best way to be confident about one's own ability! From the rating agencies to the industry awards, it is always a challenge to be among the leaders!

## 15.7  Become More Organized

The preparation for the report may take several months and include numerous collaborators and reviews. A little help is needed to stay organized throughout the year. Hopefully, some **tools** exist for this purpose, and the good news is: some of them are free!

## 15.8  Reduce Stress

The road towards sustainability sure is a long one, and the reporting world is no exception. Try not to be drowned under too much pressure, convey the benefits of reporting and **have fun** along the way!

## 15.9  Save Money

The reporting budget may vary from one company to the other, but having it approved by our CFO is always kind of the same story. To make sure the report tops our company's agenda and priorities, it is necessary to prove that CSR reporting and **ROI** can walk hand in hand.

# 16

## Summary

Now the model for managing corporate responsibility has been addressed thoroughly. An attentive reader has hopefully got a clear picture on the following questions:

1. What subjects are now the most topical as concerns corporate responsibility?
2. Which parties – in addition to the companies – influence the development of these issues at a national and international level?
3. What kind of a steering group should be set up to develop the CR management model if such a system has not existed earlier?
4. Which stakeholders have we identified, what are their expectations of our responsibilities and how have we responded to them so far?
5. What are the boundaries of our CR, what does our CR value chain cover, which parties do we include in it?
6. Which subject areas and performance indicators should we choose among the suggestions in the GRI recommendations, being material for our own responsibility and reporting?
7. What kind of measurable promises should we make in our management principles, as to improving our responsibility performance?
8. What is our action plan on our fundamental development subjects; in which schedule will we carry out the reporting on our actions, targets and results of the material subjects; are there other ways of communicating our CR work to our stakeholders and other interested parties?

© The Author(s) 2017

J. Kuisma, *Managing Corporate Responsibility in the Real World*,
DOI 10.1007/978-3-319-54078-8_16

As I have estimated, a committed and devoted CR steering group can get the management model ready in about six months by following my suggestions. Taking an experienced consultant into the steering group will bring integrity and useful external opinions into the group's work. Support and motivation from top management is crucial for success; without it, no results will be achieved.

There are very few training programmes offered on managing CR. Therefore, the persons in charge should network actively, taking part in as many events on the subject as possible. And fortunately there are immense amounts of information about this subject on the Internet. Almost daily surfing pays off, but you must remember that everything you find on the web is not always true nor useful. But very soon you should be able to separate the wheat from the chaff.

Reading is over, now you can get to work! I wish every success to all new CR experts!

# List of interviewees

**Bhunya, Nilambar** independent CSR consultant, auditor and trainer, based in Kolkata, India, associated for example with Wethica as their Lead Compliance Auditor.

**Elkington, John** Co-founder of four companies, among them Volans Ventures and SustainAbility.Ltd. Founding member of the B Team advisory board, author or co-author of 19 books. John lives in London.

**le Roux, Corli** Head of Sustainability in the Capital Market Division Johannesburg StockExchange, South Africa.

**Lund, Peter** Professor at the Department of Applied Physics of Aalto University, Finland.

**Peitsalo, Anne-Maria** Martela's corporate responsibility specialist. Martela is a listed Finnish company manufacturing office furniture.

**Pietikäinen, Sirpa** Member of the European Parliament, former Finnish Minister of Environment.

**Räsänen, Merja** Partner and director of consumer goods trade at Nikolai Sourcing Ltd. Nikolai Sourcing has offices in Beijing, Shanghai, Hong Kong, New Delhi, Dhaka, Stockholm and Helsinki.

**Ronkainen, Janne** Executive Director of The Trade Union Solidarity Centre of Finland SASK.

**Vuori, Timo** Chief Executive of ICC (International Chamber of Commerce), Finland.

© The Author(s) 2017
J. Kuisma, *Managing Corporate Responsibility in the Real World*,
DOI 10.1007/978-3-319-54078-8

# List of useful web pages

## United Nations

*Sustainability Goals*

http://www.undp.org/content/undp/en/home/sdgoverview/post-2015-development-agenda.html

*Global Compact*

www.unglobalcompact.org

*Business and Human Rights*

http://www.ohchr.org/Documents/Publications/GuidingPrinciplesBusinessHR_EN.pdf
http://business-humanrights.org/en/un-guiding-principles
http://business-humanrights.org/en/updated-assessments-of-national-action-plans

*International Labour Organization (ILO)*

www.ilo.org

*ILO Convention ratifications*

http://www.ilo.org/dyn/normlex/en/f?p=1000:10015:0::NO:10015:P10015_DISPLAY_BY,P10015_CONVENTION_TYPE_CODE:1,U

*UN Principles for Responsible Investments*

www.unpri.org

© The Author(s) 2017
J. Kuisma, *Managing Corporate Responsibility in the Real World*,
DOI 10.1007/978-3-319-54078-8

## Other international organizations

*OECD*

www.oecd.org

*International Standardization Organisation (ISO)*

www.iso.org

*International Chamber of Commerce ICC*

www.iccwbo.org

*Transparency International*

www.transparency.org

*Global Reporting Initiative GRI*

www.globalreporting.org

## European organizations

*European Commission*

http://ec.europa.eu/growth/industry/corporate-social-responsibility/index_
en.htm.

*BusinessEurope*

www.businesseurope.eu

*CSR Europe*

www.csreurope.org

*Business in the Community UK*

www.bitc.org.uk

## Other continents

*Business for Social Responsibility (U.S.A)*

www.bsr.org

*The Business Ethics Network of Africa*

www.benafrica.org

## National ministries

*Finland*

http://www.tem.fi/en/enterprises/corporate_social_responsibility_(csr)

*Denmark*

http://web.archive.org/web/20140703201148/http://eng.mim.dk/the-ministry/

*The Netherlands*

https://www.government.nl/topics/corporate-social-responsibility-csr

## Auditing/consulting companies

*PwC*

http://www.pwc.com/gx/en/services/sustainability/sustainable-development-goals/sdg-research-results.html

*KPMG*

https://home.kpmg.com/xx/en/home/insights/2014/10/materiality-assessment.html

*BeyondBusiness (consulting company)*

http://www.b-yond.biz

*Kesko's risk management*

http://www.kesko.fi/en/investor/corporate-governance/risk-management-and-audit/
http://www.stockmanngroup.com/documents/10157/17245/CSR±2013±ENG.pdf

*Carbon emissions etc.*

http://www.ghgprotocol.org/
http://www.cdp.net
http://lipasto.vtt.fi/en/index.htm
https://www.rijksoverheid.nl
https://www.gov.uk/government/policies/transport-emissions
http://www.cefic.org/
http://www.cofret-project.eu/Library-Info/Calculation-Tools/

https://www.wttc.org/mission/tourism-for-tomorrow/hotel-carbon-measurement-initiative/
http://www.ecompter.co.uk/benefits-hotels/
http://energy-base.org
https://wbcarbonfinance.org/Router.cfm?Page=Funds
http://ec.europa.eu/clima/policies/ets/index_en.htm
http://www.fao.org/news/story/en/item/196220/icode/
http://uk.businessinsider.com/these-6-countries-are-responsible-for-60-of-co2-emissions-2014-12?r=US&IR=T

## Calculating carbon footprint

http://www.ccalc.org.uk/software.php
https://www.simulationstore.com/sulca
www.pef-world-forum.org
http://www.iso.org/iso/home/news_index/news_archive/news.htm?refid=Ref1643
http://martela.com/carbon-footprint

## Videos about climate change

http://www.circularecology.com/what-is-1-tco2e-video.html#.VMNrkjgcSM8
https://www.youtube.com/watch?v=CvBMVOTiLSo
https://www.youtube.com/watch?v=UatUDnFmNTY
http://www.newrepublic.com/article/120310/nasa-video-shows-carbon-dioxide-pollutions-path-across-planet

## Water footprint

www.waterfootprint.org/?page=files/productgallery
www.waterfootprintkemira.com
https://www.iso.org/obp/ui/#iso:std:iso:14046:ed-1:v1:en
http://www.theheinekencompany.com/sustainability/focus-areas/protecting-water-resources
www.coca-colacompany.com/setting-a-new-goal-for-water-efficiency

## Product declarations

http://www1.ruukki.com/Construction/Environmental-product-declarations

## Environmental auditing of suppliers

*Business Environmental Performance Initiative BEPI*

www.bepi-intl.org

## Safety, equality at work

*Zero Accident Forum (Finland)*

http://www.ttl.fi/en/safety/occupational_accidents/zero_accident_forum/
pages/default.aspx

*Equality material bank (Finland)*

http://www.yhdenvertaisuus.fi/welcome_to_equality_fi/

*Work-life balance*

http://www.borenius.com/2014/06/17/crowded-years-from-paper-to-practice/
http://www.borenius.com/2014/06/16/balancing-acts-by-the-dutch/

## Social auditing of suppliers

*Auditing schemes*

www.sa-intl.org
http://www.saasaccreditation.org/?q=node/23
www.ethicaltrade.org
www.sedexglobal.com
www.bsci-intl.org
www.fairwear.org
www.fairtrade.net
www.wrapcompliance.org
www.fairlabor.org
www.icti-care.org
http://www.eiccoalition.org/
www.gscpnet.com

*Supplier lists*

http://sustainability.hm.com/en/sustainability/downloads-resources/
resources/supplier-list.html

http://manufacturingmap.nikeinc.com
http://www.kesko.fi/en/media/news-and-releases/news/2015/purchasing-chain-of-clothes-and-shoes-made-transparent/
http://www.stockmanngroup.com/en/supplier-and-factory-list.

*Minimum wage/living wage*

http://www.ncsl.org/research/labor-and-employment/state-minimum-wage-chart.aspx
https://www.youtube.com/watch?v=5-ImoKhymL4.

*Human rights*

http://www.ohchr.org/Documents/Publications/GuidingPrinciplesBusinessHR_EN.pdf
http://www.bghr.org/
http://business-humanrights.org/en/videos

## Community engagement

http://www.storaenso.com/about/download-center?topic=2cb0d995-9de2-4a27-af55-2bbaa7e91a29
http://assets.storaenso.com/se/com/DownloadCenterDocuments/Sustainability_Report_2015.pdf
http://assets.storaenso.com/se/com/DownloadCenterDocuments/Policies_Wood_and_Fibre_Sourcing_and_Land_Management_2016_english.pdf

## Political relations, corruption

http://www.transparency.org/cpi2015#results-table
https://www.microsoft.com/about/csr/transparencyhub/political-engagement/

## CR Management Principles

*Code of Conduct*

http://www.vaisala.com/en/sustainability/responsiblevaisala/codeofconduct/Pages/default.aspx
http://martela.com/files/media/Responsibility/martela_corporate_code_of_conduct_2016.pdf

*Environmental policies*

http://www.lassila-tikanoja.fi/en/company/corporate-responsibility/code-of-conduct/Pages/environmental-policy.aspx
http://cdn.ek.aero/english/images/environment_policy_tcm233-658143.pdf
http://www.finnairgroup.com/linked/en/yhteiskunta/Finnair_Environmental_Policy.pdf
https://www.jal.com/en/csr/environment/vision/
http://www.burberryplc.com/documents/corporate_responsibility/global-environmental-policy.pdf
http://company.marimekko.com/sustainability/environment
http://www.kesko.fi/en/company/policies-and-principles/environmental-policy/

*HR policies*

http://www.orion.fi/en/Orion-group/Sustainability/policies/human-resources-policy/
https://corporate.vattenfall.com/sustainability/policies-and-management/human-resources-policy/
https://www.neste.com/fi/en/node/18049
http://www.kesko.fi/en/company/policies-and-principles/hr-policy/
http://www.veolia.com/en/veolia-group/careers

*Sourcing principles*

http://martela.com/files/media/Responsibility/martela_social_requirements_on_suppliers_2011.pdf
http://www.fortum.com/SiteCollectionDocuments/Corporation/Code%20of%20Conduct%202012/suppliers_CoC_eng.pdf
https://www.neste.com/en/corporate-info/sustainability/sustainable-supply-chain/supplier-requirements
http://www.novonordisk.com/sustainability/actions/Responsible-Business/Responsible-sourcing.html
http://eu.patagonia.com/pdf/en_US/Patagonia_COC_English_02_13.pdf
http://www.woolworths.co.za/store/fragments/corporate/corporate-index.jsp?content=../article/article&contentId=cmp205999

*Action plans*

http://www.lassila-tikanoja.fi/en/company/corporate-responsibility/
http://www.ngk.co.jp/english/csr/web/environment03.html
http://www.itochu.co.jp/en/csr/activities/actionplan/

https://www.marubeni.com/csr/group/action_plan/
http://www.nikon.com/about/csr/environment/promote/action_plan/index.
htm
http://www.toshiba.com/csr/env_5th_environmental_action.jsp

## Reporting

*Global Reporting Initiative (GRI)*

www.globalreporting.org

*GRI Index*

http://www.lassila-tikanoja.fi/en/company/annual-report-2015/responsibil
ity/reporting-on-corporate-responsibility/Documents/GRI_Index_2015.pdf
http://www.stockmanngroup.com/documents/10157/19127/Stockmann
+CSR+2015.pdf/9747e232-32fe-4ba7-9177-23d93dc3a791 (GRI Index is
at the end of the report)

*EU directive on non-financial reporting*

http://eur-lex.europa.eu/legal-content/EN/TXT/?uri=CELEX%
3A32014L0095

*Integrated reporting*

http://integratedreporting.org/

## Videos in communication

http://www.kesko.fi/en/company/responsibility
http://www.martela.fi/vastuullinen-valinta
http://www.vaisala.com/en/sustainability/Pages/default.aspx
https://www.youtube.com/watch?v=wTdkHPeemME

## Introducing persons in charge

http://www.fortum.com/en/sustainability/contact-us/pages/default.aspx
https://www.neste.com/en/corporate-info/who-we-are/contacts/sustainabil
ity-safety-and-environment-contacts-0
http://www.vaisala.com/en/sustainability/contacts/Pages/default.aspx

# CR News, articles, discussions

www.csrwire.com
http://www.theguardian.com/uk/sustainable-business
http://www.mckinsey.com/insights/
www.linkedin.com

# List of people I have quoted in my book

All the quotations I have in this book have already been in the Finnish language version. They have all been taken out of public material and do not require permissions. I have marked all the sources in the text before the quotations.

## Corporate values

**Tapio Aaltonen** consultant, Novetos Ltd – text published on Novetos' website as an advertisement of Novetos' services.

**Martti Puohiniemi** consultant, A3 Interaction, text published on their website, advertising their services

**Laura Honkasalo** journalist, interviewing Martti Puohiniemi for a Finnish magazine Fakta.

## Corporate responsibility in corporate strategy

**Lasse Kurkilahti, Toivo Äijö** survey report published in Talouselämä magazine 35/2014.

## Essential issues in materiality assessment

**Elaine Cohen** consultant, BeyondBusiness, Elaine's blog in 12/2014

© The Author(s) 2017                                                    **241**
J. Kuisma, *Managing Corporate Responsibility in the Real World*,
DOI 10.1007/978-3-319-54078-8

## Use of energy...greenhouse gas emissions

**Benjamin K. Sovacool** professor, Aarhus University, article published on sciencedirect.com.

## Transports are Is Only Part of the Life Cycle

**Adrian Williams** professor, University of Cranfield, research published on the website fairflowers.de.

## Working Hours

**Doug deRuisseau** Senior Advisor, Social Accountability International (SAI), Q&A-section of the SAI website.

## Corruption and bribery

**Ravi Venkatesan** consultant, International Social Venture Partners, article in McKinsey Quarterly, Jan. 2015.

## Typical weaknesses of stakeholder cooperation

**Wayne Dunn** former professor at McGill University, post in a LinkedIn discussion group (CSR).

## New Year's Resolutions

**Marion Enzer** consultant, her WiznessBlog, Jan. 2015.

# Index

**A**

Absentee rate, 112, 114
Accidents at work, 108, 167
Action plan, 21, 39, 40, 54, 60, 61, 62,
    149, 169, 174, 183–185,
    187, 191
Animal welfare, 7, 16–17
Assurance of the report, 188, 198–199

**B**

Biodiversity, 19, 78, 89, 106, 166
Boundaries of value chain, 64–65, 191
Bribery, 16, 21, 29, 75, 107, 156, 157,
    158, 159, 166, 176, 219
BusinessEurope, 31
Business Social Compliance Initiative
    (BSCI), 12, 106, 122, 125,
    140–141, 145, 146, 150,
    175, 182
*Business travel*, 103

**C**

Carbon compensations, 86–87
Carbon disclosure project, 83, 85

Carbon footprint, 26, 97–100, 104,
    176, 182
Carbon free electricity, 84–85
Chemicals
    European Chemicals Agency
        (ECHA), 14, 80
    REACH regulation, 14, 80
Chief Financial Officer, 1
Child labour, 3, 7, 12, 20, 22, 55, 65,
    121, 124, 125, 134–135, 143,
    152, 166, 167
Climate Agreement, 88
Climate change, 8–9, 19, 51, 72, 80,
    81, 83, 86, 87, 89, 97, 99, 103,
    104–105, 122, 179
Code of conduct, 43, 124, 141, 170,
    171–172, 174, 175, 212
Collective bargaining, 20, 22, 124, 125,
    127, 152
Communication policy, 170
Compensation, 15, 86, 108, 110, 128,
    130, 193
Corporate governance, 7, 58, 59,
    176, 180
Corporate strategy, 42, 43, 61
Corporate values, 43–46

© The Author(s) 2017                                                    **243**
J. Kuisma, *Managing Corporate Responsibility in the Real World*,
DOI 10.1007/978-3-319-54078-8

Corruption
    anti-corruption, 6, 21, 26, 157, 158
    Corruption Perception Index, 16
CSR Europe, 31, 32
Customer satisfaction, 164

D

Discrimination, 7, 20, 22, 112, 117,
    124, 127, 128, 152

E

EcoEnergy label, 85
Economic responsibility, 41, 61,
    69–75, 101, 117, 148, 191
Economic value, 70
Electronic Industry Citizenship
    Coalition (EICC), 143, 145
Emission permits, 86, 87
Emission trading, 86–87, 193
Employee turnover, 4, 15, 111–112,
    122, 167, 193
Energy
    efficiency, 2, 10, 11, 80, 87, 167,
        183, 193, 213
    efficiency reviews, 2
Environmental impacts of products, 93
Environmental responsibility, 4, 6, 7,
    20, 41, 61, 77–106, 166, 171,
    175, 204
Equality, 18, 19, 110, 116, 117, 124,
    156, 200
Equal remuneration, 116–117
Ethical Trading Initiative (ETI), 139,
    141, 175, 182
European Union EU
    EU Commission, 28–31, 35, 101,
        201, 202
    EU Directive on non-financial
        reporting, 35, 181, 187, 193,
        198, 201–202

EU Multistakeholder Forum on
    CSR, 28, 35
EU Parliament, 17, 28

F

Factor Four, 10, 78, 87
Factor Ten, 10, 78, 87
*Fair Labor Association*, 143
Fair Trade Labelling, 141–142, 214
Fair Wear Foundation (FWF), 141,
    145, 182
Fixed-term employees, 110–111
Forced labour, 22, 124, 125, 135,
    136, 143
Freedom of association, 7, 20, 22, 124,
    125, 127, 152

G

General business principles, 43
GlobalG.A.P., 93
Global Reporting Initiative (GRI), 6,
    24–25, 29, 46, 62–64, 66, 70, 71,
    72–73, 75, 78, 79, 82, 84, 89, 91,
    105, 108–112, 114–118, 123,
    150, 151, 152, 155, 157–161,
    163–164, 165, 167, 169, 176,
    177, 181, 184, 187–192, 194,
    196, 198–199, 201–205, 214
    GRI G4 Guidelines, 203
Global Social Compliance Program
    (GSCP), 106, 143, 145
Greenhouse gas emissions, 8, 9, 10, 52,
    65, 80, 83, 86, 104, 193
Greenhouse gas protocol, 83, 85
Grey economy, 16

H

Hazardous waste, 91, 194
Health care, 2, 108, 113, 114
    precautionary, 2, 15, 108

Health and safety, 42, 108, 112, 117, 118, 124, 125, 133–134, 160, 163, 170, 174, 179

Human resources policy, 108, 170, 173, 174

Human Rights
  Business and Human Rights, 13, 21, 132, 152, 172, 188
  declaration, 13, 130, 151, 172

I

ICTI Care, 17, 143, 145, 175

Indicator protocols, 194

Integrated reporting, 190, 193, 204–207

International Chamber of Commerce (ICC), 6, 26, 35, 158, 163, 172

International Organization for Standardization ISO
  14001 (environment), 6, 26, 77, 93, 173, 179, 182
  14046 (water footprint), 12, 26, 90, 100
  14064 (greenhouse gas accounting), 9, 26, 83
  14067 (carbon footprint), 98
  26000 (social responsibility), 26, 29, 180–181, 202
  31000 (risk management), 58, 180

J

Job satisfaction, 54, 67, 107, 108, 109, 111, 112, 113, 116, 118, 119, 122, 163, 171, 200

L

Labour conditions, 12, 121, 122, 189

Labour rights, 13, 22, 47, 69, 74, 121, 123, 131, 151, 153, 176

Labour standards, 20, 182

Lifelong learning, 19, 114–115, 167

Living wage, 73, 130, 131

Lost workdays, 114

M

Management principles, 2, 6, 27, 41, 43, 58, 60, 61, 62, 169, 170, 175, 177, 183, 188, 191, 211, 212

Material aspects, 2, 62, 64, 66, 67, 69, 75, 77, 189

Material efficiency, 10–11, 78, 79

Materiality, 8, 24, 34, 40, 41, 43, 61, 62, 63, 67, 118, 165, 166, 169, 187, 192, 200, 223, 224
  assessment, 8, 40, 41, 43, 61, 62, 63, 67, 118, 165, 169, 187, 192, 200

Materials used, 78, 79, 148

Minimum wage, 72–73, 117, 129–130, 132

O

OECD
  Guidelines for multinational companies, 25, 172
  National Contact Points (NCPs), 25, 32

Own present state, 60

P

Paris Agreement, 8, 88

Part-time employees, 111, 118

Payback time, 2, 193

Performance
  indicators, 7, 8, 26, 29, 39, 40, 46, 54, 60, 61, 66, 93, 108, 114, 150, 165, 181, 184, 188, 191, 195, 202

Performance (*cont.*)
  reviews, 108, 110, 116
Political contributions, 159–160
Product
  policy, 170, 176–177
  responsibility, 7, 163–164, 174,
    182, 211
  statements, 170, 176–177
Promises, 8, 45, 62, 80, 108, 169–174,
    183, 185, 187, 211, 219
Public procurement, 16, 29, 33,
    101, 157


R

REACH regulation, 14, 80
Recycling, 11, 64, 78, 79, 90, 91, 92
Remuneration, 12, 73, 116, 117, 124,
    128, 129, 131, 132, 133, 140
Reporting software, 192, 194
Responsible sourcing, 27, 73, 121, 124,
    140, 144, 170, 174
Responsible supply chain, 12, 121–153
Risk assessment, 40, 43, 56–60, 72,
    143, 153, 158, 176, 191
Risk management, 7, 13, 42, 43, 56,
    58, 59, 64, 106, 170, 175–176,
    180, 198


S

SA 8000 standard, 127, 131, 138–139,
    144, 182
Screening of suppliers, 105–106
SEDEX database, 139
Sick days, 15, 108, 109, 112, 167, 193
Social Accountability International
    (SAI), 129, 135, 138, 140
Social auditing, 131, 132, 137,
    138, 182
Social certification, 12, 137, 138, 141,
    182, 214
Sourcing principles, 146, 174–175

Sponsoring principles, 170, 177–178
Stakeholder
  assessment, 40, 41, 47, 52, 54, 55,
    56, 61, 169, 191
  engagement, 52, 66, 189, 217
  influence, 3–4
Standard entry level wage, 117
Steering group, 39–43, 47, 49, 54, 61,
    63, 67, 170, 188
Strategy, 29, 30, 32, 35, 39, 42, 43,
    47, 49, 50, 51, 52, 58, 61, 64,
    67, 94, 177, 178, 179, 189,
    190, 191, 196, 198, 199,
    205, 211
SWOT analysis, 40, 60, 191


T

Tax footprint, 13 14, 71
Training, 2, 7, 34, 102, 108, 114,
    115, 116, 128, 134, 139, 140,
    152, 153, 157, 158, 167,
    170, 193
Transparency International, 16, 157,
    219
Transports, 2, 16, 176
Triple Bottom Line, 4, 5, 7
Turnover of staff, 108


U

United Nations UN
  Global Compact, 13, 20, 21,
    23, 188
  International Labour Organization
    (ILO), 12, 22–23, 32, 130, 135,
    143, 172, 174, 182
  MIllennium Development Goals
    (MDG), 18
  Principles for Responsible
    Investments, 23–24, 172, 212
  Sustainable Development Goals
    (SDG), 19

UNDP (United Nations
  Development Programme),
  20, 23
UNEP (United Nations
  Environmental Programme), 23,
  24, 86

V
Value chain, 64, 65, 105, 191
Values, 7, 43–46, 51, 61, 177, 178,
  200, 211
Vision of corporate responsibility,
  47, 211

W
Waste
  handling of, 91–93
  hazardous, 194

hierarchy, 91
management, 65, 77, 91, 92, 106,
  136, 183, 193, 195, 211
Water discharge, 90
Water footprint, 11–12, 26, 90, 100,
  182
Water use, 11, 87
Weak signals, 48, 49
Welfare at work, 2, 62, 108, 113, 118,
  167, 171, 200
Working conditions and terms, 125,
  130, 136, 139, 142, 144, 150,
  182
Working hours, 12, 15, 35, 111, 119,
  124, 125, 128–129, 130, 140,
  143, 150
WRAP (Worldwide Responsible
  Accredited Production), 133,
  142–143

The manufacturer's authorised representative in the EU is Springer
Nature Customer Service Centre GmbH, Europaplatz 3, 69115 Heidelberg,
Germany. If you have any concerns regarding our products, please
contact ProductSafety@springernature.com

Printed and bound by CPI Group (UK) Ltd, Croydon, CR0 4YY
27/04/2026
02097633-0003